FOR LOVE OF THE BROKEN BODY

FOR LOVE OF THE BROKEN BODY

A SPIRITUAL MEMOIR

JULIA WALSH, FSPA

To Jani: May the brokenness always be beautiful ♡ S.
S. Julia Walsh

Monkfish Book Publishing Company
Rhinebeck, New York

For Love of the Broken Body: A Spiritual Memoir © 2024 by Julia Walsh

All rights reserved. No part of this book may be used or reproduced in any manner without the consent of the publisher except in critical articles or reviews. Contact the publisher for information.

Paperback ISBN 978-1-958972-27-4
eBook ISBN 978-1-958972-28-1

Library of Congress Control Number 2023040636
Contact the publisher for Cataloging-in-Publication Data

Cover portrait by Julia Walsh
Book and cover design by Colin Rolfe

Monkfish Book Publishing Comany
22 East Market Street, Suite 304
Rhinebeck, New York 12572
(845) 876-4861
monkfishpublishing.com

To my Franciscan Sisters, thank you for loving and receiving me,
blessed and broken, and showing me how to share
as a member of the Body of Christ.

To all the men I love.

This is a work of creative non-fiction. To the best that my memory allows, this is a true story based on actual events, although some names and details have been changed to respect the privacy of people. Some characters are conflations of real-life persons who influenced my path. Besides memory, other sources for this material have been interviews, medical records, emails, instant message (G-chat) conversations, and journal entries from the time period covered (mainly 2007-9). Instant message conversations, emails, and journal entries included in the manuscript have been edited to improve clarity and readability. Quotation marks are used for dialogue.

CONTENTS

Part One: Shattered 1
Part Two: Repaired 105
Part Three: Held 169

Acknowledgments 237
Permissions 239
Glossary 241
About the Author 249

PART ONE
SHATTERED

1

Saying goodbye could kill me, but it doesn't. I'm alone, face-down in a stream on the farm in Iowa where I grew up. My body is soaked. I taste blood in my mouth. What happened? Oh my God. I fell off the cliff, twenty feet onto the rocks. And I'm not dead. God, help me.

In each direction, hills rise and fall across sweeping farmland: pastures of grass and forest, corn and soybean fields. I roamed this land freely as a child, tangled blond hair bobbing and thorn-scratched white freckled arms all-flailed about. In a nearby park, I learned to cross-country ski: I learned how to fall and protect my head. That falling lesson may have saved me just moments ago. As I fell, I lifted my hand to my forehead: my wrist a cushion for my skull, as my body rammed into the creek bed, face first. My whole body crashed into the limestone, sharp stones jabbing into my soft flesh. Glasses jammed into the bridge of my nose, piercing open my skin. My body tremored: my jaw wobbled, cracked, split. Two lower front teeth ejected from their roots. Right above my chin, my teeth are shattered, my tongue feels edges of bone and pieces of teeth rolling around in the metallic, warm blood mixing with saliva, flooding my mouth.

I gasp, spit, lift my head out of water.

I hear my voice moan, weakly, as a blur of water, blood, and teeth fall from my mouth. Glasses fall from my face, quickly disappearing downstream. All is blurry. This body, my body, is broken; I'm soaked with water and blood.

The water is shallow, six inches deep: enough to drown me. My mind says: Julia, get up!

I need to fight for my life or accept death—an unexpected outcome for this day of prayer, when I'd hoped to make peace with this farm no longer being my home. I came back to ritualize goodbyes to the land, as a fresh new novice, a Franciscan Sister. Ritual erupts out of us, though; the spiritual made physical, I'm learning. Blessed? I'm broken and bloody at the bottom of a creek bed. I still could die.

Somehow, I turn over. I'm lying on my back, face up to the green tree canopy, the blue sky. Clear water flows 'round my curvy body. Face, knees, and breasts poke through the stream like islands. Water washes my wounds clean. My tongue feels jagged teeth. I taste mucus and blood. My cheek muscles tighten, my jaw hangs open. A hot pain bursts across my chin.

Am I going to die out here? I'm only twenty-five years old. What I know of death is that it can come at any moment; mortality's power is greater than our humanity. What I know of death right now is that I'm not afraid of it, I look forward to an eternity with Jesus; but I'm afraid of how my death will hurt those I love, who love me.

God, it's a little early, don't you think? I don't want to die. Not now. I know God hears me, is with me.

Gasping, I breathe, feeling my belly move up and down, feeling the air flow into my mouth, throat, expanding my lungs. I groan and exhale. Everything is blurry, but I can feel what's happening in my body. I can assess what my body can do. Another exhale, inhale. Ribs broken? No, I don't think so. My mouth moves but feels its jaw loose and wobbly—broken. I take a deep breath and try to yell for help. But my voice only echoes back to me garbled, muddy, soft.

Around my ears, I hear the water washing over my body, over stones, rippling through the channel above my head, downstream. I hear leaves rustling in trees, birds chirping.

I hear Milton, my family's cocker spaniel, running through bushes and grass at the top of the cliff, his chain jangling like wind chimes.

Mainly though, silence. No one is nearby. The closest person is probably Uncle Enoch, milking his cows. How would he ever hear my cry for help over the murmurs of the cows, the hum of the milking machinery, through the walls of the barn?

If I want to live, I know, I must try to save myself. Or pray.

I could be paralyzed, so I check what works. Toes wiggle: yes. Feet have feeling, yes. Legs lift: all good. I scan every part. Most of the pain: in my face, especially in the gap between my chin and left ear, above my lips. My left wrist, my left hand. All over: beaten up, bruised, sore. But I'm alive. I have strength. I can do this, I hope. I must try. Come on, Julia!

Trying to stand, I wobble back down into the water, sharp rocks pressing into my skin. Rolling onto my side, I look back at the cliff. How high do I need to climb? Everything's a haze. Tan (rocks) and greens (trees) wash together creating a wall. The cliff up; too high, might as well be a mountain. Can I climb back up without falling again?

"God help me!" I holler as loud as I can, eyes squeezed together. I'm surprised to hear my voice boom back. I blink my eyes toward the cliff, then, my vision becomes clear: as if my glasses are on my face for a moment. An escape route? Yes, yes, a clear path, a space for crawling, just big enough for my body to slide into, meandering along the cliff's face, up to the top. I see the way, thank you.

I hear myself panting and groaning as I crawl through flowing water, toward the face of the cliff, that gap. I stay on my knees, my soft palms gripping hard rocks. My left wrist stings. Muscles tighten. One-handed crawl, here I go, avoid another fall. My heart is racing. God, help me, God, help me. Slow. Slow.

Eventually I make it to the top of the cliff, and, very slowly now, get to my feet.

I see a brown blur in the green: the log I love, where I prayed through my teen years. Moving out of the trees, I see a blur of blue— my tent, I set it up just a few hours ago, knowing nothing of what would soon happen. Something is dripping off my face, near my eyes. Is this sweat? I lift my aching hands to wipe: all red. More blood! Don't panic, Julia. Keep going.

Milton scrambles over, panting. Then he bolts back to the farmhouse, barking fiercely. Does he smell my blood and know I'm hurt? Is he running to get help? Oh Milton, no one is home!

At the tent, I struggle to find the zipper. I put my face right next to the fabric, trying to see where the zipper pull is. All I see is my blood on the nylon. Shaking, I find the zipper pull, pull open the tent. More colors and blur: purple backpack inside the door. I reach inside and fumble for the cell phone. In the blurs, I see blood dripping, coating everything I touch. I flip the phone open, hold it close to my eyes so I can see the power button and press it on. Blood pools around the keys. The phone is unresponsive.

God, help. I press again. The screen lights up. The phone chimes and rings, rebooting in my bloody hands. I press 9-1-1 but nothing happens. I want to lie down. Oh God, I'm so tired, but I better move up the hill so the phone can connect. *God, do I have enough strength to make it back to the house and call 9-1-1 on the landline? Help me God, help!* I re-zip the tent and stand, wobbly, try 9-1-1 again. Nothing.

Breathe, pray. I know the formula for situations like this; it's the stuff I'm learning from my elder Franciscan Sisters. But now I feel my jawbone dangling loose, blood still dripping off my brow, from my nose. In the distance, up the hill, I hear Milton barking, running around the farmhouse. I take a few steps through the tall grasses, toward the sounds of Milton's barks. I hold the phone close to my face again, press 9-1-1 again. Bloody fingerprints. Bloody screen.

I hear a human voice, a woman's voice. "9-1-1. What is your emergency?"

My voice wails, everything in me awake. I'm crying because I hurt. I'm crying because I'm alive. I'm crying because I hear another human voice, because now another human can know what happened to me: I'm broken and alone.

"Ma'am, try to take a breath." The woman's voice is kind, concerned. I try to stop crying, gasping for air between sobs.

"Ma'am can you talk? What is your name?"

"I'm Julia," I cry. My voice is garbled, my speech sounds slurred.

"Where are you, Julia?"

"18566 April Avenue." I can hear that I'm hard to understand, with my broken jaw, my bleeding lips, my swelling mouth.

"Can you repeat that?"

I try to, slower.

"Did you say 1576 Agate Road?"

"No!" I take a few more steps, through scratchy tall grasses, lifting my sorest arm over my head, stooping my body forward. The phone goes silent: disconnected.

Where am I? Oh God, I'm going the wrong way. Downhill? How am I going to make it back to the house without my glasses?

I try to slow my breathing, stop my sobs. Where are Milton's barks? Move toward those. I listen, redirect my body, inching forward, through the blurry and scratchy grasses.

All I want is to curl up on the ground and close my eyes. But again, I taste blood and feel the jagged edges of broken teeth in my mouth. From now on, everything will be different in my life, nothing will ever be the same again. This moment changes everything. I suddenly understand. Surprised by the thought, I'm jolted from my stupor.

I try to stand taller, to look up the hill, to focus on moving toward Milton's barking. Squinting, I see the red barn not far away and I move forward. Again, I press the keys for 9-1-1 on my cell phone. This time, a man's voice. "9-1-1. What's your emergency?"

My broken jaw moves around; my voice comes out garbled. Tension and pain radiate through my body. I feel so hot.

"I already called, talked to someone else, we got disconnected," I yell at him. I repeat my address. "I fell off a cliff and broke my—"

"Ma'am. I'm sorry, I'm having trouble understanding. Can you speak more slowly? What address did you say?"

I groan. I repeat again. He hears me this time.

"Help is on the way," he says.

"I'm in the pasture behind the house, trying to make it to the backyard."

"Good," he says.

I step forward. The call disconnects. Oh God.

This goes on again and again: I take a few steps, stand still to dial and connect, speak to a 9-1-1 operator, move toward the sound of Milton's barks, then get disconnected. Redial and repeat. The same information to a different person each time. Will anyone ever come find me?

Finally, a voice sounds familiar. It's the first woman I spoke to, the one whose kind voice caused me to sob when I heard her. "Help is on the way, to 18566 April Avenue," I hear her say.

"What were you doing on the cliff?" she then asks.

"I wanted to go swimming," I say. "The cliff crumbled when I tried to climb down."

"How steep was the cliff?"

"I don't know. Maybe twenty or thirty feet?"

The grasses are shorter as I approach the edge of the pasture, where the goats graze. I squint and make out the familiar red farm gate. I know I don't have the strength to climb over it now, like I have done hundreds of times before. I fumble and find the chain. I unlatch the gate, move through it, re-latch it—because the last thing my parents need today is for the goats to get out. My legs wobble, knees collapse. I fall onto the mowed grass at the bottom of the hill, on the lawn.

"Julia, are you alright?" The phone is still pressed to my ear and the 9-1-1 lady is speaking.

"I'm on the lawn now. I can't stand anymore."

"Can you make it to the door of the house?"

I begin to crawl up the hill, through a patch of lawn along the driveway where my brother and sisters and I used to slide down. Did the hill get bigger? I can see the grass close to my face, now speckled with blood. I don't know if I can keep holding the phone in my hand and crawling. Oh God, everything hurts.

"Help is on the way, Julia," the 9-1-1 lady says.

Finally at the back door, I'm done: too weak for anything else. The thought of climbing the cellar steps and making my way through the kitchen and living room to the phone feels impossible. I'm dizzy.

"I'm at the back door of the house. I don't think I can make it inside," I say into the phone. I stare at the grass, watching my blood pool.

"Stay right where you are. Help is on the way." The woman's voice remains chatty, comforting, encouraging. I listen and moan.

I'm alive. And I will never be the same.

2

Two years out of college, living in a convent, I don't know other women my age doing this.

At daily Mass, on a wooden pew surrounded by my gray-haired elders in mismatched blazers and skirts, heads bowed in prayer, my sandy brown hair hangs over my eyes in a side bang. In t-shirt, sweatshirt, and worn jeans, I wonder how I fit, if I do. My mind wanders, but I bow, stand, sit, and recite responses during the worship service too.

I trace the line-up of events that got me here, starting with the awe I felt for God in preschool. By adolescence, though, I see men and their charms, how they tug at my heart. It suddenly dawns on me: it is because of men that I am here. Let me explain.

The summer before college, at seventeen, in a college-prep program, I'm kneeling beside a bed in a quiet dorm room, hands folded in prayer, I'm talking to God about the latest boy I like. God knows what is best for me, I know, and I want to make choices that line up with God's plans for my life. I've been concerned with a divine plan since toddlerdom, since first becoming dazzled by God's power and love. Ever since, I've wanted to know, love, and please the One I could never see.

Prayer opens me to God, helps me tune in. I've felt this in the past: how prayer helps me listen more truly. I could use some guidance now, on my knees in the dorm room, as I think of this current cutie—his thin and lanky frame, spikey blond hair, and loose cargo jeans—and I feel a flutter around my heart. God, he is so cute! I don't know what to do. *Could I, should I, ask him out?*

I know what I want to hear, to sense: assurance from God that of course I can date, be normal, have fun, and be giddy with my girlfriends when they chatter about their flings. In those conversations, I'm sick of being a spectator; I feel so behind. I want to catch up, prepare for college, somehow, get rid of my innocence maybe. I've never really *heard* God's voice before or anything, but I believe in the possibility. A childhood filled with Bible school, Bible camp, and Catholic Catechism class has convinced me that God communicates with each of us, after all.

My hands press together, feeling warm as I pray. I hear my own voice, muffled quietly, as I mutter aloud my prayer-thoughts in the solitude. My eyes are squeezed tight. My head bows toward the pink-and-green-patterned quilt on the bed. *God, do you even want me to date? Do you even want me to get married? What is your will for me, God?*

I hear my questions and know what I want, but a thought crosses my mind, quietly, like a stream of bubbles stirring under the waterfall of these muttered prayers. At first, I ignore it. But then it keeps repeating, nudging for attention, like a song in my heart demanding to be sung. *Be a nun. Be a nun. Be a nun.*

This bizarre thought could be coming up from my childhood. Maybe I'm hearing these words because I decided I was open to nunhood long ago. I was raised to be a faithful Christian by the adults in my life: my Lutheran grandmother, my cradle Catholic dad, my converted-to-Catholic-at-marriage mom, aunts, uncles, neighbors—all faith-inspired. Regular church attendance and reception of the sacraments made up the tapestry of my childhood, youth. Conversations about faith, meal prayers, and concern for the poor were part of the family rhythms. I knew there were women clergy in other denominations, but I never thought about being a priest, a worship leader. Nunhood, though—I've been curious about it for years.

In fourth grade during lunch one day I asked whoever I was sitting near what they wanted to be when they grew up, wondering if anyone else was thinking about being a nun, trying to figure out if

I was odd. "If God tells me to be a nun, I'm going to say yes," I said, thinking of how I strained to hear the divine summons in the night, like young Samuel in the Hebrew scriptures. Our tiny public school was surrounded by Iowa cornfields; the thirty-six people I graduated with just a couple months ago were also my kindergarten classmates: Liz, Amanda, Carol, Lori.

At the start of our senior year, last fall, we acted out the senior predictions we wrote for each other during a variety show. Hundreds of farmers, parents and grandparents, sat on hard bleachers and cold folding chairs in the school gym with necks strained toward the stage, as I walked across wearing all white, the spotlight warm and bright. Carol's voice projected through the speakers: "Ten years after her graduation from Valley High School, Julia Walsh became a nun. Then she came back to visit her family and was driving by the high school, got in a car accident in front of the school and died. Now Sister Julia is a ghost that haunts Valley High School." The crowd laughed and clapped, knowing my reputation: a bad driver and a committed Catholic.

Be a nun. Be a nun. Be a nun. In the dorm room at the college prep program, my own voice is a whispered rumble on repeat, like a song in my head that won't shut up. My throat aches. *God, I don't think you understand. I want you to say it's okay for me to kiss boys, for boys to kiss me, like others get to do.* I feel my face droop, thinking again about how I could be a college student in a couple months, and I still haven't been kissed. I close my eyes tighter, as if that gesture could shift what I'm hearing in my heart, as if God will hear my reasonable request to have permission to make out with cute guys.

But all I hear is: Be a nun.

Still praying, I feel my shoulders and head convulse. Tears and snot run down my cheeks. Terror ripples through my body as I cry, as the emotion erupts from a deep place—as if the hollows of my heart are cracking open. Apparently, my heart knows what I'm meant to do, even though I don't like the plan.

Be a nun.

Is it me saying this? Or God? I suppose only God would direct me away from dating, physical affection, romance. On the other hand, maybe God was involved and there's good reasons why those prom dates never turned into anything, and why long phone calls with high school crushes never became something real.

I'm not sure. So, a few days later, I decide to resist, to allow myself to experience dating like I want, to not yet surrender to God. Besides, I don't actually even know any nuns. I have no idea how to start figuring out how to be one.

I shelve my feelings and work hard in the college prep program, and within a week I ask my crush—lanky frame, blonde hair—out. Soon, he and I are snuggled together in a chair in a dorm lounge, chatting with a group of friends. The conversation turns to "firsts" and someone offers, "Julia's never been kissed!" Then another tells the lanky guy I'm snuggled with, "Kiss her!" Every eye is on the two of us. I squirm, appalled and embarrassed. I really don't want my first kiss to happen this way. How is this romantic?

But he kisses me. I feel his saliva. And although I try to slow the moment down and enjoy it, there is no bliss or thrill. There's only disappointment.

* * *

Away at college a few months later, I rarely date. Every now and then I find myself alone with men who might be trying to make moves on me, such as the guy who works at the theater and takes me during off-hours to watch a movie in an empty house. But no one kisses me and I don't kiss anyone. I simply enjoy making friends. I don't really get close to anyone that I want to date. I'm too busy to care much about it all.

Then, one evening during senior year, at a casual Wednesday night Mass, I'm sitting with others in a circle in a dim and cozy dorm chapel, singing along with a guitar in the glow of candlelight. Some of us are on big pillows, others on soft chairs; the priest sits among us. I'm listening to the readings and participating in the shared homily along with everyone, but my face is twisted in concern as I look around for Andy and Greg, who are usually here too.

By this time, Andy—compassionate, goofy, and often dressed like a middle-aged professor—is one of my best friends. We met at a picnic I hosted along with others on the resident life staff at the start of the school year, and we quickly clicked. Andy transferred to Loras as a junior and came to the picnic along with Greg.

After the picnic the three of us go back to my dorm room because I offer to share some Amarula liquor I brought back from South Africa with them. We are animated as we talk about our favorite Catholic devotions and saints. They know more than I do, even though we're all cradle Catholics. I tell them what it was like to attend church and volunteer in South Africa, where I just spent a semester abroad. I'm going through reverse culture shock frustrations about American consumerism, and even though I need to process a lot out loud, they get me laughing and help me lighten up.

Greg and I have been friends for over a year by this point. When I first transferred to Catholic liberal arts Loras College from Lutheran Wartburg College—as a history and education major—the first class I attended was "The History of U.S. Catholicism" with four other students—all of them young men. That's when we met.

The classroom door creaks open and in walks Greg, meek and contrite. He tries to enter quietly despite his tardiness, but his tardiness can't be unnoticed in a small group. He's wearing a faded red t-shirt and has a short, shaggy, brown beard. When he sits in the wooden desk next to me, I feel my body pull toward his small frame. Once I realize I'm staring at him, I look at the syllabus in my sweaty hands.

While working in the campus ministry office a few weeks later, I overhear someone say that it is too bad the guys that live in the pre-seminary house can't date. I am surprised to learn that there's a pre-seminary on campus and ask who lives there. "Have you met Greg, yet?" someone asks. "Yeah, I have class with him," I say, my heart clenching with disappointment.

Whenever I see Greg around campus—in the chapel or library—I'm cheery and chatty. I sit with him and other pre-seminarians in a booth in the coffee shop and delight in hearing Greg talk about his love of saints, Christian history, and hear blunt critiques of modernism. He is both sarcastic and rude and also completely reverent and gentle; his complexity is beautiful to me, somehow. Over the semester, a deeper friendship starts to bud, but not enough for us to stay in touch when I move to South Africa the following January. So I'm surprised—and a bit delighted—when I see his name on the list of dorm residents a year later, while working with the other resident assistants getting ready for move-in day. I guess he's decided not to be a priest after all.

Along with Andy, Greg and I get into the habit of meeting up at Wednesday night Mass, so now I am looking around the carpeted candlelit circle chapel, feeling confused, concerned. Where are they?

After Mass, I rush across campus to the dorm building where we all live. I find the two of them in Andy's room. They greet me with slurred speech and start snuggling up to me, putting warm hands on my arm as they speak. Liquor bottles and beer cans are littered among the books, rosaries, and saint statues cluttering Andy's room. The stench of alcohol is strong.

"We are getting drunk because girls are mean," they say. I'm on the floor, Andy is on the bed, Greg is near me, leaning against the bed. I'm disappointed that they skipped Mass to get drunk, but mainly I feel a warm sadness toward them both. I feel an urge to comfort and assure them that not all women are bad. Greg is especially depressed, I find out, because Lily, the girl he'd mentioned he was dating, dumped him. Andy suggested they drink the misery away together. Soon, Andy becomes sick, throwing up all over himself, and together Greg and I haul him off to sit in the shower while we clean things up.

After Greg and I get Andy into bed, we're together in the stairwell before going back to our separate rooms. Greg holds me in his arms, giving me a long tender hug goodnight. He whispers, leaning into my neck, "Can I kiss you? I want to kiss you."

I want to say yes, of course. I want him to kiss me. But I also want to maintain the principles I established for myself back when I was a teen determined to be a good Christian girl: I will only let boyfriends kiss me, not drunk men—not even if they are my friend. No matter how I feel in the moment.

"Not while you're drunk," I say. "Come see me tomorrow and we'll talk about it." I give him a final squeeze and go off to bed. It takes me a long time to fall asleep.

The next night, Greg, now sober, comes to my dorm room and tells me all about his sad breakup with Lily. I listen for a long time because I care for him, feeling scared that we aren't going to come to any resolution about us. So, I remind him of what he said to me in the stairwell.

"Greg, I've liked you ever since our Catholic history class together last year," I say.

He smiles. "You've always made me happy, Julia. Remember how you came over that one time to work on that project?" he says. I nod, remembering how I'd been at the pre-seminary house sitting next to Pat at the dining room table, our laptops and books open. While we were deep in a discussion about progressive Catholic movements, Greg came down the stairs with his hair a mess, seeming drowsy, as if he had just woken up from a nap. I greeted him with a giant smile.

"When I saw you, my awful mood shifted immediately. I felt so happy. I hadn't been to class in weeks," he says.

"Awww," I say, leaning into him, grinning. He has his arm around me. We're sitting on my bed.

"Julia, seeing you motivated me to start going to class again. To start living again." I nod, knowing that he struggles with depression.

I look into his chocolate eyes through his dark-framed glasses, framing the deep dimples under his beard. We start to kiss. Our glasses awkwardly crash into each other. Then I pull away.

"Wait, am I your girlfriend now? I only kiss guys if we're dating," I say, squirming out of his arms.

He laughs and pulls me toward him. "Yes, Julia. I'll be your boyfriend." He kisses me again.

I feel his warm lips on mine and my body hums with electricity. Then we take off our glasses and kiss for several hours, well into the night.

Once Greg leaves my room, I feel like I'm burning with fluorescent light. In the dark, trying to sleep, I imagine that anyone passing by would know that I have a boyfriend now because of the light pouring from under the door.

In class the next day, I draw exclamation marks and smiling faces in my notebook and barely listen to the discussion. *I'm Greg's girlfriend! I'm Greg's girlfriend!* I doodle and delight in the happy, repeated thought.

When I see him in the student union, though, he keeps his distance. I flash a smile, but he continues to frown. My throat feels tight. Why won't he look at me? What's going on?

That night Greg shows up in the doorway of my dorm room, his shoulders slumping, a frown across his face.

"Lily called," he says. "She wants to get back together with me. I told her yes. Sorry, Julia."

* * *

The love I feel for Greg, even as a friend, is deep and strong, but his dismissal of me tests my feelings. Weeks later, when one of our mutual friends throws a party and I'm not included, I confront her and she mumbles that she didn't want both Greg and me to be there. I understand, knowing the tension between Greg and me can be uncomfortable for others to be around.

He hurt me and I'm trying to forgive him, but I'm mad.

I accept the fact that it is easier for my friend to leave me off the guestlist than him—after all, I'm the one working three jobs and trying to write my thesis. But a gloom sinks into the cracks of my broken heart—a gloom that stays with me for months.

* * *

The year prior, while studying in South Africa for a semester, I fly to Namibia to visit Justin and Erastus, two men I came to know a few years earlier when we were counselors at a Lutheran Bible camp. At the end of that summer, I told them I would try to visit them before my thirtieth birthday, and meant it. So, when I ended up studying abroad in South Africa, I *had* to reach out to them. For the first part of Easter break, I visited Erastus and his family; they took me on a beautiful camping trip across Namibia, showing me the Atlantic Ocean and sand dunes and the wonders of the silent desert.

After traveling with Erastus, Justin and a few people from the church where he was pastor picked me up in Windhoek and drove me to northern Namibia to stay with his family for Holy Week. There I ate fresh guava from a backyard tree, heard roosters at sunrise, and saw the sunrise over the desert while stumbling to the outhouse. Family and friends delivered gift after gift to his home for me: homemade pots, baskets, live chickens. Throughout the week, we went from feast to feast in one simple home after another and I came to know the richness of people who live as subsistence farmers in sub-Saharan Africa: their wealth is made of generosity, warmth, graciousness, and they can give endlessly of themselves and their time, no matter what materials they possess. Hospitality comes from scarcity, not abundance, I discovered.

A year and half later, during the extra fall semester while I'm student teaching, Justin comes back to Iowa to study at the local Lutheran seminary across town. We have so much history together. One Sunday, I'm in the car with him, driving through the hills back from Dubuque to Mom and Dad's. Attempting to reciprocate the hospitality I experienced in Namibia, I invite him to come home with me to visit my family, see the farm. Driving through the hills and alongside the steep cliffs near our farm, I tell Justin about my happy childhood memories playing in the rocky pastures and rolling fields. And I start pondering the future.

"Justin, what do you think about me becoming a nun?" I ask tentatively.

"I don't think that would be good for you," he says. "You're too happy and outgoing. I think it'd be awful for you to be stuck inside praying and being quiet all day—"

"No, no. I don't think you get it. I don't want to be that type of nun," I say. I feel a burning in my heart, a crispness in my mind. "I want to be the type that's out in the world, serving the poor. I want to live in community, to live a life of prayer and simplicity. I want to do peace activism and stuff. I really think the best life for me is to be that kind of nun."

I'm surprised to hear confidence in my voice. But I realize right way that I mean what I say. I pause before I speak again.

"I think I'm gonna do it," I say, a few moments later, realizing I don't care that much what Justin thinks.

* * *

Back on campus that afternoon, distracted from grading papers and writing lesson plans, I think about what I told Justin in the car and how it conflicts with my lingering feelings for Greg, who is single again. It seems like Greg still likes me, based on the sweetness of his letters last summer, when we wrote back and forth and rebuilt our friendship. I forgave him for hurting me during his on-again-off-again-with-Lily that left me in the middle of the fiasco. Now I think about him often and each time I do I feel my chest tingle, longing for the next time we're together. God, I feel so alive around Greg.

I'm thinking this through, feeling like I'm tuned into God too. Yes, I just told Justin I want to be a nun, and that felt right and true. At the same time, I love Greg, I think I do. I don't understand why, exactly; he's not very nice to me much of the time, but I think I feel real love for him. Whatever it is I feel, I know it's a steady and deep affection that pushes aside his flaws. I wonder if it's based on the gentleness I observe when he prays, and the reverence I admire when he assists the priest during Mass. I see him bow his head, his eyes closed, his face peaceful.

God, you know I've daydreamed about getting back together with Greg and having a real relationship. I imagine what we would be like as a couple. And you know that every time I think about this, I feel the logical part of my mind win out: there's something about the dynamic between us that's not good for me. Would he stunt my growth somehow? Yeah, I know he pulls on the part of me that likes to please people, and I've encountered a strange new side of myself around him—a kind of subservience. I feel you making it clear to me: Greg and I aren't made to be together. But, wow, I love him, don't I? Love is a mystery to me.

Later, at Sunday evening Mass in the main campus chapel, I kneel in a pew, hands pressed together after receiving communion, thinking and praying about my talk with Justin in the car. As I remember what I said, it feels like a light is flowing through me, pouring in fresh clarity. This is how I want to give my life to you, God. I kneel in the pew and scrunch my eyes shut. God, I mean it. I'm happy to do it. I'll be a nun for you.

On my way out of the chapel, I see Greg, looking adorable like always. He and I stand between the pews at the front of the church and chat. He is melancholy as usual, shoulders hunched, face serious. I'm excited, though, my smile is bright; I'm practically dancing, trembling with joy. "Greg, I realized something big this weekend," I tell him. "I think I want to be a nun! I think God might want me to be one too!"

No words come out of his mouth, but his eyes widen and brighten, his face turns red. He smiles and reaches out, squeezing me tightly. It feels like he is vibrating with joy now too. I've never seen him so happy.

The following day, I'm at mass praying about the recent conversations. God, I think that you and Greg are the greatest loves of my life right now. If the idea of me being a nun makes Greg so happy, then it will probably make you really happy too. I know I want to make you happy, God—more than I want to make him happy. I want you to be pleased with me and my choices. I want to honor you with my life—even if that means giving up dating, kissing: no chance for physical relationships anymore. For you, I will do this.

Around campus afterwards, I start "coming out" to my friends, telling them one by one that I think I will become a nun. I feel nervous, but each time I seem to hear the same response: "Yeah, I know, Julia. I've known for a long time."

It turns out that people have been expecting this of me, and I had no idea.

3

After finishing student teaching and graduating from Loras College, I move out of student housing and temporarily into my parents' place. Andy comes to the farm to get me and now I'm in his car, sitting in the passenger seat. The wheels are crunching over the frozen streets of La Crosse, Wisconsin toward St. Rose Convent, headquarters of the Franciscan Sisters of Perpetual Adoration (FSPA).

Andy met the Sisters the previous summer while his mom was studying at Viterbo, the college the Sisters founded. Shortly after I admitted to friends that I wanted to be a nun, it was Andy who said, speaking of the Sisters: "They're social justice activists who serve the poor and value the arts and academia, plus they're prayerful, devout." I nodded, agreeing that they sounded pretty much like everything I was looking for. I visited a few other convents during college and knew that I wanted a community both contemplative and involved in the world—in touch with both Christ and people.

I called the vocation director, Sister Dorothy, and arranged a visit for a week after December graduation. Although I had my own car and could drive myself just fine, Andy wanted to drive me. I let him, because I love being with Andy, and was touched by this gesture of support.

The river bluffs rise in the East and the Mississippi River lies to the West, as frost forms on the car windows and cheerful chatter exists between us. Andy's mixtape of surfer music, Moby and Morrissey, has been the soundtrack for the hour and one-half since he picked me up at my parents' farm.

We park the car on a La Crosse street, then ring the doorbell at St. Rose Convent. Buzzed in, we climb concrete steps to a receptionist desk where I ask the woman there to please call Sister Dorothy and tell her we've arrived. My body is vibrating with anticipation.

Within a few minutes, a tall woman with permed gray hair wobbles toward me pushing a walker. Her eyes crinkle with light, her face bright with a warm smile. Within seconds I find myself in her long arms, trying to not knock her over as we hug; I feel so bouncy with happiness. "Hey, calm down. You don't want to push me over," she teases. I laugh and apologize. Later, she tells me that, in that moment, she felt her gut say "yes!" She deeply sensed that I would fit in this community of Sisters on the Mississippi River.

Andy promises to pick me up a week later. I tell him thanks and we hug goodbye; then I follow Sister Dorothy through the carpeted hallways of St. Rose to her office.

We settle next to a blue stained-glassed window and I study the itinerary for my visit, a schedule that includes daily Mass, check-ins with Dorothy, meals with different Sisters, a visit to the community archives, a chapel tour, a visit to the Villa St. Joseph (housing the infirm), prayer in the Adoration Chapel, and a tour of the free clinic across the street that the Sisters started. I notice I already feel joyful and relaxed, excited to be here.

An hour or so later, in the formation house—called Chiara House—I join the rhythms of community meals and evening prayer, peppering the women with questions about everything I can think of: daily routines, handling finances, works of ministry, prayer and spirituality, community values. The only novice (a beginner, or newbie) at this time, Sister Sarah, is home from the Common Franciscan Novitiate for her Christmas break. I notice that she seems free and comfortable; she asks me to help move a desk out of storage and into her bedroom, and she puts her feet up in the living room with ease. In fact, one evening after supper and evening prayers, the two of us go to downtown La Crosse to a coffeeshop and sit in a wooden booth gripping warm ceramic mugs, swapping stories. I notice that her teeth are crooked, and she looks plain without makeup, yet comes off as confident and comfortable—beautiful in simplicity and nonconformity to usual codes of beauty. We talk about our attraction to Franciscan Sisterhood and as I get to know her, I can't shake the feeling that I'm with someone familiar, like an old friend. "The more I learn about other communities and hear how other novices are treated, what they're struggling with, the more I believe that FSPA is really the best," she says to me.

That experiential week, I wander around St. Rose Convent and the nearby Viterbo College campus whenever I can. I stop and stare when I come upon a life-size statue of St. Francis of Assisi. His swirling habit is frozen in time, along with his joyful dance. Over his head, he lifts a giant wispy bowl with the shape of a man cut out of it: the body of Jesus Christ. I walk around the statue and study it from each side and notice how sunlight shines through, enlightening St. Francis with the image of Christ. The frosty gray steel glimmers.

Seeing the statue glow, I feel enlightened and frozen in time, both. I'm stunned, realizing that I'm not seeing this statue for the first time. I recognize it as a copy of a statue I danced around at Wartburg College—where I was a student for my freshman and sophomore years. It was at Wartburg that I first was introduced to the depth of Francis of Assisi, where I learned that he was more than an animal lover and nature freak; he was also a model peacemaker and lover of the poor. My college friends told me I was "so Franciscan"; I never understood why, but I felt known and accepted when I heard it. I felt embraced.

I feel the warmth now of this belonging—a groundedness and embrace—as I study the dancing saint and absorb the joy, light, and exaltation of Mystery.

* * *

Later, back in Sister Dorothy's office, I'm sitting next to the stained-glass window when she hands me a small pink book to read. Its matte cover is printed with a sketch of St. Francis and a monstrance on an altar. I recognize the altar as the one in the Adoration Chapel, where the Eucharist is exposed behind glass and upheld by a decorative gold stand—the monstrance—where Sisters keep vigil, taking turns praying every hour of day and night. I felt calm in the silent space of the Chapel earlier. This booklet is the FSPA constitutions, Sister Dorothy explains. "You can borrow this and read it while you're here," she says. I'm distracted by the title on the cover: *Unity in Diversity*.

I tell Sister Dorothy that at Loras I came to value this very phrase, "unity in diversity" as an element of Christian life when I studied the pluralism and diversity in the church. During my first semester at Loras, in that class with Greg and others, I naïvely asked many questions. How different would the Bible be if it had been written by women? Why can't women be ordained priests? I felt confused when one of the men turned red in the face and said I was a heretic and stormed out of the room. I turned to my professor and stupidly asked what a heretic was. The professor laughed. As the course continued and we read books about divisions between Christians with titles like *What's Left?* and *Who's Right?* I understood that the division was so intense in Catholicism that many of its members were essentially praying for peace in the midst of a civil war, and I hated it. My experience in that course, combined with what the Bible taught (diversity is good, meant to enrich us!) led me to put a rainbow button on my backpack emboldened with the words "Unity in Diversity."

Sister Dorothy listens and smiles and agrees with me that the resonance of the constitutions to my own values could be a sign.

Then I meet the famous FSPA sister. In the basement below the main chapel, a feeling of warmth covers me as I encounter the collection of items related to Sister Thea Bowman: paintings, photos, clothing, a wheelchair, robes, and plaques from honorary doctorates she earned. I listen to Sister Jolyce explain that Sister Thea is the only African-American who ever entered the community and she was a gifted preacher, teacher, scholar, and singer. She died at age fifty-two, in 1990, from breast cancer. Illness didn't stop her from serving and living until she died, Sister Jolyce explains; she spoke to the United States Bishops Conference about the Black Catholic experience, and miraculously got them to stand, hold hands, and sing "We Shall Overcome!" I can tell that Sister Thea had a fiery spirit. I do too, I think. If Sister Thea was able to be herself and share her talents as a member of this community, maybe I can too.

At the end of the week, I'm with Sister Anita in the kitchen, helping her make kolaches, a Bohemian sweetbread and her family's

Christmas tradition. My mouth is watering from the scent of baking dough, and her friendly spirit warms the room. I stand at the counter island and spoon poppyseed and apricot filling onto the dough while listening to her stories about life in community, teaching high school science, serving as a pioneering youth minister, and leading a global education program at Viterbo. She speaks with confidence and clarity; I feel her strength and certitude in the cadence of her voice, in how she stands next to me at the counter. Something occurs to me as I listen: both Sister Anita and Thea's lives show that community life allowed them to follow their passions and interests, to offer their gifts in service of the world's needs. No one hides their lights around here. After a while, Sister Anita raises her dark eyebrows and smiles, thanks me for staying in La Crosse to help her bake instead of going back to Iowa to be with my family. "I don't think I would have been doing much at home anyway," I say with a shrug. This feels so natural. And, until she said that, it hadn't occurred to me that I could be anywhere else.

* * *

The week now over, back in the car with Andy, riding over a snow-covered landscape I chatter excitedly about my experiences. I like the Sisters. I know I do. I can imagine my life with them. I think I will apply to join them one day. Maybe when I'm thirty?

"Julia, as I drove here, I imagined all the possible moods that I might find you in, and I thought of all the different ways I might respond to you," Andy says. I laugh, thinking of how he knows all my moods. "But I was unprepared for this. Julia, you're beaming," he says.

"Really?" I say. Then I become silent and look out the window, examining light shining through snow-covered tree branches. Jesus, I know you're up to something with me. I feel the shifts happening in my heart. If I join these Sisters, I'll belong, I'll be free. Won't I? But Jesus, I don't know if I'm ready yet. I need more time. Don't I? I'm not sure, but it's amazing to think I've encountered something that made me glow.

4

I'm not yet sure where I belong, with whom I want to live my life, but I know where I'm from. I'm Elsie and Kevin's daughter. Mom and Dad met as night nurses in an ICU in Alaska in the early 1970s, both far flung from their roots. Dad hitchhiked with a friend from Massachusetts for nursing school; Mom moved there from Iowa to work, because my Uncle Enoch was stationed in Alaska on an Army base.

    I imagine Dad as a hippy, driving a Volkswagen van, sleeping at a commune in the woods. Pictures show Mom smiling into the camera brightly, boots firm on the earth on a hiking trail, a short blond bob and blue eyes, a down vest hanging off her thin frame. I wonder how much they went hiking together while dating in Alaska. They must have fallen in love quickly; I've heard the story that six months after they met, Dad showed up on the Iowa farm to ask Grandpa Hanson for Mom's hand in marriage. Grandpa said yes. Mom came two weeks later. Grandma made some calls; they were married by the Lutheran pastor in Mom's home church on Saturday, and the simple ceremony was followed by coffee with homemade cake.

    Even when he was in his early twenties, Dad looked like he does now: bald, brown beard, thick glasses. He told me he was into transcendental meditation during those days, and that he isn't proud he ventured away from his Irish-Catholic roots. I pretended to understand, wondering why meditation could ever be bad. Before I went to kindergarten, Dad sat in a wooden rocking chair in the farmhouse, with me snug in his lap, a Bible open. He read aloud slowly, pointing at every word. Later, when my teachers realized that I could already read, I told them Dad taught me.

When he was home from work at the hospital, he never seemed too busy to listen, pausing from milking the goats in the barn or unloading wood from his truck. I'd interrupt and ask about whatever was on my mind. Where does water come from? Why are leaves green? Why are other kids so mean? In response, he'd tell a joke, story, offer a philosophical tidbit or a science lesson—sometimes connected to Christian principles. I couldn't have said it in those days, but Dad was—and is—an informal pastoral minister, happy to muse on the meaning of life with anyone, swap stories and wisdom, share compassion. He taught me how to offer quality presence, to be a host.

Tickled by one of Dad's jokes or something that crossed her mind, Mom could erupt with laughter at any time of day. The sound of her joy filled the house, echoed across the farm; her spine convulsed; she wiped snot and tears from her red face. What's so funny, Mom? Oh, I can't explain, but ooooh, I'm going to pee my pants! Struggling to breathe, still laughing, she'd grip her lower stomach and rush out of the room. In quieter times, she'd summon me to her side in the kitchen and show me how to measure flour and sugar, sift, stir—make dough. Cookies, breads, bars would go into the oven, and then come out warm and gooey, filling our mouths, bellies. House-cleaning wasn't as regular, but Mom taught me that too: I learned how to polish floorboards, make sinks sparkle, dust wooden windowsills. I understood that everyone had to do chores. Everyone had to pitch in.

A sloping yard surrounded our farmhouse and spilled down the hill into the barnyard, pastures, then a creek below a cliff. Built into a hollow, the farmstead included fruit trees, bushes, a large barn, a summer kitchen (used as a woodshed), a welding shop, windmill, and a crumbling granary and stable. Along with surrounding pastures, woods, and nearby fields, each building provided the safest playground that my siblings and I could want.

In my earliest memories, I'm four years old and studying the grass under the clothesline on a bright sunny day. Probably prompted by a lesson I learned at the public library story hour, I'm thinking about the number of languages in the world. *There are more languages in the world than I can count! Can I know all the languages when I grow up? No, not if there's hundreds or thousands of them, numbers I can't even count to. Is there anyone in the world that knows every language? No one could. Except, God does. God can understand everyone!* My heart and mind were burst with wonder.

I ran to the house to tell the nearest person I could find the good news. Skipping through the front porch into the kitchen, the screen door banging behind me, Mom stood over the stove stirring something in a pot. "Mom! God knows every language in the world!" I proclaimed. "Yes, that's right," she said, smiling. "Very good, Julia."

On an ordinary day, Mom didn't hesitate to take breaks. Was she praying while boiling tea water in the middle of the afternoon? While selecting her mug? Was she showing me how to contemplate when inviting me to join her on the couch and sip hot herbal liquid? We'd look through the window, up the hill and into the lilac bushes: Do you see the blue jay, Julia? Don't the bleeding hearts look pretty dancing in the sunlight?

Dad was a goat farmer, nurse, husband, and father of four, but none of that made him too busy to join the cast of *The Music Man*, performed on the high school gym stage during a town festival in July. As a second grader, I tagged along, singing and dancing in the community scenes. Along with county fairs, summer festivals and musicals, the social texture of our farming community consisted of extracurricular art and sports activities. The whole district, preschool through twelfth grade, was on one campus: cornfields and pastures nestled beside playgrounds and athletic fields. Crowd-filled bleachers for Saturday wrestling tournaments in the middle of winter. People young and old sitting on metal folding chairs for band and choir concerts, speech tournaments, plays, musicals. At a basketball game, track meet, or football game it seemed like every high schooler was either a spectator or playing a part: if not competing then in the pep band, running concessions, on the dance squad, or part of the cheer team. I wasn't the only cheerleader who marched with the band during halftime shows in my cheerleading uniform, gripping my flute in chilly temperatures.

I wanted to be sporty, but my myopic and asthmatic body made me into a pathetic athlete, so I became serious about cheerleading, considering it my sport from seventh to twelfth grade. As a cheerleader I felt powerful, influential: the better I flipped and twirled my body, the louder I yelled, the more people stood and clapped.

But I grew up in the shadow of Hans, my older brother. A star pitcher on the baseball team, a fast running back, decent trumpet player, he was also respectful, smart, popular, and playful. I liked him, but in many ways, my brother was a mystery. I never doubted Hans cared for me, and would stick up for me if I wanted him to, but I never told him how my throat tightened and my chest squirmed when kids chanted "Walsh! Walsh! Walsh!" stomping on the bleachers during pep rallies. I knew they were cheering for him, as I clapped my pom-poms and swirled my short blue cheerleading skirt. I was proud of him and his talent, but did people know me?

If the threads of community social life consisted of school extracurriculars, then the Christian churches dotting the intersections of Elgin, Clermont, Wadena—and country roads in the valleys and hills in between—created the loom of spiritual life. The whole school district had one Catholic church, in the center of Clermont, where Mom and Dad took us each week.

I've been going to church every Sunday my whole life. Crowded into a pew, saying the prayers, holding hands, singing songs, receiving communion, right alongside Mom, Dad, Hans, Ellen, and Colleen. We would discuss the Mass as a family in the van on the way home, asking questions, saying what we thought about the homily, as Dad drove along hilly pastures and alfalfa fields back to the farm.

As a high schooler, I wanted to be good, to please God and my parents. Alone in my bedroom, I underlined verses in my Bible that gave me moral guidance, helped me know I needed to respect authority, obey laws, not steal, be pure. I wanted to be popular, like Hans, but was uninterested in what other teens did for fun. I was afraid to mouth off to adults, to drink, smoke, swear. When friends at school tried to pressure me to join them, I said "my parents will kill me," without thinking about how the phrase was violent, my fears overly dramatic.

More than religiosity, Mom and Dad emphasized forgiveness, faith, kindness, inclusion, and other Christian values—feed the hungry, shelter the homeless, live simply, be a peacemaker—in the way they coached us to handle conflicts and to be grateful instead of materialistic. They made do and got by; reminded us that other people couldn't afford luxuries and trendy toys; the hand-me-down clothing and off-brand toys could work fine, right? Each summer they took us to a cheap motel on the outskirts of a midwestern city for a few days—Minneapolis, Milwaukee, Chicago—and exposed us to the vibrancy of urban life. We spent hours enthralled with the size of public libraries, visited parks, free zoos, skyscrapers. When we were in restaurants, we didn't pray together before meals, but we did when we sat together around the kitchen table in the farmhouse. Like bedtime prayers, meal prayers were simple and sweet, part of the rhythm of a day.

* * *

When I was student teaching in Dubuque, Hans lived with a friend in Arizona. I called him to say I was thinking about being a nun, that I was going to visit the Franciscans in La Crosse after graduation. Hans, what will you think if I join the convent? I'll support you, he said, and I heard the sincerity in his voice. What if I end up leaving, will you be ashamed, think of me as a quitter? No, whatever you decide is fine. Julia, I love you, I'll always support you. That's how I remember it.

Before and after I visit the Franciscans in La Crosse for a week, I talk to Mom, Dad, Ellen, and Colleen too. "I think I found the group I'm going to join," I say, excitedly, "I just don't know when." They listen, ask questions, encourage me to follow my heart; no one seems surprised. I think about how I may have found the right community, but I'm not sure yet. I tell everyone, "I want to have a few more experiences first, more adventures before I settle down." I can't really tell what Mom thinks of this, but she agrees it's a good idea to wait, to get a job or travel or something. Dad tells me that he's asked his hospice patients to pray for my vocation.

I do get a job, briefly, an internship with the Iowa Catholic Conferences in Des Moines, where I live in a simple furnished apartment for a few months. There, I fill out the application for the Jesuit Volunteer Corps (JVC) and as I do I check my motives. Joining JVC is a way to give religious life a trial run, I figure. The structure of JVC (and other service programs like it) is based on religious life: a group will live simply in an intentional community, serve the poor, and pray together. I expect JVC to look and feel like Catholic Sisterhood, but I'm glad it's only for a year. Much easier than giving up my whole life. So, I pack my bags and go to Sacramento, California in August for a year, excited to meet new people, experience a new place, see what God has to show me.

5

After an orientation retreat, my new housemates and I arrive to a fully stocked, crumbling and stained house. We laugh and holler "Look what I found!" opening cupboards and closets, discovering all that's been left behind by the previous year's volunteer community: books, candles, notes, snacks, tacky house décor. Our house is called Casa Jane Addams, for the social worker, activist, and founder of Hull House in Industrial Revolution-era Chicago. I look through the dining room window and see an old fire station across the street repainted with bright colors. I look closer and see that it's been converted into a social services center. The first weekend, I take a walk around the Sacramento neighborhood of Oak Park, feeling amused by handmade "No Hooking" signs hanging on light poles.

Casa Jane Addams is made up of six women full of ideals: each raised Catholic, everyone up for adventure. E-Beth, Tines, Peg, Mayr, and Trishy are all from the East Coast, recently graduated from schools whose names intimidate me: Fordham, Georgetown, Boston College. Because of my midwestern and working-class roots, I often feel like an oddball. They start calling me J-Ballz (because of my courage?), making me laugh.

Our shared values (spirituality, community, social justice and service) and weekly rhythms (taking turns cooking supper and leading spirituality and community nights) make for a meaningful life together. In many ways, we pray and party hard: we drink, dance, date—all while accompanying people on the margins of society. The communal beats of joy energize our full-time volunteer work for different nonprofits. I serve with formerly homeless young adults and their children at a transitional living program at a place called Tubman House.

Within a few weeks, we realize that an awkward group of guys live next door, students at a nearby Bible college. One night during a drunken 2 a.m. cab ride from The Press Club downtown, we are talking about how funny it is that we don't associate with these guys who are about the same age as us. So when we get home, Tines scribbles a note saying, "We really want to be friends," and leaves it on their doorstep. We laugh and wonder if anything will come of it. Months later, they show up with expensive coffee drinks on a Friday night and sit around our dining room table, talking about the Bible—trying to convert us away from our Catholic faith and questionable morals.

Mid-September we pile into a van and go to San Francisco for a party hosted by another JVC community. In the crowded apartment, I feel myself looping back toward a cute man: he's small framed and thin, his choppy dark hair hangs over his eyes. I feel curious about his funky style: he's wearing a snug, faded t-shirt along with unique vintage jeans. He isn't in JVC—"I heard from my friend there was a party, so I came over," he says. I keep returning to the drink table and each time I move through the apartment I look for him. His face says that he notices me too.

We get to talking. His name is Brandon. He is a math teacher at a fashion school. My cheeks get warm. I say I need to find my friends. But, going back for another drink, I look for him again, wondering what type of math fashion students need to know, what's the strangest clothing his students ever made? I never make it back to E-Beth and Mayr, but they see me talking with Brandon and smile, raising their eyebrows.

We sit together on a couch in a dark living room. He leans in. "Julia, can I kiss you?" he asks. I say sure, and enjoy the kiss, although all the while I'm thinking about God. Have I misunderstood God's guidance until now? The kissing doesn't last long, but Brandon and I exchange numbers and start talking a lot on the phone.

A few weeks later he drives to Sacramento and comes to Casa Jane. Omigosh, my first real date, finally! I run out to his car, forgetting my keys. He tries to open the car door for me, and I say I can open and close my own doors, thank you very much.

We drive to a fancy restaurant where I order creamy pasta and we both argue and flirt: how can men be chivalrous *and* not make assumptions about what women want and need? We end up at the theater watching a movie that neither of us care about: we kiss and kiss, instead, in the darkness. Walking back to his car, Brandon suggests that he could pay for a hotel room for the night. I could stay with him. My shoulders clench and my brain feels mushy. "No thank you," I say, but then can't stop wondering what's going on. I don't think he'll hurt me, but I know I better explain some of my morals to him. Do that later, I decide. Now, I want to have fun. So, Brandon spends the night snuggling with me in my twin bed at Casa Jane, and I delight in feeling him close.

* * *

My Casa Jane housemates are applying to grad school: we celebrate every acceptance letter that comes to our mailbox. One evening, E-Beth asks me what I think I'll do after JVC ends in August and I feel dizzy thinking through the options. She sits on a couch and listens while I spin in circles on the stained living room carpet. I stand in one spot and tell her that I want to go to graduate school, but I'm not sure how I'll afford it. Then I move to another spot and say I want to backpack in Europe and might go if I can find work abroad. "But, I think I could end up poor and pregnant if I did that," I sigh. Then I spiral across the room and speak about the option that feels like a destiny I want to avoid: "Or, I could enter the Franciscan Sisters. But I'm not sure I want to, yet."

Away from everyone and everything familiar in California for that year, my heart is filled with longing: not for family, friends, or the farm in Iowa, but for being with the Sisters. When a newsletter comes in the mail from the convent, I read the whole thing as fast as I can, my heart racing, happy. Then I re-read it again, trying to memorize details so I can ask Sister Dorothy about them during our next phone chat.

When I'm driving around Sacramento in the dusty and worn-out van, I daydream about the chapel in La Crosse. I don't know what I want, but I *do* want to go back to pray with the Sisters. Sure, Brandon is cute, but my heart is already in La Crosse.

* * *

In April, my Casa Jane housemates and I go to a Catholic social justice conference in Sacramento. With the freshness of spring in the air, we sit in the back of an auditorium filled with old people and listen to a theology lecture. I am enamored, enthralled, impressed: listening feels like guzzling a nutritious nectar; intelligent words of poetry, ancient wisdom, and hope float over me like a curtain of peace, commission me to advocate for change, accompany the oppressed. It feels as if I'm within a flow of invisible coziness, a warm shower of sunlight. A strength fills my bones, I breathe deeply. I listen with my ears, my mind, my heart: I feel Jesus near, like his hand is resting on my leg. I stare at my jeans: What's up, Jesus?

The next morning, I'm barely awake as I stupor toward the shower. Standing under the water, I hear a steady voice mutter, "I want to begin formation." What? That confidence is *my* voice. I'm startled awake. I know this message has bubbled up from a quiet corner inside my heart, the shy space where Christ provides plans. It is time to apply to the Franciscan Sisters. Is this really me talking? I call Brandon and tell him I don't want to see him anymore, trying to dismiss the guilt that stirs—but he doesn't sound fazed by my decision.

Every step in the extensive application process puts me into conversation with Jesus. I feel Jesus nudging, checking, even flirting: "Are you sure, Julia, you want to give up dating and the chances of ever being married, all for the love of me?" I can hear it, but without sound. I don't know how else to process it. No, I'm not sure, Jesus, I pray simply back, but I'm sure I want to start formation with the Sisters. I feel like he is encouraging, agreeing: yes, that's right.

Then, after months of waiting, when my phone rings and I finally hear Sister Lucy Ann say, "Yes, you're admitted to the Franciscan Sisters of Perpetual Adoration"—I'm overjoyed, ecstatic. I understand the gladness I feel to be a confirmation that my life is moving in the right direction. So shortly after Christmas I move into Chiara House in La Crosse and begin a formal trial period called the Associate Phase.

6

Less than two weeks after settling into Chiara house in La Crosse, I'm with Sister Anita in the living room, journaling in the glow of the soon-to-come-down Christmas tree on a quiet January afternoon. A simple prayer ceremony was held to mark my entrance, to ritualize that I was starting my formation. I'm slowly immersing into the life, living with the Sisters and developing relationships. This quiet moment in the living room is a rare pause in an otherwise packed schedule. Most days I rush around between theology classes, Mass, meetings, a part-time job at a deli downtown (since I'm not a member of the community, I have to cover my personal expenses), and meals in the convent dining hall or in Chiara House with Sister Anita and our other housemate, Sister Mary Louise.

Most days, it feels like my mind and heart are stuck in a constant spin, as I try to adjust to convent culture. Sisters can be so quiet and serious, I often feel like a misfit. I'm only twenty-four years old and they are much older than me; most are *at least* triple my age. Though things are new and exciting, it's boring too—nothing like living with my friends in Casa Jane.

Questions, frustrations, and irritations boil in me as I think about conversations I've already had. Comments like "Balance," "Love the creation that God made as you," and "Pray a lot"—feel condescending, belittling, annoying. Do they think I would have come, and given up my independence, if I didn't already have a regular prayer life, already have a life oriented to God? The worst thing a Sister said to me: "When I was your age, I too was concerned with holiness and sainthood." Isn't that the point? Or was there a judgment—"hush, patience child"—coming through? I'm unsure, struggling and wondering if I really fit among these women, scribbling tangled thoughts onto the pages of my journal to gain a bit of release.

When I let myself think about it, I know I can learn a lot from women who have accepted me into their life, who are letting me live with them as I try to figure out if I want to stay. They have evolved with the Catholic Church and Franciscan Sisterhood during decades of commitment: they know what it means to stick with something good no matter how confusing or messy things may be. Their advice comes from the sanctity of their memories and experiences.

But in this January moment, in the quiet living room with Sister Anita, I only want to scream. I'm sick of being talked to as if I don't know anything, as if I haven't lived before coming here.

So I close the journal and study its cover. There's the blue of a waterfall photo, an artistic image of three overlapping women with arms outstretched in shades of orange and pink. I ponder the quote pasted next to the pictures, in shades of blue, white, black, and gray, a magazine clipping and a Virginia Woolf quote that reads, "And that was what she often felt the need of—to think; well not even to think. To be silent; to be alone. All the being and doing, expansive, glittering, vocal, evaporated; and one shrunk, with a sense of solemnity, to be oneself…. When life sank down for a moment, the range of experience seemed limitless."

My Casa Jane housemates gave me this homemade journal as a gift for my birthday. Tines made the collage on the cover and the first five pages are brightened with each of their colorful handprints and a cheery birthday blessing written in bright magic marker. As I flip through the pages, my face falls into a frown. I miss my friends and the life we had together.

I came here because I want my life to have more depth, to feel deeply rooted; deepness and roots often felt lacking in Casa Jane; we were only a temporary intentional community and our commitments were fleeting. My hunger for more is part of what inspired me to apply to become a Sister. I want to learn how to be alone, to be fully myself. Now that I'm here, though, I long for peers.

The night that Casa Jane gave me the journal, a construction paper crown was crammed on top of my choppy dyed hair when I got home from work: the words "Birthday nun" in a banner across my forehead, my glasses removed, a blindfold pressed over my eyes. When I could see again, I was overjoyed to be at the Cheesecake Factory and able to feast on my fatty favorites. There was a surprise party back at our house when we returned, where I couldn't stop smiling while dancing and singing along with the soundtrack to *Sister Act*. I can't imagine the Sisters here ever being that fun.

The Christmas tree glows, and I write in my journal. Sister Anita sits quietly nearby, her eyes closed and a half-smile across her face—probably praying. I never say anything to her about my doubts because I don't want to disturb her peace. I don't want to disturb the calm in the convent.

7

Sometimes on weekends I borrow a community car and drive a few hours to visit my college friends, Hillary and Angela. I go out to bars with them, get a little tipsy and roll my eyes at anyone who tries to flirt with me. Away from the Sisters, I remember how when I was about to enter the community, the Sister-psychologist interpreting my psychological tests recommended that I be able to remain in frequent contact with old friends, that peer support would remain important. I think of this a lot. Am I trying to justify my behavior, though? Am I escaping from something I don't like? With friends, I'm able to do things I don't do with the Sisters—go to bars, browse in shops—things I miss having as regular parts of life.

St. Patrick's Day weekend, I take the train to Chicago to meet up with Casa Jane friends for a wild reunion. Everyone else flies in from their grad schools on the East Coast, or from Sacramento where they are living and working. All six of us pile into a hotel room downtown. The first night, Friday, we cram into a cab and ask the driver to take us somewhere good for dancing and try out a few bars. Saturday, we mix in with crowds drinking on the streets and marvel at the weirdness of the Chicago River dyed green. Then we take a cab to the Hull House Museum, to honor the patron "saint" of our community, Jane Addams. It was the birthplace of social work, Trishy reminds us (she is always full of facts).

Saturday night, I drink gin martinis in the hotel lobby and listen as my friends talk about their boyfriend dramas, graduate studies, and jobs. I smile and laugh, feeling happy, yet my mind drifts in and out, as does my heart. I feel different, out of place again. My new life is poles apart from drinking with age-mates in an elegant hotel. I realize I suddenly feel drained and miss the quiet, simplicity, and solitude of Chiara House.

"I'm going to go find somewhere to pray alone for a little bit," I say to the group. "I'll catch back up with you in twenty or thirty minutes."

I find my prayer book and go into an empty stairwell to pray the Divine Office, the evening prayer of the worldwide Catholic Church, like I'm learning to do with the Sisters. I recite the psalms aloud and chant the Magnificat—Mary's song of justice and peace that I am falling in love with—that inspires me to be a woman who uplifts the poor and lowly, like her song says.

> My soul magnifies the Lord,
> and my spirit rejoices in God my Savior,
> for he has looked with favor on the lowliness of his servant.
> Surely, from now on all generations will call me blessed;
> for the Mighty One has done great things for me,
> and holy is his name.
> His mercy is for those who fear him
> from generation to generation.
> He has shown strength with his arm;
> he has scattered the proud in the thoughts of their hearts.
> He has brought down the powerful from their thrones,
> and lifted up the lowly;
> he has filled the hungry with good things,
> and sent the rich away empty.
> He has helped his servant Israel,
> in remembrance of his mercy,
> according to the promise he made to our ancestors,
> to Abraham and to his descendants forever. *(Luke 1:46-55, NRSV)*

But back in La Crosse, a few days later, I find it difficult to engage in community life. The few other young Sisters don't seem to have much in common with me; they are serious and quiet. They already have their established groups. I'm unsure they want me around. We talk. I'm polite and friendly at community gatherings, but I spend more time alone or talking on the phone with old friends who live out of town than getting to know these Sisters. When friends on the phone ask how I'm doing I say, "Actually, I'm pretty miserable."

8

I have always loved two movies about nuns: *The Sound of Music* and *Sister Act*. They introduced me to religious life. More than anything else, they first put the thought in my head that "If God wants me to do that, I'll say yes," as I admitted to classmates in the fourth grade.

In both movies, I saw nuns—women with diverse personalities living together, praying together, focused on God. That was attractive to me, and the value of such a lifestyle made sense. Watching them over and over as a teen, I eventually realized that the picture painted in *Sister Act* was the more attractive: Sisters living among the poor, serving the marginalized of society, even though it took an intruder, an outsider—Whoopi Goldberg's character—to spark life into them. I liked the idea of serving and being among the poor better than being cloistered and removed from society, like the nuns were in *The Sound of Music*.

There were problems with me being introduced to religious life through these films, though. Both were Hollywood depictions of religious life and emphasized nun-ish stereotypes: there's great piety and purity, there's a token grumpy Sister, they always wear habits, and are interested in conformity. None of these realities, I am learning, are actually true.

A lot changed after the reforms of the Catholic Church in the 1960s, after a Church council called Vatican II reformed much about how Sisters live (veils and habits no longer required; Mass no longer in Latin; the Church no longer an institution, but the Body of Christ serving the world). I have a lot to learn and have to take stock of my stereotypes, to evaluate how they are creating certain expectations. For example, very much a post-Vatican II cradle Catholic, I was initially shocked that not all women in religious life wore habits and veils.

It also takes me a while to catch on to the fact that "nun" and "sister" don't mean the same thing. Nuns live a life of prayer and work, *ora et labora*, mostly behind monastery walls, away from the world. Sisters live "in the world," with service and simplicity, to witness God's love to others, while also sharing a life of prayer together. As I learn more about this, I pray for openness and curiosity so that I won't become disappointed, because real religious life isn't much like the movies.

More challenging to my process is how both *The Sound of Music* and *Sister Act* involved themes of hiding and self-discovery, of gaining a better understanding of who the character is and what lifestyle is the best fit. *Sister Act* presented a convent as a place to hide, since the community agreed to take in Whoopi Goldberg's character as part of a witness protection program. Now that I am inside a convent, I sometimes find myself wondering if I am trying to hide from something too.

For its part, *The Sound of Music* complicated my search for belonging, with its themes of coming and going, of discovering love outside the convent. I always identified with the character of Maria, her carefree playfulness—*she climbs a tree and scrapes her knee, her dress has got a tear*—and creative, fierce determination to what is best for the children in her care. I could easily imagine myself in her shoes, especially in the early part of the film when she leaves the convent to be a governess and then causes an upset to the norms of the household with her joyful, nonconforming behavior. She teaches the children to sing and sews them play clothes out of ugly curtains. She stands up for the children to their father, the captain: *they want you to love them!* In many ways, I am probably hoping I might become a strong woman like her.

The trouble is that Maria's time outside the convent as a governess and caring for the kids has drastic implications: she falls in love and leaves the convent, ends up becoming a completely different person. Then she resists the romance too: desperately wanting to remain a

Sister, trying to escape back to the convent—again a hiding place—once she realizes she is falling in love with a man.

Now inside the convent myself, I wonder if a desire to be like Maria is influencing and complicating my discernment. Do I so much want to be like the strong woman Maria was, that I am avoiding figuring out who *I* am, who I am meant to be? Am I looking around for the man I will fall in love with, who will take me away from the convent and make me into a mother and wife?

When I am honest, I can admit that these questions are often humming in the background of my heart and mind, nudging at me for attention. I hate these questions, though, so I don't let myself think about them. I hate how the questions reflect my main fear: misunderstanding God's guidance. I am not willing to admit that some film narratives shape my ideals and dreams and are distracting me from being fully present to this new religious lifestyle. I don't want to think about it. So I don't.

9

Shortly after Easter, I'm back in Chicago for a week-long social justice workshop called Urban Plunge. Along with a couple dozen other men and women, most of whom are also young adult Catholics starting their life with different religious communities, I'm learning from speakers and field trips around the city designed to teach us about social justice and ministry. We cram into mini-vans and visit community centers, urban gardens, shelters.

In this group is Mike, a Franciscan postulant. In his brown Franciscan habit, bearded face, and slightly balding head he looks like a stereotypical religious, almost iconic—like a monk cookie jar I once spotted in a gift shop. With that look, I assume he is probably terribly traditional, unlike me. So I don't think much of him, at first.

Then, during a casual dinner, Mike is listening while Sister Anne—a young Sister in another community—and I chat over the table about the challenges of adjusting to religious life culture and meeting our Sisters' expectations. I tell her I am shocked to learn that my elders dislike the fact that I wear blue jeans to daily Mass, and ask if this is her experience too. We devour guacamole, salsa, and tortilla chips and our conversation broadens: could God desire that religious life become something more radical than traditional, in order to respond to the needs of our communities? Mike and others around the table start chiming in, sharing hopes and struggles; we become animated and energized, leaning in, standing up, our volume increasing.

At one point, Mike turns and speaks quietly only to me, a sad grin coloring his heart-shaped, chalk-colored face. Behind dark-rimmed glasses, tears flood his deep brown eyes. "This is the first time since I entered, that I feel like I fit. I really am struggling with religious life. I'm not sure about the vow of celibacy."

I'm surprised to hear this, and even more surprised by a sudden need to hold him, comfort him, which I resist. I'm saddened by his ache and touched by the vulnerability he offers me so quickly. I realize that I have been completely judgmental; his traditional monk-look has little to do with who he really is. His questions are the same as mine, and I feel an immediate intimacy.

As the week continues, I'm drawn toward Mike. I want to be near him as much as I can, I realize, my throat tightening with guilt and confusion. On the last night, a small group of us—two Jesuits from southern Africa, Sister Anne, Mike, and me—camp out in a nearby Starbucks having a hearty discussion. We end up moving from there to a park, then on to a bar. We spend the whole evening bonding, drinking coffee and beer, laughing, telling stories, and sharing our hearts.

Saying goodbye the next day, I promise to stay in touch with everyone in the new little group. "Have you joined Facebook yet? Find me on there and be my friend!" I ask Mike for his address and tell him I will write him a *palanca* (Greek for "wedge," meaning, to open a door), a spiritual letter of support that I was introduced to during retreats in high school and college. I give everyone in our group my phone number, even though I really just want to know Mike better. I don't want the others to think I'm singling him out and treating him differently.

Riding the train back to La Crosse, I think about Mike's beauty. I'm surprised by the attraction I feel to him because his body is shaped differently than other men I've crushed on. Even so, I feel shimmery, happy, as I think about him. My shoulders soften as I remember how I felt warmth exude from him toward me too. I write in my journal about sexual chemistry, wondering how I'd know if we have it. Why, God, have you put Mike in my life when I'm already feeling doubt? What is your will for me? Is my future supposed to include this man—this Franciscan friar?

* * *

Months later, I'm on the phone with Mike, hearing the sound of his deep, gentle voice. If I was nervous after the phone rang and I heard him say hello, now my nerves are soothed; my face stretched into a cheery grin, feeling glad for attention from him. He's saying he's decided to leave the Capuchin Franciscans—the Caps—and move back to his home state of Colorado.

"Oh yeah?" I try to sound cool. But in my heart and mind I feel an avalanche of questions rolling around. What's really going on? Do I have anything to do with his choice to leave?

Afterwards, I think more about the change in Mike's life and find myself daydreaming about leaving the Sisters to date him. Immediately I feel dumb and start praying: Am I ridiculous and irrational, God? I don't know how he feels about me. I'm not sure how I really feel about him. I *do* know that I'm lucky to be with the Sisters, and I don't really want to leave the convent. So, I'll stay.

Yes, the first few months living with the Sisters have been tough and confusing. I wonder if Sister Lucy Ann, the Sister supervising my formation, realizes I've been unhappy when she suggests I go live with other Sisters in Minneapolis for the summer. But then, quickly, I look forward to the suggested change. And in the heat of June, I arrive at the house where Sister Sarah now lives with Sisters Eileen and Linda.

On the sunlit porch, Sister Sarah greets me warmly, exposing crooked teeth as she smiles. She helps me put things in my new bedroom and then shows me around. "Here's where we watch TV and movies together… Here's where we eat together… Sometimes we pray here, but most of the time we pray on the porch or in the living room." With Sister Sarah, I feel like I'm with a friend again; she is so much closer in age to me than Sisters Anita and Mary Louise. I feel a hope move into my heart, a lightness upon my shoulders. I know I can be happy here.

As the days and weeks unfold in Minneapolis, the Sisters show me how Franciscan Sisterhood is a life of freedom and discovery. Sister Sarah shows me how to be honest about my struggles each time she admits something that weighs on her during our weekly house meetings. Sister Eileen, a nurse with spiky brown hair and a recent graduate from acupuncture school, shows me that it's possible to be innovative and try new ways to serve the poor. Sister Linda is a bit older—"a late vocation"—who came to the community after being married twice and having two sons and converting to Catholicism; she always looks good in fashionable clothes and makeup; she helps me see that it is possible to remain myself and still fit into community.

I get a summer job as a summer program instructor for the University of Minnesota Upward Bound program, using my teaching degree and working with low-income youth again. For the first time since entering community, I feel like I am doing meaningful work that matches my experience and education, that I'm sharing my gifts. I love it. I feel happy again.

It doesn't take long to realize that with Sisters Sarah, Eileen, and Linda I've found the type of intentional community that I came to the Sisterhood hoping for. We share our cooking and meals, share prayer and chores, and have weekly house meetings. I get to contribute to the community and be an equal participant and not just adjust and try to meet the expectations of others. I get to give my input about how things work. I feel free to be myself. After 8pm I'm not consumed by loneliness like I had been in La Crosse; I'm often with one of the Sisters, talking or watching TV, playing board games and laughing. I'm living with friends. Plus, it is great to live with Sisters who share my desire to become a peaceful presence in a neighborhood of need.

The large house we share is on a drug corner in the inner city, not far from Lake Street. Our neighbors across the street have painted the words "Pagans unite!" over the door of their forest green house. Nearby, Hmong and Latino children often play together. Once, while Sister Sarah and I are grilling our dinner in the backyard, we witness a police raid at the house next door, including assault rifles. They tell us to go inside. Another time, I hear Native American music echoing down the street coming from the home of the Elvis impersonator whose costumes hang on the clothesline at the end of the block. Feeling curious, I ask him about the music and learn that his next gig is to dance at a pow-wow. Among the diversity and activity, I feel energized and alive; I have found a home.

I'm not expected to pay rent or contribute groceries, nor pay tuition at the graduate school where I'm taking a theology course.

Anything that is part of my formation process the Sisters pay for, freeing me up to learn the way of life, be immersed in the community—but still come and go as I please. In a way, this freedom means I'm able to save up enough money to do something I wanted to do for years: get a tattoo.

* * *

When I was eighteen and working at Bible camp in Iowa, I started doodling Christian symbols on my foot with Sharpie markers, trying to decide what sort of tattoo I wanted. Most of the time, I doodled an *Ichthys*, the fish symbol that contributed to the spread of Christianity in the early church when it was a subversive, illegal movement in the Roman Empire. Legend says that when Christians would encounter others in public they would doodle with their feet in the sand and draw a fish on the ground. If the other person noticed and was also a Christian, they would interpret the code and draw an image in return while continuing the conversation. Then, each would know that the other was Christian, a safe person to talk to about matters of faith and life and death. The symbol was a fish because the word for fish in Greek, *Ichthys*, was an acronym for "Jesus Christ God's Son and Savior," which is itself a bold, subversive statement from an era when Caesar was considered the Son of God and the government mandated he be worshiped as such.

Over the last thirty years or so, the Jesus fish was popularized by capitalistic Christianity. It was the type of Christianity that was excessive in the United States and encouraged believers to declare their faith with a car decal, or as jewelry around the neck, or on a wrist as a WWJD (What Would Jesus Do?) bracelet—any trinket that a well-intended Christian could purchase at a Christian bookstore. I was one of those well-intended ones. I had an Ichthys pasted on the back of my rusty car during college. I wore my purple and white WWJD bracelet into threads after keeping it steadily on my wrist for a year, then transferred it into my Bible as a bookmark. I found some security in my identity as a Christian, some sense of belonging among the Christian brand.

But when I lived with my Casa Jane housemates in Sacramento,

I discovered that, although my faith was genuine and real, it wasn't the typical evangelical type. I wasn't out to convert anyone; my desire was to accompany as a loving companion, as I believed Jesus would do. Even so, I was unapologetically Catholic (still am), grateful for the sacraments, energized and steadied by ritual and structure, passionate about diversity—the broadness and variety that make us a truly universal Church. That year in JVC, I admitted to my supervisor at Tubman House, Bridget—a Catholic, lesbian, and mother to triplets—that I wanted to get a Jesus fish tattooed on my foot once I could afford it. I found her response challenging, provocative.

"You aren't one of those types of Christians. You aren't a Bible thumper. You should get something else, something more symbolic and unique, like a cup of wine or loaf of bread," Bridget said.

Before I moved to Minneapolis, I started to schedule myself away from community less and less, as religious life was deepening within me. I noticed this and made a remark to Sister Anita as I stood in front of the kitchen calendar. Sister Anita responded, "Find a way to ritualize the change within you." So I started thinking about the tattoo. A permanent marking on my body would show that sharing life in community has changed me, that I am OK with how my experience so far can't be undone.

I hadn't yet decided if I would enter the novitiate next May and go through the formal ceremony, marking my entrance into the next stage of incorporation. I was still daydreaming about Mike and wondering if I should leave the community to date him. Yet, I wanted to invent my own ritual, to mark an acceptance of the shifts I was feeling inside. No matter what was going to happen—stay with the Sisterhood or leave—a tattoo of bread might remind me how living in community is its own type of holy food. Whatever the future is to hold, the impact of sharing my life with the Sisters could never be erased. But my tattoo wouldn't be a Jesus fish. It would be that loaf of bread.

* * *

A few weeks after my twenty-fifth birthday, two college friends, Hillary and Angela, come to Minneapolis to visit for the weekend. I'm happy to have people who really love and get me be part of the night when I permanently mark up my body. Before leaving for the tattoo parlor, we all gather in the dimly lit living room, a candle burning on the coffee table: Hillary, Angela, Sister Sarah, and me. Someone points out that we probably shouldn't do the wine-drinking part of our ritual in the tattoo parlor, so we snuggle into couches and recliners and sip red wine out of clear, tall glasses.

I share a little. "Thanks for being part of this night," I say. "It means a lot to me that you are here. I don't know if I'm going to stay with the Sisters, but the past nine months have changed me, and I want to ritualize this change with this marking on my body."

I tell Angela and Hillary about the Franciscan community's practice of constant prayer, adoration, happening 24/7 in La Crosse. I explain that in our adoration chapel at St. Rose Convent there are always two people praying before the Eucharistic host—a piece of bread that we believe is the body of Jesus Christ—in a monstrance on a high altar. I've come to see that this devotion is the heartbeat of our community life, the rhythm of prayer grounding, energizing, and moving the Sisters into compassionate action.

They listen to my impromptu litany of love for bread, my belief that Jesus really is the Bread of Life. I explain that I believe God unites us as one body when we consume the Eucharist during Holy Communion and I tell them that the image I chose to have tattooed, a black-and-white image of a loaf of bread, was inspired by the logo for JVC. (Bread representing simplicity.) I want those JVC values to direct my life now in a more committed, rooted way. The image of the baguette has three curves at the top to represent the Trinity. I explain that the image will be open at one end to represent my desire to be open-minded, open-hearted, with open hands, able to give and receive. As we sip our wine in the candlelight, Sister Sarah, Hillary, and Angela all nod in understanding.

"It's nice to know what your thinking is behind all this, where this idea came from," Hillary says. Then we finish our wine, collect the Bible, baguette, and a tattered copy of a poem, and head out into the night air.

As we walk from the car to the tattoo parlor, the September wind rustles leaves, swirling my ruffled denim skirt, whipping Hillary and Angela's long blond hair around in circles. Once inside, we all sit snugly onto a red vinyl couch in the waiting room, our shoulders and hips touching. I feel cozy tucked next to Sister Sarah, slightly leaning into her fuzzy blue sweater and long, thin body. I stare at the brightly colored art hanging on the black wall. My heart is racing. I'm excited *and* terrified at once.

"Let's read the poem now," I say. Soft smiles and the reverence of prayer creases into our faces as we pass the paper between us and let words shape our mouths, vibrate sound through the peaceful room:

> Bakerwoman God,
> I am your living bread.
> Strong, brown Bakerwoman God,
> I am your low, soft, and being-shaped loaf.
>
> I am your rising bread,
> well-kneaded by some divine
> and knotty pair of knuckles,
> by your warm earth hands.
> I am your bread well-kneaded.
>
> (Alla Renée Bozarth, "Bakerwoman God")

A thin man dressed in black enters the room and tells us he is ready. He's the tattoo artist. I jump up like a nervous bunny and we all follow him into the back room. A large solid man is lying face down on a chair, his back exposed, as another tattoo artist bends over him, focusing on an elaborate design. The buzz of the tattoo needle fills the brightly lit room.

The artist in black gestures toward a chair. I explain that my friends are with me for support; that we are going to pray. I take off my sandals as he sits on a stool near my feet next to a tray of supplies: a gun-like needle, paper towels, cotton swabs, a bottle of black dye. My friends stand around me, like nurses ready with their own tools: Bible and bread. The artist puts on rubber gloves and rubs ointment over the top of my foot; his gentle touch and the feeling of cool ointment relaxes me.

Hillary breaks the baguette and gives each of us a piece. We silently chew and swallow the soft bread while watching the artist work his craft. It occurs to me that what we are doing is likely bizarre by tattoo parlor standards; I want to laugh loudly and marvel at how the artist remains focused and unfazed by us, but I remain still and quiet.

The needle buzzes and a permanent black mark starts to take shape on the top of my foot; an ache steeps deep past my skin, into my muscles. I want to scream, to kick the man in the face, to jump out of the chair. Instead, I squeeze Hillary's hand, take a deep breath, and focus on the sound of Sister Sarah's voice proclaiming the bread of life discourses from the Gospel of John, chapter six. I let the mystery of my faith calm me:

> So Jesus said to them, "Amen, amen, I say to you, it was not Moses who gave the bread from heaven; my Father gives you the true bread from heaven. For the bread of God is that which comes down from heaven and gives life to the world." So they said to him, "Sir, give us this bread always." Jesus said to them, "I'm the bread of life; whoever comes to me will never hunger, and whoever believes in me will never thirst." (John 6:32-35, *NABRE*)

Before long, it is finished. I tell the tattoo artist I love it. Four curvy lines look like the baguette we broke and shared. The artist rubs cream on my foot, wraps the wound in plastic wrap, and gives me care instructions. As I get up from the chair, my foot aching, I notice there are crumbs on the floor and apologize for the mess.

"Don't worry about it. Happens all the time," he says, remaining cool. I laugh, say goodbye, and thank him again. Along with my Sister and friends, I limp out of the parlor, forever changed and toward an unknown future with my love, Jesus, the Bread of Life.

10

When Mike joins Facebook, he starts sending me friendly pokes. We email and talk on the phone, all while I continue adjusting to living with the Sisters in La Crosse and Minneapolis. Then we begin instant messaging on Google email, G-chat, while we both are multitasking at our desks.

The first time I send Mike a G-chat message, I see the colored dot lit up next to his name in the margin of the screen, indicating he's online. In the conversation box, I send him a *HEY*. Then an email pops into my inbox, a short message: *I can't figure out how to do this*. I type step-by-step instructions for him, amused and laughing, for IM is nothing new to me.

April 3, 2007 G-chat
11:36 a.m.

Mike: so do you have any apprehension about the goings-on in your life?
;)
Julia: hmmmm
in a way
i'm so complicated, so multi-dimensional
and although my gut, heart, spirit, etc, are totally down with the upcoming novitiate
i can't stop my mind from reminding me that i never got to really enjoy my 20s like i wanted to

	but, yet i am
	i'm enjoying my 20s, probably most authentically to who i am
	i guess it's like i'm partly jealous of my friends that can date, party, go on rando trips to europe, have 3 day hang-overs.... ;)
Mike:	don't be jealous of three day hangovers. seriously.
Julia:	although i know that if that's what i was doing i would be just wishing i wasn't running from my call, most deeply
Mike:	i do know exactly what you're saying.
	i don't really have any advice for you, though!
	not like you need any...
	except that you NEED to follow through with it until you reach an end, one way or another.
	and you'll KNOW when you get there. either you'll be an 80-year-old sister, or a stripper.
	well, maybe not a stripper...
	[...]
	if you ever want to talk about it, let me know!
	i don't know if i can help at all...
	plus, i don't know if they would want me talking to you anyway...
	i could be a bad influence!!!
Julia:	ha, not at all
	i think all the sisters I'm close to have heard about "my former franciscan postulant friend"
	and they really seem to want me to keep having all the friends i do
Mike:	yeah, i agree with them.
	i don't think that keeping distance from people you care about is good for anybody, celibate or not...

We log off, and my chest tremors with excitement. I love how happy I feel. And I'm confused. It felt weird—and disturbing—when he suggested I would become a stripper if I left the Sisters, even as a joke. My mind and heart are filling with questions—about him, and about what I'm doing with my life. The questions filter into my prayer.

Mike and I talk again the following day.

April 4, 2007 G-chat
3:21 p.m.

Julia: omigosh, so i think, partly as a result of our conversation yesterday, i sorta had a breakdown during prayer last night.....
we were meditating on the cross and having a heart-to-heart prayerful discussion
and all i could think about is how i want to be a mom
and i wish that i wouldn't have entered fspa so early
and then when it was my time to share i started to cry and talk about how i wished i would have at least had one guy who really thought of me as his girlfriend before i entered all this
the sisters i live with are so wonderful though
they were so caring
and talked to me about call and choice
and how even though we are called, god loves us just the same
and provides the grace no matter for what we choose

Mike: yikes... it sounds like you had a really emotional night!
have you ever considered taking a little "time off" before going into novitiate?
could you take a break?

Julia: gosh
i don't know
i'm so confused about all of it right now
so, why did you leave the capuchins anyhow? you never really told me the depths of it, i don't think

Mike: probably not...
it was very multifaceted
basically, i just decided that, at that time in my life anyway, i had other things to take care of before i could really consider a vocation
"personhood" stuff before vocation stuff
there were other things too
postulancy really helped me discover all kinds of stuff about myself
i think there was a big part of me that realized that i didn't live community life very well.

	basically, when i left, i just said "i have to take care of this stuff. i can't do anything else until i do…" and they agreed with me.
i figured i'd give it no less than two years, and i left on good terms
i think they'd "take me back" if i approached them later on, although i have absolutely no plans to do so.
…at this point, anyway
Julia:	wow, yeah
i might have to have a real conversation with you about it all sometime
but, it makes me think of what the sisters said last night
and how even though God calls us, God gives us the grace even if we don't choose yes

Mike is available. I know God would give me grace if I don't choose yes, if I don't keep moving forward with my life with the Sisters. And yet, when I pray about leaving, I keep hearing "Stay." This makes sense to me. The longing to go deeper is stronger than my questions about Mike. So I ask the FSPA leadership team for permission to enter the novitiate, feeling excited to begin the next stage of the process. At the same time, I'm not ready to back away from the intimacy I share with Mike. I want to have it all.

11

A chance to explore my questions and deepen my prayer life: that's what I figure the novitiate will be, that's why I want to enter it. I sense that many of my questions about religious life can only be answered by spending more time with the Sisters, and better inserting myself into the community. But even though I decide to take the next step toward becoming a Sister—beginning the "canonical novitiate"—I still face challenges in community life. Mike remains a close confidant.

May 8, 2007 G-chat
1:22 p.m.

Julia: hey, when you were in formation did you struggle with being bossed around and feeling like your emotions weren't respected? or anything like that?

Mike: i think it's just part of it.

Julia: gosh. why is it part of it?
i just don't get this obedience thing
is that what obedience is?!

Mike: i don't know.
once i wanted to just go to my room and skip dinner because i wasn't feeling good and got "in trouble" for it.
i was expected to be at every meal.
whether i wanted to be or not.

	i think it's about "tearing down" the old person and building up the new person.
Julia:	gosh, really?
	like, how in trouble?
	why the hell would ministers want to tear us down?
	aren't we good to start with?
Mike:	not big trouble. but it was definitely made known that i was expected to be there.
Julia:	wow
Mike:	sure, we're good to begin with, but if we're going to be living in community with others, we have to leave some of our old stuff behind.
	what's going on with you?
	what are they not respecting?
Julia:	i'm frustrated with my incorporation director because she doesn't communicate very well
	and she leaves me guessing a lot, or asking follow-up questions
Mike:	what do you mean?
Julia:	well, to be specific
	my parents' house and their restaurant is only an hour and a half from la crosse
	so, like a week after my reception into the novitiate they are hosting a concert at the local opera house
	and my dad is emceeing and stuff
	so, of course i want to go and i asked her if i could and she could go with me
	and she knows that it is really difficult for me to miss out on family stuff
	and she responded by simply saying something like:
	i'm thinking that you are just getting into the canonical experience and that it wouldn't be helpful for you to be going away so soon, so i'm saying no to your request.
	i think it pissed me off because she didn't say anything like, "i imagine this will be difficult for you, but we shouldn't go" or "i know how much you value your family and it would be hard to miss out on this, but we shouldn't go"

	i guess it just seems cold to me
	i don't know
	maybe i'm hypersensitive about it all
Mike:	i think that novitiate is meant to be a sort of "retreat" time where you don't go out
Julia:	right
Mike:	i think they want you to be immersed in religious life
Julia:	and i get that
Mike:	i think, at least at first, if you're going to be in a religious community, you'll have to make certain sacrifices. it's not like being a carefree bachelorette anymore
Julia:	and they don't really remember to communicate the expectations to us
Mike:	i know...
Julia:	i feel like i have been making lots of sacrifices
Mike:	i think that was one of the things that went into my decision making process. i didn't want to live in that kind of environment.

***

Much later, I realize that my frustrations with my incorporation director, Sister Lucy Ann, have nothing to do with her. My people, my home, my identity: everything in my life is shifting and I'm struggling to feel control. I want solid ground beneath my feet; I long for smooth transitions and easy answers.

I'm not sure I want to be a Franciscan Sister, and I'm not sure I want to profess vows.

Prayer can be tough; I struggle with sitting still. I still enjoy things that don't seem to line up with simple living: fashion, fine dining, evenings out. Plus, the thought of giving up my independence and desires isn't attractive right now. I doubt I'm Sister material, that God designed me for these purposes. I want my doubts to recede from the path I'm on as I approach the novitiate ahead.

On a May afternoon, I'm tucked into a recliner inside a hexagon shaped prayer hut, a hermitage, my legs crossed under me, my torso tilted as I lean into one hip. To the right, a twin bed; a kitchenette, behind me; a small writing desk tucked into a corner. I stare through the giant picture window and into a valley, praying and thinking. Sunbeams glimmer through young, spring leaves; budding branches reach upward.

Upon my lap: an Afghan blanket, a pen, a journal. Left to right my hand moves quickly, the pen scribbling words upon the blank page. Words of honest truth, prayer. Words that remind me again how conflicted I feel about becoming a Sister. Distractions churn. Yet, in this rare moment of focus, I write for nearly an hour, filling pages in the smooth, firm book. I list the stirrings and desires that made me, got me here. I'm in the middle of a five-day silent retreat. Thoughts meander and are half self-centered, half God-directed.

My words dip in and out of confusion, agony; they fall out as floppy prayers. *Why am I so strange? What am I getting myself into, by following you Jesus into an unknown future, by entering into such an unusual lifestyle?* Eventually, I feel a shift: I know I'm eager to move forward with my life, with my journey with Jesus. There's a lot of mystery ahead, but my experiences so far have taught me that God is trustworthy. My fingers and wrist begin to cramp from clenching the pen after scribbling my thoughts onto the page. I pause and gaze through the window again, into the valley of gaping trees. Ash, maples, oaks; the brown wood is dotted with the bright spring green of new, opening leaves, vibrating in the breeze, stirring the sun rays and shadows into a dance. A bird jumps from one branch to another, and its song echoes.

In this hut designed especially for contemplation, I pray on what I consider to be holy ground. The ground is holy because Franciscan Sisters have been praying here for decades—possibly a century. I heard that when Sister Cecy was part of the FSPA leadership team in the 1980s she helped build these hermitages to offer a space for private prayer and meditation to the public. Now there are three hermitages all the same shape and spaced a fair distance apart, on the backside of a cornfield and on top of a Mississippi River bluff in southwest Wisconsin. The valley below is an erosion-formed coulee, a geological feature found between the rolling hills in this driftless area—a region of the Midwest unlike the prairie land that was smoothed flat by the glaciers of the Ice Age. Consisting of parts of northeast Iowa—the farm I grew up on is only ninety miles away—southwest Wisconsin and southeast Minnesota, the land is made of steep hills and wooded valleys, streams and rivers, with fields and pastureland tucked in.

The hermitages on the bluff side are available to retreatants through the Franciscan Spirituality Center in nearby La Crosse, a small city of about 50,000 along the Mississippi, twelve miles away. All sorts of people come here to pray, rest, or enjoy solitude and silence. Nearby, the newly plowed black earth sloped uphill toward a four-story, stone complex with a full-size chapel, various parlors, nursing stations, private rooms for sisters and a dining hall—a space called the Villa St. Joseph.

* * *

Later, I climb the hill to the Villa to talk with my spiritual director, Sister Janet. We sit in soft mismatched chairs in a parlor and have a lively spiritual direction session focused on transition. "I had a vision you were becoming bread in Jesus' hands, that he was about to break you, and share you with others to help others become more whole and connected as one body," she says.

I like how she envisions my future life as a novice. I am tickled by the image she offers, and how it connects to the theme for my upcoming ceremony: walking with the Bread of Life. I think of my tattoo.

Sister Janet has heard me ramble about how important bread is to me, how I understand God as bread, how I hold dear the image of God as baker woman. But when she speaks of Jesus breaking me and sharing me with others, I feel tense, uncomfortable. It sounds painful and violent to be broken by God. Why would God want me to be broken?

Back in the hermitage, I'm alone in the silence, yet feel connected. I'm aware that there are likely other Sisters, holy women, snuggled into their recliners, up the hill and across the field, in their rooms at the Villa right now, praying too. Or sitting firmly on a pew, gazing toward the altar in the dim chapel, breathing deeply. At least two are in the adoration chapel at St. Rose Convent, I know, praying where the Blessed Sacrament is exposed in a monstrance upon a high white marble altar, between old paintings of saints and angels, under a domed, blue ceiling dotted with painted stars.

I think of saints I have learned about while preparing to become a Sister—for the approaching day when I will become a novice, preparing to profess my first vows of poverty, celibacy, and obedience as a Franciscan. I think of how many of the holy ones throughout history would be overtaken by unexplainable religious experiences, words that feel foreign, clunky, and slightly humorous to me: *levitation, ecstasy, bilocation*. I believe (want so desperately to believe) in such manifestations of the Spirit in the lives of holy folks in the same sort of way that I once believed in Santa Claus—with a vibrant hopeful eagerness that it could be real, a trust that good folks would never lie to me. But imagining some of the scenes I've studied makes me giggle. The story of Blessed Juniper who so exuberantly wanted to demonstrate the freedom he found in God that he preached with a pair of underwear on his head. The story of Francis of Assisi so consumed with passionate love for God that he burst out of his hermitage and into the winter weather, ripped off his tattered brown habit and rolled around in the snow naked.

Such stories make me remember the times in my life when I felt enflamed with awe and gratitude, that my body stirred with desire to manifest the feelings in the physical, human world. Passion can erupt in each of us, even spiritual passion, but I have chosen to restrain myself and keep my clothes on.

In the 1200s, they thought St. Francis was holy, saintly for his ecstatic outbursts. *Do such things happen to people today?* I wonder, dismissing my doubts, remembering how I heard a Sister say that mystical experiences are common, but most people keep them private.

I also remember hearing the story of St. Faustina as a girl in my home parish in Iowa, where the priest hung a poster of Jesus on a closet door in the sanctuary. In the image, Jesus stands in a white robe with red and blue glowing wounds bursting forth from his chest. Faustina had several visions of Jesus. As a girl I would pray to God: I want to see you, feel free to visit me, if I'm good enough.

Tucked into a recliner in a hermitage on the edge of the Wisconsin woods, I wonder if I'm good enough for God now; if I ever could be good enough to have a vision, to be close to God, for Jesus to come and visit. I wonder if I'm I capable of being a saint. I wonder what I need to do. Then, slight vibrations of shame and terror remind me of my unworthiness and fear, choking my daydreams.

My focus returns to the view of the trees rising from the earth, to the green specks backed by bright blue sky. I feel the Afghan in my lap; my body nestled into the recliner on the bright May day.

I decide to pray a different way. I want to try out some of the meditation skills I gained since I moved in with the Sisters. I find the red prayer shawl draped over the recliner, its yarn soft between my fingers, and place it on my shoulders. The red embraces my pale arms and white t-shirt. I put the meditation bench on the carpeted floor in front of the wide picture window, washed with sunlight and warmth. The small, sloped panel of wood is slightly padded; I thought another one that I saw was an odd footrest until someone demonstrated its proper use. I kneel on the floor, my calves settled onto the smooth white carpet. The bench angles toward me, I rest my bottom on the panel, hold my spine upright. I feel my back straighten, more secure and solid than when in a chair. I lean forward, light the candle. I close my eyes and take a deep breath, first gulping in air with a desperate desire to calm myself and unite with God, as the mystics of history have done. I try to focus on my breathing, on my physical sensations, the feeling of my hips settled upon the meditation bench, my hands settled upon my lap, half open as if a bowl.

Gradually, my breathing slows and my mind sharpens in on the present moment. I feel air flow into my nose, through my airway and into my lungs. My belly expands, billowing in like a balloon widening, then narrowing as I breathe out through my mouth. I breathe like that for a while, perhaps the most focused and longest meditation I've ever done. My mind fills with images of Jesus: his gentle shoulder, his worn feet.

My mind wanders into a mantra, *union, union*. My body pulses with a desire for union with God, to be as close to my love, Jesus, as I can be. My body begins to vibrate with a subtle shift in energy, with the type of energy I've felt when snuggled next to an attractive man on a couch; my sensations feel more awake, more engaged. I'm alive and excited. I continue to breathe, return my focus to my breath, to the mantra, *union, union*. My body rocks forward and back. I feel big and small all at once: the surroundings both solid and crisp, yet distant and blurred. I'm flesh with a desire, with a groaning to be in full communion with everything that I'm suddenly, passionately in love with: God and all of God's creation. *Union, union.*

I slowly open my eyes, lean forward and blow out the candle resting on the windowsill. I continue to focus on my breathing as I stand, let the red prayer shawl fall to the floor, and move through the screen door of the hermitage. My feet find the path to the woods and feel the dark brown earth beneath my bare toes. My eyes take in every sight; colors seem brighter, shapes sharper. I move down the hill into the trees. Tiny twigs crunch under my feet, the decay of last fall's leaves feel cool and wet on my toes, as I move deeper into the woods and down the hill, as if trying to locate a lover calling me into his home.

My prayer shifts. *Jesus, Jesus.* I breathe slowly and let my body move between the trees. I mutter and groan, only half aware of my actions, yet conscious that I feel one with love. I know that if I feel this way for a human man, I might crawl between sheets with him, free myself of anything that could be between us and abandon myself to whatever he'd have with me. Yet, this feeling is for a spiritual being—for a God, for a savior, the source of all love itself. *Jesus, Jesus.* He who is beyond—and yet completely part of—the physical world I move through. I continue to breathe and enter deeper into the woods and further down the path. I can't make love to God, I know, but I can roll around in the woods, so to speak; I can absorb every speck of God's creation by entering into it with all my senses.

Eyes open wide I see dark earth dotted with fresh green plants bursting into life. *Jesus, Jesus.* I sit on a bench built into a tree, hanging off the path above the deep valley of woods below. Looking up the hill, I see tiny violets waving their simple purple petals in the subtle breeze. I squirm with delight, with bliss. I roll my head back and look up into the bottoms of the treetops, the lacy opening revealing the bright blue sky. I hear a bird call from a distant branch, behind me, farther downhill. I continue to breathe deeply, in the fresh forest-tasting air. *Jesus, Jesus.*

I breathe deeply, slowly; noticing my heart, throat, torso filling with heat, an electric energy flow. *Jesus, Jesus.* In my mind, I moan like a lover, with joy and ecstasy. Outwardly, I'm quiet. I close my eyes and listen to the sounds of the woods, to the trees creaking in the breeze, to squirrels jumping through branches, to birds chirping, their song echoing through the valley.

Eventually I rise from the bench and return to myself. My mind stirs: What was that? What did I just experience? I slowly walk back to the hermitage, up the trail. Everything appears the same, yet I feel changed. Twigs crack under my feet. Cool earth stirs. I move my body over ground that feels holy. I'm in love and in awe, and I flood with gratitude.

Suddenly an image crosses through my mind. I see myself moving up the hill, in my white t-shirt and black yoga pants, my light brown bob bouncing over my pale neck. I see myself completely surrounded by Jesus, as if his body were layered larger upon mine. A mystical body and a human body connected, moving together. I see a golden glow in the places where we merge: head, shoulders, hips, knees, feet. I see all this in the back of my mind as I climb up the path toward my hermitage, and back to a reality coming quick: I'm about to become a Franciscan Sister.

12

Peeking into the chapel at St. Rose Convent, I feel a happy tingle in my shoulders, a wide grin stretching on my cheeks. My family and friends are sitting in the pews with the Sisters: my worlds are merging! Everyone is waiting for my novitiate entrance ceremony to begin.

At the front of the church, I see Earl standing at the podium, a guitar strapped around his round belly. His bald head gleams as he studies the music, looking relaxed, comfortable. As a professor in the religious studies department across the street at Viterbo, I got to be his student a year ago during my first semester in La Crosse. He helped me appreciate the sacraments that connect us to God's grace through ordinary elements such as bread, wine, water, and oil. That semester, Earl encouraged me in my journey with simple kindness: he gave me a CD of prayer music for Lent; he asked me for my thoughts during discussion; wrote notes like "FSPA is lucky to have you" on my essays. As I got to know him as a teacher, I also got to know his wife, Marci, who worked at the convent, and his young daughter and son. I came to know him as an FSPA affiliate and leader and loving presence in the La Crosse community, a Catholic Worker, someone who the Sisters have known and loved for decades. I've heard Earl play guitar and sing at Mass and other prayer services, his deep, folksy voice, his prayerful croon. I could think of no better person to play guitar for this moment in my life.

The song I picked for Earl to play was unknown to the Sisters, but it mattered to me: I sang it at campfires at Bible camp before college, sang it to God when I prayed alone. While studying Franciscanism this past year, it occurred to me that the song expressed our spirituality, that the lyrics are about the self-emptying poverty and prayerful focus that I'm hoping to gain as a novice:

> *Lord, fill my life with you alone*
> *Empty myself of all that's my own*
> *Lord, fill my life with you alone*
> *Jesus, keep my eyes on you.*
> *Help me stand, stand for what's right.*
> *Help me walk, walk in the light.*
> *Help me run, run for the prize.*
> *Jesus, keep my eyes on you.*
> *Jesus, keep my eyes on you.*

My eyes are wet with tears, my cheeks tight as I grin. I feel giddy, practically ecstatic. I lean against the chapel wall and gaze around the room at friends and family and all the Sisters, feeling an urge to run around and give people hugs and cheery "hellos," but I feel a tap on my shoulder. Sister Lucy Ann, my about-to-be novice minister, hovers above, very tall, asking me to follow her. My heart starts racing and my shoulders tense. What's happening?

We go into a curved room on the other side of the chapel narthex, where I see the entire FSPA leadership team together, along with Sisters Sarah, Cecy, Karen, and Laura. Everyone is dressed up, in nice blouses and long skirts, a variety of colors and patterns. Standing among them, I wear my green dress printed with white flowers and a white cardigan. Someone says, "Let's stand in a circle." Another closes the heavy gold doors, separating us from the narthex, where the ushers continue to hand out worship aids to people trickling in. The room falls silent as I look around, uncertain. Then another Sister begins to pray out loud, asking God for blessings upon my novitiate experience. As I hear the loving words, my breathing slows, I feel my chest warm with love and gratitude.

I stand at the threshold of the chapel a few minutes later, holding a ceramic bowl filled with ordinary cooking Crisco emitting an odor as it melts below a flame: the tissue tucked into the shortening like a wick on fire. The burning flame dances brightly in front of my heart. I gaze into it, thinking about how I'm holding a lard light, a community tradition dating back to 1865 when a novena to St. Joseph—and a vision of the mother superior, Mother Antonia—disturbed the local priest at night, allowing the Sisters to gain permission to begin the practice of Eucharistic Adoration. Since they were given permission to begin the devotion so quickly, they didn't have a sanctuary lamp. The novice said that she knew how to create a simple light from lard and tissue. Mother Antonia prayed: "Dear Lord, accept this poor light. It is the best we can give You now, but if you will help us and bless the community, we will one day establish the perpetual adoration of the Blessed Sacrament and build for You as beautiful a chapel as our means will allow." The promise that was made that day, on the Feast of St. Joseph, eventually led to the building of this very chapel a century ago. It is unique, iconic in its architecture; there are dozens of angels decorating the space, plastered pillars are painted gold and green to look like marble. Every month, hundreds of tourists come from all over the world to visit and savor this sacred space.

Piano music swells into the room and Earl starts to strum and sing. Voices old and young sing the hymn "Table of Plenty," and I begin to walk down the aisle, following Sister Karen. She's carrying the San Damiano crucifix, the icon that St. Francis of Assisi was praying in front of when he heard Christ say, *"Francis, rebuild my Church which is falling into ruin."* I follow the cross with burning lard light in my hands. Behind me Sister Laura carries a basket of bread filled with loaves: I baked one, Mom brought one from Iowa, Hillary brought a loaf too. Behind her, Sister Cecy carries the Gospel book. The five sisters in the community leadership team follow, with Sister Linda at the end: she is playing the role of presider for this prayer service. We sing about the table uniting heaven and earth, the table offering an abundant feast. I want to trust God more deeply, to have hope that my needs really *will* be provided for, as the song says. But I'm not sure what I'm getting myself into.

I sit next to Sister Lucy Ann in the pew, across the aisle from my friends and family. We listen to the Scripture readings proclaimed and sing the responsorial psalm. Sister Cecy reads the Gospel, the story of the Blind Bartimaeus leaping up and following Jesus without any questions, once he was able to see. She sits back down and now it is my turn.

I stand, step into the middle aisle, and bow before the altar. Standing behind the ambo, I begin to read the reflection I wrote during my retreat at the hermitage. I tell everyone about the leap of faith challenge on the ropes course at Bible camp, where I would jump from the top of a forty-foot pole and into the air toward a trapeze, only to quickly fall toward the ground and come to a sudden stop. Snapped in place by the belay, I would dangle and be pinched between my legs as I was slowly lowered to the ground. Once on solid ground again, I felt different: transformed by the rapid fall, by the courage, by the adrenaline still rushing through my veins.

"Right now, I'm at the top of the forty-foot pole in the middle of the beautiful woods. I love it here! I love the view and being eye-level with the birds in the treetops. I can stand up tall without fear and hear the cheers of my loved ones all around me. It's so fun on top of this pole that you might have to remind me to keep moving.

"Jesus calls me to take the leap of faith. He uses the voices of the community to get me moving like he did with Bartimaeus. Suddenly I'm anxious. Can I have the faith like the blind Bartimaeus and leap up and go toward Jesus with no questions? Will I receive new sight and follow him on the way?

"I don't even know how I'll land! At camp, the friendly belay would pull me to a sudden stop eight feet above the ground. The harness would pinch me uncomfortably while I was lowered slowly to the soft earth. I think part of me enjoyed the fall. But all of me hated the sudden, uncomfortable stop.

"I believe that this time the belay is Jesus. That should make the leap of faith easy if Jesus is the one that catches me! I look at your faces, my friends, family, sisters and community who are so dear to me, and I'm warmed with gratitude and peace.

"And so, I leap."

* * *

I sit back down in the pew, joining the congregation in a pregnant pause, a sacred silence. Sister Lucy Ann and Sister Marlene, the FSPA president, stand on the steps in front of the altar and face the assembly. Sister Lucy Ann holds a wireless microphone in her hands.

"Julia, it is with a joyful and grateful heart that I invite you to present yourself for reception into the novitiate of the Franciscan Sisters of Perpetual Adoration." Sister Lucy Ann summons me.

She passes the microphone to Sister Marlene who asks, "Julia, what do you ask of the Franciscan Sisters of Perpetual Adoration?"

I stand and read from the script in my hands, lifting another wireless mic to my mouth. "I ask to enter the novitiate of the Franciscan Sisters of Perpetual Adoration. I desire to live out the Franciscan Spirit of Eucharistic presence in communion with you."

I move into a spot between Sister Lucy Ann and Sister Marlene, as we rehearsed. I hand Sister Marlene the mic. She looks into my face, smiling. "I welcome you into our novitiate. May the Spirit continue to bless you on your journey."

She gives me the mic and I read my next line from the script, "Sister Marlene, what does the community ask of me?"

"As a community we ask you, Sister Julia..." and then she pauses as I feel my body jolt, hearing my new title: *Sister*. I hear some of my friends and family chuckling; they noticed me jump. I try not to laugh, too, but keep listening. "...to be open to the blessings of the novitiate as you continue your journey into deeper relationship with God, yourself and your Franciscan Sisters."

Sister Marlene hands the wireless microphone to Sister Lucy Ann, who says. "Julia, I invite you to come to the fire that burns in your spirit. I invite you to embrace God's loving presence. I invite you to continue to allow the breath of the Spirit to nourish you and speak to your heart."

The piano begins to ring a harmony through the pillars and Sister Beth, the cantor, starts leading the assembly in a song of blessing, praying that love and peace and the presence of God remain with me. I feel my body beaming, a bright smile upon my face and tears in my eyes, as I look into the sea of faces in the pews, my family and friends and now *my* community of Franciscan Sisters. So much love has made me into who I am and got me to this moment. I'm now Sister Julia.

* * *

Talking to Tines on the phone a few days later, she asks me, "What does it mean to be a novitiate?"

"I'm a novice, actually," I say. "Novice is the person. Novitiate is the phase of formation, or the place where the novices live."

"OK, got it," she says. "You're now a novice. In the novitiate."

"Right. Yeah, so I guess I've been thinking it's kind of like nun boot camp," I tell her, even though I have no clue about real boot camp and hate the military metaphor. Like boot camp, though, I know that the novitiate will be a time for a full immersion into FSPA with stricter, more demanding expectations, like intense self-work and spiritual exercises. I tell her I'll pray and study more, have a lot of meetings with Sister Lucy Ann and other sisters, and meet with my spiritual director. I explain that it is a time to focus on getting ready for vows.

"Oh yeah, the vows. What are they again?" she asks.

"Poverty. Celibacy. Obedience." I tell her that I'm not sure what it all means, but I know I can't own any private property—the Sisters and I are to own everything in common and share our money in one common pot and live simply, so we can share more with the poor. I remind her of what feels obvious: "I can't have sex, date, get married. The idea is to give my whole body to God," I say. I tell her that obedience means I must do whatever God and community say, basically. I must listen, because my life isn't my own. I tell her that if I decide to take vows and am approved to do so, it will probably happen in about two years.

"Maybe I should start looking for a green dress," she says, remembering how when I was applying to the community, I told my Casa Jane housemates I wanted them all to come to my vows wearing green dresses, like a group of bridesmaids.

"Ha, I don't know. I'm not sure what will happen. Of course, I want to make vows though!" I say.

"What else will you be doing?" she asks.

I tell her I hope to learn how to live as a Franciscan Sister. I'll try to focus on being more present to the sisters. I'll volunteer, because I wouldn't be allowed to work or earn any money, at least during the first year—the canonical novitiate year. I explain that I'll have to take a "hermitage day" once a week and be silent, working on my relationship with God in solitude.

I explain that after the first year, I'll become an apostolic novice instead of a canonical novice, so the expectations will shift. I anticipate volunteering or working nearly full-time, while integrating into community and deepening my prayer life. The first year, the canonical year, will be the strictest, though. It will be a time to figure out who I really am, and whether being with the Sisters is a good fit or not.

"I'm a bit terrified—dreading—what this will do to my social life," I admit.

"Hmmm, I think I get it. That's kinda cool." Tines' voice sounds relaxed. She's quiet and thoughtful for a moment before she speaks again. "I kinda wish everyone could take a year off to figure out who they are and where they are going with their life in the middle of their twenties. I'm kinda jealous, I could use some time like that," she says.

"Oh gosh, that's a really good point," I say, sighing. "Now that you say that, I'll try to take advantage of this time." I feel challenged to see the novitiate as a blessing, a privilege—I know this could be better than worrying about how everything will go: what a big shift in my mindset.

* * *

Since I don't have a classmate my community leadership decides to send me to a program in Joliet, Illinois called the Common Franciscan Novitiate for most of my canonical year. I will live with novices from other Franciscan congregations, Sisters from other parts of the country. Together, we'll participate in the program that two novice ministers—Sisters from other congregations—will facilitate. And since my entrance into the novitiate ceremony was in May and the program there won't begin until late August, I'm glad to spend the summer with my Sisters in La Crosse before I go. I'm glad I can adjust to being a novice while living with my own community.

Before long, I fall into a groove of holy activity. I take bike rides around La Crosse and pray in the marsh. I spend hours journaling in the adoration chapel. I help out with chores and cooking in Chiara House, attend daily Mass, volunteer in the communications office, study FSPA history, visit Sisters around the convent and at the Villa St. Joseph, and meet with Sister Lucy Ann for regular instruction and guidance. I quickly decide I like being a novice, even though I can't run off to my friends and family on the weekends anymore. I'm feeling how the rhythm, space, and structure are inviting me into learning and growth. I know this time is an opportunity that I don't want to waste.

At one ordinary Mass at St. Rose Convent, I reach out to a Sister in a nearby pew, grinning, to say, "Peace be with you." She pulls me toward her. "Peace be with you," she says, smashing me with a hug, my glasses bending into my cheek. When we let go, I turn to another Sister, one that I don't know as well, who gives me a hearty handshake and says, "Peace be with you."

At the front of the sanctuary, the priest stands behind the altar and quietly holds up the host. The white, flat, circular bread appears as a moon rising on the horizon. Quietly, and unnoticed by many, he reverently breaks the bread. The sound of crisp cracking is heard slightly under the sound of breathing, praying people, as the words "Peace be with you" float throughout the crowd. He takes a piece of the bread and puts it into a vessel of wine and says some prayers silently.

As I watch, I think of how we are connected to the time when Jesus' body was bloodied and broken on the cross. We are connected to that time when his resurrected body stood before his disciples with his wounds exposed. With God, though, time is not linear, I'm learning. Mysteriously, amazingly, every moment is happening; seconds are layered upon seconds like lines on the face of a cliff. A priest at an altar in the middle of the United States in the early part of the twenty-first century is as real and current as the bread broken in Jesus' hands, as Jesus' body broken upon the cross.

Piano music rings through the sanctuary, giving the cue that it is time to begin a brief call and response prayer: we admit our sinfulness and ask for God's mercy. Across the aisle, I see Sister Dorothy standing by her walker, and mouth "Peace be with you" as I flash her a peace sign with my fingers. She grins and does the same. I turn my gaze to the front, to the altar.

We sing in unison. My mouth makes music along with others. "Lamb of God, you take away the sins of the world, grant us peace." The sound of bodies moving together and kneelers thudding to the floor follow the song. I gaze upward in observance. Others gaze downward in reverence.

The priest holds a piece of the broken bread in front of his heart. "This is the Lamb of God who takes away the sins of the world. Happy are those who are called to his supper," he says.

We respond reverently; our voices blend together. "Lord, I'm not worthy to receive you, but only say the word and I shall be healed." My folded hands rest on the pew in front of me. I'm thinking of how, after his resurrection, Jesus was made known to his disciples through his wounds, the brokenness in his body, *and* in the bread he broke with them.

I think about how the church community is the broken body of Christ as well, and at this ritual, we are broken so we can unite into one. Christ's body, the bread, has been broken so we can each consume parts of it and become one. We connect as a community through our shared partaking of the holy food. This might be what Sister Janet meant when she said she saw a vision of me being broken during my retreat. This might be why it feels right to be a novice even though I'm so confused, uncertain, and weak.

I hear the communion song begin, and flip through the hymnal so I can find the words to sing along. I follow my pew partners to receive communion, to consume Christ, to take him into my body. Person after person receives Jesus into their mouth: they taste the bread; they swallow and allow the body of Christ—the bread—to enter them, to become part of their digestion. I bow as I approach the Sisters who are distributing the host. I hold my hands flat in front of my heart, like a little altar.

"The body of Christ," the Sister says.

"Amen," I respond, meaning yes, I agree, I believe it is so. I taste bread on my tongue, I believe it is more. I step forward, examine my hand for crumbs and lick where I see them.

Then I move my body to the communion cup, to the Sister holding a chalice full of wine—Christ's blood. I bow again when I approach her. "The blood of Christ," she says.

"Amen," I say, reaching for the metal cup and lifting it to my lips. I see the red liquid flowing toward my mouth. I taste and swallow. I can see all the ways I'm imperfect and not confident about being a novice, but I'm offering my broken self to the Franciscan community, just as Christ is offering himself to me, and each Sister offers her brokenness to others. I can see how growing closer to God could allow me to grow closer to my new Sisters.

We are nourished by this body, this blood. We are fed and connected, we are in communion. Our humanity has already made us into a family, and consuming this bread makes us into Christ's body. We are given the grace and energy to share in Christ's divinity. I don't understand it, but I believe it: through our consumption of the bread and wine, God's nature is stamped into our cells and shapes who we are, how we live with love. Or, how we could.

Walking back to my pew, I look around at my community and feel only love. Some Sisters hold their hymnals and sing. Others fold their hands in prayer. Some sit and gaze forward, smiling. As I move, I pray in thanksgiving for this gift, this grace, that will make me new again.

13

Formation for my elder Sisters—forty, fifty, sixty years ago—was drastically different than what I'm going through. FSPA now calls formation "incorporation" meaning we are received as women that God is already forming and then are incorporated into the community. The Franciscan sources that I'm studying were only translated into English within the past thirty years. But decades ago, when my elders were in formation, twenty to thirty Sisters would sit in class together, listening to lectures about history and tradition, taking notes, not asking questions. They were expected to fit in and not stick out. This is how they describe their novitiate to me when I sit with them at lunch in the convent dining room. I want to groan, overwhelmed by the contrast. Even if I want to hide, to not stick out, everyone notices me: I'm the only novice.

Plus, for my elders, much of their formation emphasized "the pursuit of perfection." What did that mean? Where did these ideas come from? I ask them.

It meant that we were expected to move in rhythm with the established patterns, they tell me. We had to walk properly, hold our hands a certain way. Our clothes and space in the dorm were inspected. We had to be at certain places doing particular things at exactly the right time. And if we made any mistakes, if we broke anything, if we were even thirty seconds late, we had to kneel before the Mother Superior and publicly beg forgiveness at the "chapter of faults." Everyone would hear us, our confessions were public, and we were expected to confess something, so sometimes we would make something up, if only to comply.

As I hear it described, I feel my face wrinkle with disgust. "It sounds so awful, why did you stay?" I ask.

We didn't know any other way, Sister Anita admits. Now we know how unhealthy it was for our lives to be focused on the external, on the outward expressions of conformity, another Sister says. It was once understood to be good spirituality, though, someone else offers. But no one asked you about what was going on in your mind and heart when you were praying. There was no discussion about what it meant to be in relationship with God.

"Did people fake it? Do you think they didn't believe in God? Or weren't praying?" I wonder aloud.

Maybe, one sister says. But they might have been one of those who disappeared, who left in the middle of the night. We never knew if that was their choice, or they were asked to leave. We never got to say goodbye. We never knew if we were going to be next.

It sounds so far from perfect to me. "How could this pressure and fear allow you to live a happy life?" I say.

We were told that if you keep the Rule, the Rule will keep you. And the Rule, at that time, was all about how things appeared.

It's so hard for me to imagine what it was like. I wouldn't have survived.

You would have been a different person; it was such a different time, my elders explain. It wasn't much different from how things worked in our families, from where we came from.

I sigh and stare at the blank space in the room as I listen, aware of the gap between me and my elder Sisters, overwhelmed by how different we are.

The worst part, Sister Anita says, was that we never knew where we stood. We never knew if we were OK or if we were going to be the next to disappear in the night.

* * *

When I'm in solitude and am probably supposed to be praying and behaving with piety, my mind wanders and I trace the events that made me a novice. I know I was a pretty odd kid, a strange teen. Sometimes it was tough for me to understand social cues, to get that others didn't want me around. I tried to be everyone's friend, but I mostly hung out with the unpopular group at school; defending those who were teased. I tried not to care what other people thought.

As a teen, I kept a packed schedule and survived on little sleep. I had several jobs and was involved in a lot: school plays, cheerleading, choir. I attended tutoring sessions and tried to get good grades. I figured I needed a scholarship to afford college and reduce stress for my parents. I kept trying to improve my chances.

My busy pace continued into college when my schedule was packed with volunteerism, various jobs around campus, clubs, and a lot of studying. I continued to try to get good grades—I wanted to get my money's worth—although it seemed like school was harder for me.

Yet, I remained strange, not doing what others did during those years. I barely dated. I didn't have my first kiss until I was seventeen and even that was staged, in that dorm lounge with others watching. When I entered the convent at twenty-four, I could count all the people I had kissed on one hand. Not exactly normal—at least compared to my friends who started having sex when they were in junior high and others who were dating seriously in high school and college.

I knew I wasn't hideous, or at least I didn't think so. I figured my personality was outgoing enough. I was kind and caring to those I knew.

But I wanted to know what my friends were talking about, to be able to relate when they were giddy about boyfriends. I was interested in knowing what it was like to date; to have a boyfriend; to be wanted, liked, loved.

During my hours in solitude, I think about all this on bike rides along the marsh trails, or sitting in the silent adoration chapel. I wonder why my life has gone this way, why dating never got to be my norm. In these moments, I feel sick to my stomach with sadness. I'm not sure that I'm OK with the sacrifice I am making.

I don't know if Mike is that man, but I wonder if he might be, and I daydream about the idea of being closer to him now and then. Then I quickly dismiss the thought. I want to joyfully make this sacrifice because I love God, but I don't know if I'm there yet.

The sadness in my stomach starts to feel like an ache that radiates and becomes a clenching in my chest and my throat, like sobs stuck inside my body. I hate the feeling. I don't want to dwell on it, so I pray. *Thank you, God, for protecting my vocation and helping to make it easier for me to enter community. I could have gotten sucked into the thrills of dating and romance. I don't know if I could have chosen this life if I had to turn down a person I loved, that loved me. Thank you, I guess, for the fact that me being here means I will remain strange forever.*

14

Lying on my back on top of my bed covers, I stare at the ceiling, talking to Ellen on the phone.

"Hey," she says, "Did Mom or Dad tell you that they sold the farm?"

"What?! Shit! No," I say, exhaling in frustration about the roundabout way I'm getting information, about the way everything in my life is changing.

"I hadn't heard," I tell her.

"I know," Ellen says, "I imagined that I'd take my future children there someday."

"Shit. This sucks," I groan.

"Yeah, I know," she says. "It really, really sucks."

* * *

I sit with Sister Lucy Ann at the little table in her office for my weekly check-in. I tell her my parents sold their farm, and they'll apparently be moving out over the winter. I sigh as I speak, looking across the sunny convent courtyard at the glistening, stained-glass windows of the chapel.

I'm concerned that my parents might move while I am away, living in Joliet at the common Franciscan novitiate. I want to return to the farm one last time, to try and make peace with the changes, with the feeling that something sacred is being ripped from my life. Where is my home now?

"Sister Lucy Ann, I feel like one of the biggest things I've learned since coming to FSPA is the importance of ritualizing changes in order to integrate them, that integration is part of our prayer life," I say, thinking of my recent novitiate entrance ceremony and the tattoo I got halfway through my time as an associate. I ask if she is OK with that.

Sister Lucy Ann's lips press together as she thinks, quietly. She moves her mouth from side to side thoughtfully, then settles into a sideways half-smile. She breathes out slowly. I pick at my hangnails. I'm tempted to fill the silence with more reasons why I should get what I want, why I think it is a good idea.

"You know you can only be away from community for a few days during this canonical novitiate year. If you go, you won't really be able to visit your family. You must promise you'll stay silent until you briefly say goodbye on Saturday."

"I promise that's what I'll do," I say, "Thank you, Sister Lucy Ann, thank you!"

* * *

I want to live my faith, radically, for my lifestyle to be like the early Christians. Being a Sister is a form of radical discipleship of Jesus Christ, I figure. It is how I can live in a committed intentional community long-term with like-minded prayerful, Gospel-centered women; women who also want to serve people on the margins of society, end injustice, advocate for peace, live simply and sustainably, close to the earth and close to the poor. That's what I think, hope for. That's why I want to be a Sister. But then there's the day-to-day: the errands, chores, tasks, and technology—not to mention the culture and commotion of intergenerational women with mixed backgrounds and beliefs living together and sharing everything. So much of the reality here feels like galaxies apart from good ideals and intentions.

Living in Chiara House, giant and elaborate, feels far from the poor. I sometimes find myself calling the house "Castle Chiara" under my breath, in secret. White walls are filled with religious art. High ceilings and glistening hardwood floors surround me with gaps and spaciousness. My secret name for this Victorian mansion probably would have amused St. Clare of Assisi (whose name is Chiara in Italian). She left her aristocratic family and slept on the floor with dozens of "poor ladies" who joined her in a life of poverty, celibacy, and obedience, all for the glory of God. In part, I joined the Franciscan Sisters for accountability; for role models and companions, for guides to help me live in solidarity with the poor. Instead, I'm now living amid more wealth than I have ever known. Our shared life offers me the comforts of an upper-middle class life, a contrast from the Franciscan poverty I'm reading about—and my penny-pinching roots. I stare at the walls in my bedroom, feeling like a fraud, far from what Saints Francis and Clare established. I'm so far from people I know and love who really *do* live in poverty, such as the youth and children of Tubman House in Sacramento. Why am I here?

Each time I'm asked to embrace another comfort and privilege I feel confused. Sister Lucy Ann talked me into getting a cell phone and I know I'm adjusting to having a new gadget. And she encouraged me to get regular massages, to budget for them and schedule one each month. Before I came here I never had a massage; I thought of them as a luxury for the wealthy, a type of unnecessary pampering. I never heard anyone say that regular massages keep people healthy, until Sister Lucy Ann said so. I can admit it, even though I'm not comfortable with it: now that massages are part of my routine, I understand what she means. I can feel the differences in my body, a looseness, renewed energy, groundedness. Still, I have trouble admitting that massages are becoming a regular part of my life. I'm not sure I'll ever fully accept the privilege.

I pray about my feelings of discontentment, and feel compelled to stick things out longer. I can't shake the struggle, though. It seems ironic that as I get closer to taking a vow of poverty, I feel wealthier. Some Sisters say that poverty is common ownership. I keep wondering if I understand poverty too literally—maybe I need to understand it spiritually. I wonder if we are truly promoting justice and living in solidarity with the poor if we are too far from the struggles of those in poverty. I don't know why you keep me here, God.

* * *

Questions keep buzzing in the back of my mind: What am I doing in this life? Why am I trying to become a Franciscan Sister in this modern world?

A simple answer comes quickly, like a response whispered back to my doubts: I'm here to live a life of community, prayer, and service. I want my life centered around those three things. With community, prayer, and service at the center of my life, I might grow into a better version of myself, a better Christian and disciple of Jesus. These are the quick answers, in this inner conversation I go through every week or so.

But then. Sometimes my quick answers are countered by more doubts, questions. I wonder why being a Franciscan Sister is the best way for me to live a life of community, prayer, and service. I wonder if it would be more radical for me to go join a newer movement in the Church. I imagine I would live in better solidarity with the poor with Christian activists in the inner city, part of an intentional community—more like Casa Jane.

I daydream about how it could work. Maybe I could gather a group of my friends and we could get a place together, then let people who are homeless live with us too. We could offer meals around our table and host prayer and workshops about social justice for the public. I guess what I want is a life like how Catholic Workers I know live. Would the Catholic Worker lifestyle fit me better? Would it feel more natural to live in a Catholic Worker house than hanging out in these old buildings, between these institutional walls?

Some friends have been sending messages, asking me if I've read *The Irresistible Revolution: Living as an Ordinary Radical*, by Shane Claiborne. Once I do, I weep as I take in Shane's story and learn about the "new monastics." I'm enamored by the description of how Shane and his friends live in an intentional community in one of the poorest neighborhoods in Philadelphia and serve their neighbors. I want to live simply with other Christians. I want to serve the marginalized too. That's what Jesus modeled for us. I want to be close to the poor, close to Jesus. How is being a novice helping me to become a more radical Christian?

How could the structures, expectations and traditions of the Franciscan Sisters offer me freedom to serve the poor and radically follow Jesus like Shane and his friends are doing? I feel stuck and confused as I try to think it through, try to imagine how being a Sister will free me.

Sitting in the silent adoration chapel, I muse about my confusion and bob my head in prayer. Then, one afternoon, something happens inside me: I can only describe it as a widening in my heart. It feels like an opening, a gap that allows some light to soften the doubts tangled inside. This is where I am. I'm here with these good women. I'm lucky to be with them. They're amazing! In the rays of light falling into me, a cavern is created for the Spirit to whisper. As quickly as I wondered why I haven't yet left, I know why I'm here.

It's the mothers. The spiritual mothers. The roots, the depth, the way that this form of religious life means I'm now in a beautiful web of connection, tradition. I'm tangled, I'm caught. I'm stuck. And I'm actually glad.

The spiritual mothers are the women I'm interacting with daily. They are the gray-haired and stooping ones, who embrace me with their hugs, prayer, and notes of encouragement and love. Yes, it is these holy women who I longed to pray with in the pews, even when I lived in Casa Jane and volunteered at Tubman House. It is these mothers for sure.

But it is also the mothers that came before them, generations ago. The founders of my community, the Bavarian immigrants who were eager to serve people in Wisconsin, the poor, the sick, the children of immigrants in the Americas.

Then my mind flips through timelines and zooms to the spiritual mothers of the Middle Ages. It is St. Clare of Assisi and her Poor Ladies, in San Damiano. The mystics, and bold voices who spoke to power and advocated for reforms. Go back to Rome, St. Catherine of Siena told the pope who was lingering at Avignon! St. Teresa of Avila, outgoing (like me), and deep and intense, who was sought after for her spiritual wisdom, for her *Interior Castle*. The martyrs, the holy mothers burned on stakes, who were jailed and tortured because of their devotion. The women who history has forgotten, but remained faithful in their consecration to Christ, to their lives of prayer, service, and community. The timeline flips more: the desert mothers in the early church, women who were contemplatives, removed and wise—hermits, monks, nuns, consecrated virgins. Yes, I love them and need them, all these mothers. All of them are my *why*.

Being part of the Franciscan Sisters means I'm amazingly part of this lineage too. It means that the roots are very deep, the foundation is strong and steady. It means that women are holding me up into the rafters of potential and possibility, where webs give me structure and allow me to reflect God's light.

These holy women are my mothers, my church, they are the reason I stay. Somehow, they help me know that I belong to this mystery, this communion. Somehow all of them are mine. I stare at the altar, the Blessed Sacrament gleaming behind the glass of the monstrance and I know: I'm their daughter, a little restless and weak, but I'm here with them, ready to learn.

15

But, there's Mike again.

June 22, 2007 G-chat
5:00 p.m.

Mike: well, to be honest, i don't believe in vocation.
i don't believe in "vocation" in the sense of a calling from god, a plan he has for your life, etc...
i don't think he cares.
as long as we follow the basic rules.
...like st. augustine said, "love, and do what you will."
that's it.

Julia: huh.
wow, really interesting.
i think it all makes a lot of sense
and sometimes and in many ways i'm with you
but, then there's this:
not that i want to debate vocation and life's meaning right now, i don't think that that's the point
but... why do you think you love learning about God and theology so much?
what does it feed in you?

Mike: honestly?
i don't think you'll like it...

Julia:	tell me
Mike:	i think there has to be something bigger and better than this out there, because if there isn't, this life is not worth living.
Julia:	indeed
	why don't you think i'd like that? that's truth.
Mike:	because it's pretty pessimistic and dismal.
Julia:	is that the whole thing though?
Mike:	what do you mean?
Julia:	see, for me, i love God.
	and God is big
	and since i love God and the mystery of God's bigness so much, that's why i love and live as i do
	it is exactly the point, the reason, the motivation, the movement

* * *

Back in the chapel, I'm sitting in a pew at a prayer service with my Sisters, a time of silent adoration. I gaze up at the monstrance illumined on the high altar. Our song of praise rings in the pillars. Many have their eyes closed and are breathing slowly—meditating, probably—while I shift in the pew, unable to shake feelings of restlessness, and enter into the peace of the place. I'm blessed to pray alongside such holy women; I'm blessed to be part of them, I know. Yet, I can't sit still.

Maybe I feel restless because knots are building up in my brain, as questions twist upon themselves. Earlier today I read an email from Mike, a message full of cynicism. Then, at the computer again before coming to this service, we got back into it—our discussion about call and choice as we G-chatted before I rushed down here. We were talking about poverty—the self-emptying poverty of Christ that all Franciscans are called to imitate through vows, service, and solidarity. We were talking about how "God is still speaking," that God's revelation continues through people and creation; God's messages are still coming, even though the Bible was formed long ago.

As I think about it, sitting in the silence with my holy women, it occurs that for as long as I've wanted to follow God's will and have tried to listen deeply to God's call.

But I also know that I once wanted to be a wife and a mother—that's how I pictured my adulthood when I was a girl. I also wanted to travel the world. But I had a sense that if I had traveled to Europe instead of joining the Sisters, I would have been only procrastinating on what was inevitable; I felt so strongly a true calling: I was meant to be with them.

God, I don't understand it, I know I want it, and I want many other things too. Thanks for helping me get here, to stay here. Please help me gain some clarity and contentment during this time in the novitiate.

I move my body onto the kneeler as I pray, hands folded, eyes closed.

God, help me to gain peace about who I am, who you are calling me to be, and all you are asking me to give up. Help me to say yes to you. And please be with me tomorrow, as I go to the farm in Iowa to say goodbye to the land that raised me, that has made me into who I am. Amen.

16

My alarm scowls at me from across the bedroom. I try to claw myself from a dream, out of layers of sleep that are keeping me snug in my blankets. I tumble out of bed, across the room and hit snooze, fall back under blankets, drifting back into dreams. I didn't sleep well and now I'm having trouble waking up.

I'm late, much later than I planned to wake up on my "hermitage day," and the morning I'm driving to the farm to pray my goodbyes. *How pathetic of a new nun am I? God, can't I ever get up early to pray?* I pull the alarm clock close enough to my eyes so I can make out the digital numbers: 8:47. *I'm ridiculous. It's almost 9!* My tired groan sounds muffled under the hum of the air conditioner.

I feel around for glasses, pull them to my face, and look around the bedroom. Bright sunlight peeks through the window blinds. An overflowing laundry basket of dirty clothes spills from behind my closet door, another laundry basket of clean, unfolded clothes waits to be put away. Against one wall, my desk is cluttered with magazines, notebooks, pens, and receipts. In my prayer corner on the floor, my candle is unlit, my prayer book open to yesterday's psalms, to the poem I read before bed.

I open my mouth and pray out loud. God, help me. I want to go to the kitchen for coffee and then light my candle and say morning prayers, but I also want to get on the road to Iowa by 10:00. *You're going to spend the whole day praying, get going!* I drag myself out of bed, grab a towel from the closet, and go to the shower.

After, I stumble around the dim bedroom and grab my prayer journal, a few pens, a book of psalms, a book of poetry. I cram it all into my backpack along with toiletries, clothes. When I see my new cell phone plugged into the wall, I hesitate. I want to spend the day in silence, praying, really talking to God about all that I'm being asked to relinquish. Can I gain peace about the changes in my life? I don't want to be distracted; I want to focus on God. I think about this, my new cell phone in my hands. I've only had it for three days, it's a toy, a new thing to live with. I throw it in my bag but keep it turned off. I guess it could be nice to try the camera and take pictures of the farm.

I find my sleeping bag and tent, grab my pillow, and go downstairs. I find some candles and matches, some fruit and snacks, a flashlight: more stuffed into my backpack. No one is in the house; everyone is already out for the day. Although they know my plans, I scribble a note on a marker board in the kitchen: *Off to Iowa. See you all on Saturday afternoon! Love, Julia*

When I step out the backdoor to the car, a wave of thick humidity clogs my breathing; I exhale slowly. I never checked the weather, and the house was cool. I feel smothered. *HOT!* I groan. I open the car door, roll down the windows and blast the air conditioner before I get in behind the steering wheel. I drive out the alley and turn toward Iowa.

* * *

June sunshine sparkles on the waters of the Mississippi as I drive south toward the farm, yet I'm not impressed by the beauty. My chest tingles with heaviness. I feel overwhelmed by each ditch weed, tree, lily pad, and blooming whatever. In the quiet car, I stare at the scenery through the car window as if everything is under a fog of never-will-be-the-same, it-is-all-going-to-die-some-day. I know that my entire life is in transition. Who am I becoming?

Thoughts gradually untangle as I drive in silence and take in the landscape. River bluffs, small towns, rolling farmland. This could be the last time I visit the farm, the last time I move toward the hills of northeast Iowa and say I'm going home. Wherever my parents live next would be their house, but not my home. Even though I've been with the Sisters for a year and a half now, it is hard to imagine I'd ever call St. Rose Convent home—how could an administrative center for a community become a place I'd be happy to come back to?

Where do I belong? I don't know if I will ever be as pious and prayerful as good nuns are supposed to be. I doubt I'll fit with the Franciscan Sisters. I know these hills well, but feel dazed as I drive toward the familiar farms dotting the horizon.

* * *

Early afternoon I stop by my parents' restaurant and sit at the bar to eat a sandwich and cheesy hashbrowns that Hans cooks for me. Mom and Dad—new restaurant owners and still nursing parttime—are at work and running errands, he says. From there, I drive to our hilly gravel road, winding around S-curves and up the hill. This is the road I walked up and down as a kid, I think, as I hear the rocks crunch under the tires. Along the way, I slow down, park the car on the side of the road and fumble with my phone, taking pictures of the scenery. The afternoon sun illumines the gray-red-tan limestone rocks along the road, the ditch of tall green grasses seems to glow, the field of knee-high corn reveals a grid. I could drive this hill with my eyes closed, but my eyes are open wide, so I can see every sight through my sad eyes. *I'm going to miss this place; I can't believe I might never come back.* Driving down our farm's long driveway, I stop the car and take more pictures: the white fence, the field, trees, our yellow and green house, the expansive lawn.

I think about childhood, playing outside in the sloping yard that surrounds the farmhouse and spills down the hill into the barnyard, then pastures, then a creek below a cliff. I remember running around with cousins and my siblings in the fields, playing in the woods. I think about the hours our family worked together under the hot sun, weeding the ball-field sized vegetable garden with Mom, everyone helping to bring produce to the farmer's market. I see the flowerbeds and remember quiet afternoons with Mom when she taught me to pay attention to the blooming flowers, the birds in the branches.

The mid-afternoon sun illuminates the empty gravel parking area next to the house; the openness and silence is offering an invitation to solitude and contemplation. I park and sit still for a minute, gazing at the lawn, staring into the weeds that are starting to take over the bushes. My chest prickles with feelings of being overwhelmed. As I open the car door, Milton, our family's cocker spaniel, is immediately underfoot, greeting me with giddy barks and jumps. I reach to pet him.

* * *

Lugging my backpack, tent, and sleeping bag from the backseat, I remember that I need some water, so I grab the empty bottle from my backpack before going inside. Walking through the front door I say "Hello!?" even though I knew the house is empty, no one is home; no cars are in the driveway, and everyone is at work.

The quietness of the farmhouse booms back at me. Some of Mom's magazines are left opened on the end table next to the recliner.

In the living room, I look up the hill at the lilac bushes. It's sad to think that potential future nieces and nephews won't be able to play in the bushes too. My eyes wander around the room, and I see the time blinking from the VCR: 3:43.

I've wasted the whole day! My body clenches with embarrassment, disappointment. In the kitchen, I find a pen and scratch paper, scribble a note for Mom or Dad or Colleen to find when they came home from work: *Off in the woods praying. I'll see you in the morning. Love, J.*

* * *

On the edge of the lawn, I throw my stuff over the red farm gate into the tall grass. I climb over and jump down and weave my body through the tall pasture, arms full of camping gear. Before long, the few goats that remain in our once-huge herd—now only six alpines—mosey over from the other side of the barn, chains clanging, to greet their guest. Since the small group of goats have several acres of pasture most of the grass is overgrown—some is even taller than me, making it tough to see where I'm going. Still, I plow through the wilting prairie. Buzzing insects swarm around my face. Milton jumps and pants nearby, happy for companionship.

It doesn't take long for me to find the spot. In this clearing at the edge of the pasture, my sisters and I once camped. The same trees hang overhead, but nothing looks like I remember. Has the land shifted? How many years has it been since I've been here? I begin setting up my tent, and as I do my muddled mind tries to collect the memories flooding. We once played house in the grove of cedars on the other side of that hill. Once we went sledding and landed together in a pile at the bottom of a sinkhole. On the other side of the barn, we raced our sleds down the hill. I wrote my first award-winning story describing one of those sledding excursions. Was that in the fifth grade? I bend down in the grass and clear rocks and sticks, putting my tent together. Gosh, I loved exploring the woods around here. I should go roam through them later tonight.

I find a rock and pound the stakes into the dry earth. Not far from here my cousin and I once picked berries, cheerfully singing "God is so good" each time we saw something beautiful in the woods. I find some rocks and arrange them into a circle and place my candle and matches nearby: all set for a campfire and a little place for prayer tonight. On the other side of that pasture was Grandma's house and we would freely run back and forth. In the summer she would pay us a dollar for each thistle we chopped in the pasture. Remembering her, I feel the prickly weight pressing into my chest with more might, the ache of loss radiating through my throat, chest, stomach. I try to think of the good memories and pray a simple thank you.

But the emotions are too heavy. I'm damp with sweat, and so guzzle some water. Then I grab my psalm book, poetry book, journal and pen from my backpack, zipping everything else inside the tent.

Into the shade beneath the grove of trees, I go: I want to cool off and focus on God. That's what I'm here to do. The dry ground stirs under my sandals. Under the trees, the air is cooler, fresh. I look around: nothing in this grove is as I remember. Am I in the right spot? Small insects buzz in the afternoon light. Decaying logs and branches are scattered among the brown soil. Green tree branches hang overhead. Where is the log I used to sit on?

There it is: the nook in the tree branch, close to the ground. I sat in that nook as a teenager. If I ever had free time after school on a clear day, I would come here to be alone and savor the quiet. I'd bring my backpack and do homework on my lap. Or, I'd sit and stare into the trees and listen to the creek gurgle farther below, at the bottom of the cliff. I sigh out loud, thinking of the peace I knew here.

I crawl into the nook and find that I don't fit anymore. I'm much bigger than I was. I squeeze in, for memory's sake, and feel the rough bark pressing into skin, the curve of the log pinching my flesh. Uncomfortable now. I feel my throat ache. I groan, disappointed that my favorite place of peace has changed too. Climbing down, I notice the volume of the creek gurgling below the cliff. Trees hang over the edge, making it hard to see the stream through the bramble and bushes. I want to see the water, watch it ripple—maybe it will help me feel some peace? I look around: where can I sit and pray? Milton happily runs back and forth along the edge of the cliff.

I find a stump in the shade, a little higher up the hill. I can't see the gurgling water, but I can hear it: good enough. I hear myself sighing, feel my body twitching, restless as I thumb through my prayer books, open my journal. I want to write about letting go: about the memories, the day, my feelings, my longing for peace. My thoughts feel choppy.

> *Journal*
> *Friday afternoon, "Silent" day, by the creek in the "Walsh woods" behind the house.*
> *June 29, 5:00ish*
>
> Good God, Holy, Awesome, Grounding, Solid.
>   On this day, this hermitage day, I'm in my head, in my body and struggling somewhat to center, to still, to listen, to be with you, live in purity and sense you in my heart.
>   I've made my camp; I've put up the tent.
>   I've been mostly quiet.
>   I've loved the birds and buzzes.
>   I've sensed you. And now I just want to swim.
>   As I move and reflect on holiness, LORD, guide me; help me; be with me. Amen!

Putting down my pen, I stare ahead, over the top of the cliff, listening to the water. It's cool in the shade, but I still feel hot and sweaty. I remember how Hans and I would try to catch minnows in that creek when we were little. Along with our cousins, we spent summer afternoons swimming in parts that were wide and deep. I remember trying to create a bridge of steppingstones with him without any luck; the water flowed over the rocks, our shoes got wet.

I want to go swimming. I didn't bring my swimsuit, though. Wait, what's stopping me from going in my t-shirt and shorts? I need to say goodbye to this water, this water that has formed me. This creek is part of this farm, the farm that has made me into who I am. The best way to start ritualizing my farewells is to go into the water like I used to do. I'll have to go quite far up or downstream to find a place where I can directly walk in. I'll have to veer through burning nettles and thorns. I've climbed down this cliff before, along with Ellen and Colleen, years ago. I can climb down again. Why not?

Leaving books and pen on the stump, I pace back and forth along the edge of the cliff looking for a place to climb down. It's a bit tough to see how I'll get to the water with all the trees and bushes blocking my view.

I spot a tree hanging off the edge. Wow, its roots actually look like steps heading right down to the water! I can't see the creek from there, where the tree is rooted, but I can hear it, I can feel the cooler air rising. This is a good place to climb down, and I face forward. My right hand reaches up, grips the tree branch overhead. My right foot steps downward, onto the tree root growing up through the brown earth over the rocks. Sliding my hand down, over the rough branch, I step down with my left foot.

17

There's one second, possibly two: a fast gap, a tiny pause in time. I know in this space that I'm about to die, could die. I know that I'm going to crash to the ground, into the limestone creek bed.

The rock crumbles under my foot. I lose my grip on the branch. I'm falling through branches. It's like an eternity is happening in a moment, my entire life is being re-lived in a blink: the memories that were trickling through my mind before are becoming like a tsunami and I don't know if I will drown. I'm only twenty-five years old; this might be when I die. *God, I don't want to. It's a bit early, don't you think?*

I fall through the air, from the edge of the cliff toward the solid creek bed below. I fall through a web of bramble, face forward, twigs scratching my face and arms and legs. My arm lifts to my forehead.

I've lived in Africa. I've been a teacher. Some of my writing is in print—a student newspaper. I'm a Franciscan Sister now. I don't want to die. It would hurt a lot of people; I'm lucky to be so loved. Help me God!

I'm screaming. The clear, flowing water and tan rock is rushing toward my face.

I gasp, spit, lifting my head out of water. I hear my voice moaning, weakly, as a blur of water, blood, and teeth fall from my mouth and my glasses fall off my face, disappear downstream. Everything's a blur.

* * *

Once I make it back up the cliff, through the pasture and to the farmhouse, I lie on my belly near the cellar door, my face inches above the grass. I watch my own blood pool into the green, red liquid gushing from my broken body. I'm getting weak as I listen to the 9-1-1 woman speaking through the phone pressed to my ear. I listen and moan, listen and moan. I'm alive.

I hear Milton. He continues to bark. He runs around the house in circles, trying every door.

"What were you doing in the woods?" I hear the 9-1-1 lady's voice coming through the phone pressed to my ear asking me unnecessary—annoying—questions as if I'm in the mood to chat. I try to respond politely, grateful for her kindness.

"Praying," I say.

"Praying?" She sounds surprised.

"Someone is coming." I hear car wheels stirring up the gravel driveway, a radio blaring happy music. I hear the car park on the other side of the house, the ignition and music turn off. I try to holler for help, but my voice comes out weak, like a quiet moan.

I hear Milton run over to the car, barking. The car motor stops. A car door opens. Colleen's voice floats through the air, sounding confused. "Milton, what's with you? What's the matter?" The dog leaps toward her, then away from her and toward me, trying to get Colleen to follow. He pulls her to the backdoor where I lie; she feels compelled to follow him instead of going in the front door of the house, closer to where she parked.

I hear her feet approaching, she's talking to Milton. "Geez. What's going on, Milt?"

I try to holler. "Colleen! Colleen!" The phone is still pressed to my ear, the operator is probably listening.

I see the blur of her standing over me. "Oh my God, Julia! Oh my God! Oh my God! What happened?" I can make out that her face is in shock, tears are moistening her red face.

"I fell off the cliff down by the creek.... Here, talk to 9-1-1." She understands my mumbled words. She takes the phone and speaks to the 9-1-1 lady.

"Hi...Yes, I'm her sister, Colleen... OK. OK. Maybe twenty feet or so... Limestone... OK... I'm going to call our parents... OK..."

I'm watching the blur of her over me. She fumbles for her own phone in her pocket, presses some buttons, puts it up to her other ear.

"Mom! Julia fell off the cliff down by the creek. An ambulance is coming... At the back door, by the house... OK... OK..."

"Yeah, she's awake. She's watching me." Colleen is speaking into the other phone. "OK. I think someone else is here... Yeah, maybe it's the sheriff."

It sounds like the car drove straight onto the lawn. I hear the sound of a man's boots hitting the ground and Milton barking again, running in circles, not calming down.

"Hello?!" I hear a man's voice yelling.

I try to holler back, but my voice is weak.

"Over here!" Colleen yells.

"Put your dog away!" The sheriff orders my sister as he runs over. Colleen hands me my cell phone and runs to catch Milton, to put him in the shed.

Through the phone pressed to my ear, the 9-1-1 woman says, "I'm going to hang up now since the sheriff is there." I drop the phone to the ground.

The man is standing over me. I can feel his anxiety, waves of hyper energy vibrating toward my misery, not helping a thing. He begins to fire questions.

"What is your name? What happened? Where were you? What were you doing?" *He is screaming.* I pick one question.

"My name is Julia," I mutter.

"Jessica, you're going to be OK. You're going to be OK, Jessica!" *Why is he* screaming at me? I take a deep breath and try to scream back at him.

"My name is Julia!" My voice comes out jumbled, cracked.

"You're going to be OK, Jessica!"

I groan in frustration, in pain, at the sight of my blood continuing to pool on the lawn in front of my face. I ignore him. In the distance I hear a siren, probably the ambulance. Several vehicles roll down the driveway, like a parade has arrived. I hear cars parking all over the place, car doors slamming, feet running toward me.

"Julia, I'm here." Dad.

"You'll be OK now, Julia." Mom.

A large white vehicle—the ambulance—backs toward me, doors swing open. I hear little wheels rolling on metal. A stretcher pulled out, more voices. I hear Aunt Trudy. I remember that she volunteers as a paramedic sometimes.

"Be careful with her neck," someone says.

"Here, let's put this collar on her." I hear Velcro and feel a padded neck brace wrapped around me, tangled into my hair.

"Keep her still," someone says. I hear people begin to count. They hold me still and put me on the stretcher, lift me into the ambulance.

"Can someone call the Sisters in La Crosse?" I holler to the people who are outside the door.

"Yes. Yes. We will. Where's her phone?" Mom is asking Colleen.

"Here, on the ground." Colleen finds it.

"Who should we call?" Colleen asks.

"St. Rose Convent. Chiara House. Ask for Sister Lucy Ann or the leadership team," I say with sudden lucidity.

"OK, OK, I'll call them," Colleen says.

"We'll meet you at the hospital. Love you, Julia!" Mom again.

"Julia, I'm taking off your shoes," Aunt Trudy says. I hear clicks, feel things fastening.

I hear someone crawl in beside me. The ambulance door slams shut.

We roll away from the farm that formed me, away from the cliff that broke me into pieces. As we bump over the rocky road, tilt and twist around corners, I feel each shift in my body. Each ache and shot of pain helps me know I'm alive, shows me what hurts. I moan, wondering if I could still die. I know the closest hospital is at least twenty minutes away in West Union. Will we make it?

When we reach the paved road, the ambulance driver starts to go faster, wailing the siren. Dad is in the back with me. I'm certain someone else is there too, someone very quiet—even though Dad will tell me later that he was the only one. I'm getting drowsy. I feel as if I could sleep forever. I close my eyes. Dad begins to chat, asking unimportant questions.

"What were you going to do down by the creek, Julia?"

I groan, the same sort of annoyed groan I made when Dad would wake me up to go to high school. "Swimming," I say, in a tone that really means leave me alone; I don't want to talk now.

"What time did you get to the farm?" he persists.

"About 4:00, I think."

"How was your drive from La Crosse?" I answer all his questions, completely frustrated, wondering why he thinks that now is the best time for an interview, why he won't let me sleep.

* * *

Dr. Myron, a long-time family friend, is on duty at the ER when I come in on the stretcher. He is usually cracking jokes but now he sounds so serious, his tone stern. He asks if I was ever unconscious.

"No, I don't think so. Always awake," I say, but I begin to doubt it, and with the doubt washes in a feeling of shame. I'm so stupid for getting into this mess.

"I'm so sorry, I'm so sorry," I begin to repeat.

I hear my Mom standing with the nurses, her voice emotional. "Julia, there's nothing to be sorry about. We're so glad you're alive," she says.

"Where do you hurt?" Dr. Myron asks as he gently moves his hands, touches and lifts my arms, bends my elbows, wrists, hands, examining what works.

"My mouth, my nose, my hand," I tell him.

The x-rays determine that my injuries aren't life threatening, that my spine isn't broken.

Dad is sitting next to me behind a curtain in a corner of a wide-open room. We need to pray, I think. Prayer will help me heal. I need everything God can provide right now. There's so much to give thanks for. I want Dad to help me, to pray for me when I'm too weak.

"Dad," I say. "Please pray with me. Please pray the Our Father." We begin to say the words together.

"Our Father, Who art in heaven, hallowed be Thy name." Dad's clear, deep voice helps me move my muffled words along, keeps my broken jaw moving.

"Thy kingdom come, thy will be done. On earth as it is in heaven," we say together.

Then I'm the only one speaking, "Give us this day our daily bread."

I open my eyes and see that Dad is leaving me alone. I hear him sobbing on the other side of the curtain.

I'm confused, disappointed. Why is he leaving? I need him to help me complete the prayer.

Once again, I'm by myself, and uncertain. Am I in worse shape than I feel? Am I going to be OK?

* * *

They are transferring me to a bigger hospital in La Crosse. This time, Dad rides in front of the ambulance with the driver. Mom and Colleen follow in other cars.

We go up and down the hills and over the curvy roads of northeast Iowa at normal highway speed, without sirens. A nurse is caring for me in the back, as I lay face down on a stretcher, a neck brace limiting my movements. The nurse, small, thin, exudes a warmth: she is kind and chatty—apparently determined to keep me awake like everyone else. She tells me about her horses, her family. She digs in her purse for Chapstick when she notices how cracked my lips are underneath the blood caked on my face. Cuts inside my mouth continue to bleed, and I find comfort holding the suction tube there, trying to reduce blood flowing to my stomach. I still have a little control.

I can hear and feel each bump on the rugged, cracking asphalt. I squirm with pain as we round curves and go through valleys. Along the way, I ask Dad if someone can call my friends and tell them what happened. I want everyone I know to pray.

"Call Hillary, Dana, Laura, Andy, all my Casa Jane housemates." One after another, Colleen tells them what's happened. I'm relieved to know that folks around the country are praying for me and my healing, that I'm being supported through this by their love. I relax a little as the ambulance bumps over hills.

At the ER in La Crosse there is no waiting, no stillness. I'm rushed into what feels like the center of a giant room. A team of doctors and nurses huddle around me. I can't see anyone's faces, but I feel their kindness and concern as they swarm, as they cut off my clothes and examine my body. "Lacerations on her eyebrows, on the bridge of her nose, around her mouth... Abrasions on her arms and legs. Four bruises on her left lateral chest anterior, above and below her breast," I hear someone say.

A blur, a body moves with something tan: a clipboard? A blur of an arm in motion. White coats. Bobbing heads. I'm relieved by the full-body exam, that they're checking me over so thoroughly. At the same time, I've never felt so exposed before, so naked. I'm glad I can't see their faces. I feel grateful they're kind and professional.

One nurse—does she have a blond ponytail? I think so—asks me if there is anything she can get me, is there anything I need. I think for a moment, then surprise myself with a mumbled reply. "Do you think there's any way I could get a rosary?" I don't know how things work in this giant hospital. I know it's not a Catholic hospital, but I figure they must have a chaplaincy department with resources for every religion; someone will tell her where the rosaries are kept in the ER? Despite my broken jaw and swollen face, she understands my request and says she'll see what she can do.

She disappears for a while and the doctors continue their exam. A hospital gown is put on my aching body and the huddle of doctors—are they all men?—leave together to discuss my treatment plan. Alone and unexposed, I pray. *Thank you, God, for letting me live, for saving my life. Help me to accept however this will change me. Thank you, God. Thank you, God.*

The nurse with the blond ponytail returns, another nurse is with her. They poke at the tubes around me, they ask me how I'm doing. One grabs my hand and holds it, telling me that I'm going to be OK. The nurse with the blond ponytail sighs. "Sorry, but I had no luck finding a rosary," she says.

"Thanks for trying," I tell her. "It's OK." The two nurses stand beside me for a while, being quiet. I can't tell what they look like, their facial expressions are all a blur, but I pick up a sense that they are deeply concerned, saddened. I must look awful, I figure, with this bloody and bruised face of mine. I hold the suction tube in my hands and put it back into my mouth to soak up some of the blood I can taste, still pooling there.

We all are quiet together for a while—me holding the suction tube and praying with my eyes closed, the nurses standing beside me, holding my hand, checking my vitals. Then the nurse with the ponytail jumps.

"I just remembered! Earlier tonight I saw a rosary on the helicopter pad, on the cement out there. I'm going to check to see if I can find it!"

I moan, "Thank you."

* * *

My bed rolls through a maze of white hallways, under brightly lit fluorescent lights. I'm brought through a heavy metal door into a dark room. They move me onto another flat surface. They leave the room. I'm, for the first moment since I was found by the backdoor of the farmhouse, all alone.

It is silent. It is dark. I lie still and wait, thinking how good it is to be alive, how thankful I am that people are caring for me. I feel, of all things, joy. I begin to sing hymns of praise and gratitude. Bible camp songs from my childhood: *God is so good, God is so good, God is so good, so good to me!* I sing loud and bold like I did as a kid on top of the gate at the edge of the pasture near the farm. Classic hymns: *O Lord, my God / When I in awesome wonder / Consider all the worlds / Thy hands have made / I see the stars / I hear the rolling thunder / The power throughout / The universe displayed / Then sings my soul / My savior, God, to thee / How great thou art / How great thou art! / Then sings my soul / My Savior, God, to Thee / How great thou art! / How great thou art!*

I hear the door open. Someone enters the room, probably the X-ray technician. He says to lay very still, that the table will move. He will speak to me through the glass, with a microphone, he tells me. I wonder if he heard me singing and decide I don't care. I overhear two voices talking behind something—a wall. The male voice says, "What pain medicines is she on?"

"None, yet. She's a nun," a female voice replies.

I snort, laughing. But I recover and become still. The metal table begins to slide around, the machines in the dark room make noises and take picture after picture of my hurting body.

* * *

Through the blur I surmise I'm back in the ER, and there are fluorescent lights over me again. Various medical machines are monitoring my vitals. In my hurting hand, I grip the suction tube into my mouth, sucking up the blood and drool around the new gaps in my teeth, where teeth are chipped, broken, and missing. Are the cuts on my lip still bleeding? I think so, but it seems that there's gauze taped to my face. My left hand is aching with pain, the neck brace wrapped around my neck is pinching.

The nurse with the ponytail comes over, stands at my side. I can't see her, but she must be smiling, her voice sounds happy. "I found the rosary. I had to look all over the helicopter pad, and I almost gave up, but I found it! It's broken a little bit, but here, you can have it." She places it in my right hand.

This is the hand that doesn't hurt so much, and I press the beads into my palm. I feel the shape of the crucifix, the small corpus connecting with my skin. I'm not sure where the idea to ask for a rosary came from; I don't have a strong devotion to this form of prayer, I only pray it occasionally. It must have been God's suggestion for me to ask for this sacramental item, to hold it close. I feel stronger, calmer, with the metal cross and the broken string of wooden beads gripped in my fist, as if I'm tightly holding the hand of my love. Thank you for saving me, Jesus.

PART TWO
REPAIRED

18

It's dark and there's a curtain separating me from a woman who is vibrating the room with her snoring. My body is sore, aching. Earlier, I asked the nurses huddled around how many bones I broke in my face. "More than anyone could count," they said. I can feel it: every bone from my eyebrows to my chin is shattered. If it weren't for my skin, it feels like all the fragments of bones would just scatter.

I don't understand why no one is with me, why all the Sisters and my family went to sleep. I can't possibly sleep tonight with all this pain pressing into my body, and that lady snoring so loudly on the other side of this curtain. But here I am. Alive. I'm so thankful to be alive, so thankful for all the kindness and help from so many people, that I feel like I might burst. I'm so thankful. So thankful.

Once, at a retreat, a group of us Sisters watched a documentary about a Japanese scientist who conducted experiments and found that when water was exposed to positive words like "thank you" before it was frozen the water crystals would be more symmetrical, beautiful. I remember I'm made of water; we all are. And my body needs a lot of positive energy for all the healing work it needs to do, that it is already doing.

I can't sleep with all this pain, with all that snoring over there—and the hospital noises I hear out in the hallway. I can't sleep, but I can tell my body thank you, thank you. I picture my cells, side-by-side on my arm, where it is hurting below the skin. I visualize each cell like science class diagrams, colored correctly. I say *thank you. Thank you.* I slowly think of cells lined up, building up this hurting body. In my mind, I zoom in and visualize each spot where it hurts on my face, my arms, my hand. I meditate this way for hours, falling in and out of sleep. Calm washes over me as I visualize my cells, feel the pain, and pray *thank you, thank you, thank you. Thank you for living. Thank you for healing. Thank you.*

I had the night of prayer I was hoping for after all.

* * *

I wake up alone in what feels like another hospital room, a white space, everything around me a blur. My entire body hurts, in one way or another, as if I fell off a cliff. Oh, right. *I can't believe I fell off a cliff and broke my face.*

My hand moves up to feel my wounds. There's blood crusted to my skin. I feel bruised, I must be black with bruises. Stitches are poking out from my eyebrows, my lips, my nose. The soft neck brace has been replaced by a stiff plastic one, and now I can't turn my head. I squint and try to look toward the window. I only see sunlight bright and glowing through the window shade. I hear footsteps, people pressing buttons on the machines next to me, the occasional feeling of someone else's skin gently pressed against my own, near my wrist, upon my arm.

The familiar voices of my family and Sisters swirl in and out of the space, but no one's face or words settle into me. Through the blur I learn that I will have reconstructive jaw surgery soon and it will take five to seven hours. I gather from the voices, somehow, that the surgery will be risky and dangerous. I feel hungry for prayers, for floods of love and grace.

At one point, a young woman stands beside my bed, a chaplain intern about my age—I can't make out her face, but she feels similar to a version of the woman I was just days ago: white, peppy, Christian, Midwestern. Although my voice is garbled and my mind hazy, we have a choppy conversation.

"Would you like to pray?" she asks.

"Yes, please." My body relaxes, grateful for the offer.

"How do you like to pray?" she says.

"In every way I can," I groan, feeling overwhelmed, unable to make a choice.

"Do you like the Psalms?"

"Yes," I mumble.

"Do you have a favorite one?" I have no ideas, I can't recall which ones are most important to me right now.

She waits quietly as I think about this and then says, "How about I just open the Psalms and we see which one God gives us right now?"

"Yes. Thank you."

She begins to read:

> Surely, I wait for the LORD;
> who bends down to me and hears my cry,
> Draws me up from the pit of destruction, out of the muddy clay,
> Sets my feet upon rock, steadies my steps,
> And puts a new song in my mouth,
> a hymn to our God... (*Psalm 40:2-4, NAB*)

My swollen face widens with a smile. Tears fill my eyes.

"Wow. Thank you," I tell her, my voice garbled. She's quiet and says little. It sounds like she might be crying too.

My mind and heart settle into the thought that, yes, God has saved my life, God is restoring me, directing me upon the path ahead: an unknown disturbing, wavering path of healing, transformation and becoming a new person. God has spared me and pulled me out of the pit. A new life song begins to form in my heart. Thank you, Jesus.

Before she leaves the room, the chaplain asks me if there is anything I want before I go into jaw surgery. I ask for the anointing of the sick.

* * *

I'm visited by Fr. Jude, a gentle, retired priest who is faithful in his love and devotion to my Franciscan Sisters. I see the blur of his black clothing hovering over my bed, worn prayer books in his wrinkled hands, a stole hanging from his shoulders. His presence is consoling.

My muscles feel stronger, my spirit more courageous. The ancient prayers he reads over me become like healing balms for my weary, blood-caked, broken body, swollen and tired in this hospital bed. The oil rubbed into my forehead, above my freshly stitched wounds, is like an anointing for the journey ahead, a blessing over my brokenness.

As I'm rolled off to surgery, Mom and Dad hover around me briefly, speaking quick messages of love. "Goodbye. I love you," I say, profoundly aware that the surgery might be complicated, understanding that I could come close to death again. Compared to yesterday, when I was falling off the cliff, though, I feel prepared: spiritually boosted for whatever might come. *God, I trust you. No matter what happens, I believe that I'm going to be OK. Please help everyone else be OK too.*

* * *

I wake up in a fluorescent-lit, windowless room, my bed crowded by beeping and glowing machines. My body feels like it's at an awkward angle. I try to look around and understand, but all is blurred. I doze away. I wake again and feel my jaw ache. I slowly lift my hand to my face and feel bandages, medical tape, tubes, puffiness and blood-caked bruises, something protruding from my nose.

I have a thousand questions; I want to know so many things. I try to move my mouth up and down but discover that my jaw is wired together, my mouth is full of metal, my teeth are behind wire, locked together, in place. My tongue tries to move around to feel the inside of my mouth, to get acquainted with the situation. I feel the smoothness of a wet plastic tube pressing on my tongue, squirming down my throat and toward my lungs and belly. The sensation of the tube feels like the middle-school game I once played of sucking unchewed spaghetti noodles partly down my esophagus. This, though, is not play; I can feel the seriousness, the intensity, of my situation. I feel pressure on my neck, restraining me from the inside. I try to talk but I start gagging and coughing.

Mom's voice comes to me from somewhere in the room, through the blur, "Don't try to talk now Julia..."

Nurses rush in, press buttons and I drift back away, somewhere.

I wake again, and this time I feel that I'm surrounded by a huddle of Sisters, friends, and family. Nurses flutter in and out, pressing buttons, speaking in hushed tones. I can't see anyone, all is blurry, but I know their voices and feel their love.

"You're in the ICU, Julia.... You're going to be OK."

Sadness colors the voices I hear, it's easy to visualize tears on their tired, worried faces. I want to assure them I'm OK, that I'm grateful and glad they're with me. But I can't speak. I can only think these things in my dazed, drugged state, and hope that they know how grateful I am that they're here with me, that they're praying, that I'm alive.

* * *

I have a few photos from this time that help me remember what things were like, how I felt, and the extremity of my condition. My face is swollen beyond recognition. A neck brace lifts my chin. My bloody nose presses into the bottom of my giant bloody upper lip, crusted and red with goo, wounds exposed. A large bandage crosses my forehead, elastic is pressed over the slits of skin, my puffy cheeks, holding the ventilator tubes in place that run down my broken nose. A blue crunchy tube extends above my head like an antenna. One eye is partly covered by the bandage that extends over my forehead, to the left side of my face. Part of the purplish flesh is visible underneath. The other eye is a slit, surrounded by puffy, purplish-red skin.

In the photos, Ellen and Colleen and my friend Laura are posing next to me, with grimacing faces, trying to smile. Their faces are wiped with exhaustion, soaked by tears; it looks like they have been sobbing. I'm grinning widely through bandages, tubes, and swollen cheeks; I believe I'm expressing joy and gratitude for the good healthcare, for the sparing of my life and the bonus of being with Laura and my sisters. Upon my lap is my Psalms book, opened to the ancient prayers. On the bed is a clipboard, scribbles of black ink are on a white page, mostly illegible, for writing was the only way I could communicate during the time, how I tried to interact, ask questions. I can make out some of the words on the page: "Where? I can't see." And "What did you say?" And something else a bit less clear—either it is "What time did I get out?" or "How much did they cut me?"

* * *

I wake again, this time a group of Sisters and Ellen huddled around me. Ellen asks if I'd like them to pray the rosary. I try to nod and they begin. I doze in and out as the voices of various Sisters make music through the mantras, through the rhythm of prayers. A few weeks later, Ellen says she noticed that my heart monitor showed I really liked Hail Marys, that my heart rate would slow and steadily decrease with the Marian prayer, that my heart rate went up with each Our Father.

Later, I awake and hear the wheels of Sister Dorothy's walker jiggling through the hall. She comes to the other side of the curtain to remind me that we had a lunch date. "Julia, if you didn't want to go to Panera you could have just told me," she says.

I start to laugh—try to—but my mouth can't grin, my vocal cords can't make the sound of laughter. My belly shakes. Since then, I have heard Sister Dorothy tell this story countless times, saying she knew from my shaking belly that I was still myself and my mind was working fine—that I would recover and be alright.

Years later, Mom told me that these times of prayer and sitting in waiting rooms at the hospital were important for her to accept the changes in my life. "I didn't understand until your accident. The time when you were in the hospital was a time when our family was able to really bond with your community," she said. "I thought about how brokenness and suffering are strange mysteries—how the goodness is often evident in the ways that people come together and lean on each other through pain."

* * *

Alone in the ICU, I stir from my doze, feeling that someone else is in the quiet room with me. Without opening my eyes, I feel a strong presence, a powerful love. I crack my eyelids, catch a blur of a body: a man. It must be a male nurse; my night nurse must be a man.

I feel waves of warmth coming from the man, a healing energy? I feel awe, amazed that this nurse is sitting with me, observing me, even loving me. I've never before felt so wonderfully, perfectly loved. I lie in bed smiling, feeling love and the gratitude mix together, swirl all around me: love more powerful than my pain. I fall back to sleep. When I wake again, I feel the presence of the loving man beside me. I'm surprised he's still there.

"Thank you for sitting here with me, but I know you have a lot to do, you don't need to do this. Thank you," I say, feeling strong.

He responds in a clear calm voice. "*This is who I am. This is what I do.*"

Confused, I fall asleep again and then awake for the third time. He is *still* sitting with me, quietly watching over me. I'm starting to get concerned. I say, "Thank you, but please take care of the others. I know you have others to be with."

"Ok, I will go," he agrees, "*but first I want to make you more comfortable. Would you like me to play some music for you?*" He leaves and returns with a CD player and puts on the perfect song—I've never heard it before or since, but it fills me with strength and peace.

"Thank you. What's your name?" I ask.

"*My name is Jesús,*" he says, moving toward the door, leaving a soft warm glow behind. I crack my eyes again as he moves out and see a glimpse of the back of his blue nurse scrubs, the back of his neck; I see brown skin, short dark hair.

I feel like I've been taught one of the most important lessons of my life: how to love and be present to suffering.

The next day, my friends Angela and Hillary flutter through the ICU, eager to offer care to my family and me through their actions and presence. They bring my family a big basket of snacks. They pop behind my curtain and offer to bring me my CD player and CDs from my bedroom at Chiara House.

"Would you like that?" I nod yes, sure. But, I'm confused. I thought that the nurse already put a CD player in the room? I don't say anything. I wonder where the other CD player went.

* * *

Out of the ICU and moved to another part of the hospital, Ellen and Colleen are with me. They rearrange my blankets and wipe my arms, hands, and face with a damp washcloth while I drift in and out of sleep.

I try to speak and learn that my vocal cords can make noise again, that there is no longer a tube in the way. But now I can't move my jaw up and down; my teeth are wired in place. My tongue moves around, feels the places where the teeth were broken, feels the wires in my mouth.

I moan a bit and say hello. Then it occurs to me: have they called all my friends? Do all my friends know what's happened to me?

"Hey," I say, "tell me which friends you called and what the conversations were like."

"I called all your housemates from JVC. A lot of your friends have been here visiting, along with a ton of the Sisters. Andy knows. Casa Jane knows. Practically all the contacts on your phone, Julia."

"Thanks," I say. "I want them all to pray for me."

"What about Mike?" I speak again, without moving my jaw, learning how to speak through my teeth.

"Who's Mike?" Colleen says.

"Oh, he's a close friend, even though he lives in Colorado," I say. "Can you please call him and tell him what happened?"

"Sure, I can call him. Who is he again? How come I've never heard of him?" Ellen asks.

"Just a really good friend," I sigh, closing my eyes. "I just...think he would want to know."

19

Five days after I fell, Mom and a nurse help me get dressed and bathed. I'm wobbly, weak, and dizzy, so I'm pushed out of the hospital in a wheelchair. I'm going to the Villa St. Joseph, where I was on retreat in a hermitage six weeks ago.

On my way through the main hospital lobby and front doors, I catch a glimpse of myself in the mirror and feel disturbed, shocked. I haven't seen my reflection in days, since before all this happened. I don't look like me; I look grotesque. The skin near my eyes and cheeks is dark purple and blue. My jaw is round, swollen. My nose is bandaged under a tiny, yellow, plastic cast. My cheeks are swollen, splotched with purplish green. My eyes only appear as tiny purple slits on my puffy face. There's thread—stitches—poking out of wounds on my eyebrows and swollen lips. A soft neck brace holds up my chin, which is wrapped in gauze and white hospital tape.

I look like Frankenstein. Or some other deformed monster. I can't believe people are seeing me like this. I hope I'm not scaring anyone. What are these strangers thinking when they see me?

We leave the hospital in two cars. Sister Lucy Ann leads, as my parents and I follow. I sit in the passenger seat next to Dad. Mom's in the back. We stop by a pharmacy to pick up some prescription pain medicine. When it's handed to me in a bottle, as liquid, I'm confused. Can't I have pills? It hadn't occurred to me that I wouldn't be able to stick a pill into my mouth with my jaw wired shut like this. I hadn't thought at all about what my diet would be in the coming months. I haven't thought about food in days. I don't feel hungry.

As we make our way through the La Crosse streets and over the country roads to the Villa St. Joseph, I feel like ducking my head down every time a car comes close, when someone might be able to see me through the windshield. Instead, I lift my hands to hide my face, I turn away and show the back of my head. No one should have to see anyone like this; I don't want to subject anyone to this misery without their consent. I'm broken, less than human; nothing that anyone needs to see.

* * *

Each morning before 7 a.m. a nurse or CNA comes into the little room and insists I get out of bed and get dressed. I don't understand why, especially after a night of restless sleep and nightmares. My jaw hurts. I'm tired and weak. Still, I cooperate and slowly get dressed, the best I can with my left hand throbbing in pain. Whatever God's reasons, if God has any reasons, one thing is for sure: religious life remains confusing. I start thinking about how this is turning into a strange novitiate experience, but there might be no better way for me to know solidarity with the sick and suffering, to become comfortable with my vulnerability, to learn that my body is, well, only a body.

My dirty clothes disappear into the common laundry bin and are later returned to me clean, folded, and with tiny hand-written nametags stitched inside, "Sister Julia Walsh." I chuckle when I notice this, aware that I'm likely the only one in the house who is wearing pajama pants, t-shirts, and jeans; I only ever see the other Sisters wearing vintage blouses, blazers, and skirts during the day; nightgowns at night. Could all this be part of God's mysterious plan, the way that God could get me to immerse myself into another part of my community's life and slow down?

I like being here, in the nursing home, I realize. There's quiet and decorum, a structure to each day that is comforting. Breakfast is early, followed by Mass at 9:00, then physical therapy appointments, lunch, afternoon naps, and activities. I enjoy walking through the long hallways and studying the activity calendar on the bulletin board. I like all the possibilities in this place. I go to pet therapy; I sit in a circle and pet a dog. I'm excited to yell "Bingo!" in the basement dining hall and win little fun-sized candy bars that I give away to Sisters who can eat. I wander into the library and pull books off the shelf and bring them to my room, creating clutter on the little desk; a pile of unread books accumulates, its own sort of comfort.

Cups of unidentifiable pureed food—applesauce? macaroni? goulash?—are rolled into my room on trays three times a day. I smell each cup and try to identify what I'm being fed. Even though a dietitian met with me and asked about my likes and dislikes, I'm told that I'm on the same diet as the Sisters with severe dementia who can't chew their food. I put a straw between my lips and suck down as much as I can. But it's hard to swallow. It's tough to eat what I can't identify by smell, taste, or texture. And, I have to be careful. With my jaw wired shut the last thing I need is to gag; I have been warned that vomiting could make me choke unless I can quickly cut the wires that are holding my jaw still.

When my aunts and cousin appear at my door with a milkshake, I'm thrilled. I can't stop smiling and gulping down the sweet, slurpy, cold liquid. Word gets out that I can eat milkshakes, and that I like them. More people come to visit and bring them to me; the freezer near the nurses' station fills with my stash. Even with all those milkshakes, though, I'm losing a lot of weight and feel perpetually hungry. My t-shirts are looser, my pants begin to droop. Nothing from my former life fits me anymore.

One quiet Friday afternoon, I sit in the recliner in my little bedroom, unable to see. Aunt Trudy recently returned to where I fell and took down my tent, gathered my journal and prayer books, and climbed down to the creek to find my glasses. Then one of the Sisters took them for repair and was told it would take a few days. So, lacking a spare set, I now sit in a blurry room trying to figure out how to pass the time without reading, writing, or watching TV.

With eyes closed, I listen to an audio recording of the Bible. I wandered yesterday into the library and squinted while holding cassette tapes really close to my eyes, trying to find something I could listen to. The Bible was the best I could do. I listened to the Old Testament for a while, but now I'm trying to enter the quick narratives about Jesus' life and ministry in the Gospel of Mark.

Until I hear someone shuffling out in the hallway, and there's a knock at the door. "Come in," I say, fumbling to find the stop button on the tape player. It is Sister Helen Esther.

"I came to visit," she says. "I heard what happened to you. I thought you'd look much worse! You look great! It's a miracle: God saved your life. God must have a great plan for you."

Behind her another blur appears. "Who's behind you?" I ask.

"Sister Elissa," the voice says.

"I was just leaving," Sister Helen Esther adds. "Come on in."

I see the colors of their mismatched outfits—likely secondhand skirts and blazers—blur and blend. I hear the walkers shift around as they switch spots; Sister Helen Esther leaves and Sister Elissa stands in the doorway. "I want to tell you that I'm praying. God's plans are mysterious," she says, "and we don't know why this happened to you, but God has saved you for a reason. God must have a great purpose for you." I can hear her love and concern in the way she is emphasizing each word.

After they go, I sit down in the recliner, feeling tense. Ever since I arrived here at the Villa, several Sisters have appeared at my door like this, telling me that God has a plan. Sister Elissa already said this when I arrived, with my jaw wrapped in bandages and wired shut, my bruises still bright. I hate the idea that all this—my accident—was God's plan. It doesn't make sense. I don't believe that God causes suffering, wants any of us to hurt; God is a loving parent who hates seeing us in pain. Also, if God saved my life because God has "big plans" for me, am I capable of living up to them?

There's something else that crosses my mind, too, something I try to brush out of my thoughts because it bothers me so much: did I survive only because my accident happened in the United States? Would I have died if my accident happened in a developing country? Across my throat, I feel a prickly weight arrive, a crushing pressure. I'm scared that these questions will break my faith.

* * *

Lying in the nursing room bed, trying to nap, my tongue explores again its new landscape, the jagged and sharp edges of broken teeth. Behind the wires and brackets in my mouth that hold my jaw still, my gums remain tender and sore; there are sockets where teeth once were. The wounds are fresh, hurting, but no longer bleeding.

I think of how much money my parents spent on braces, from thousands of dollars invested, so that my overbite wouldn't complicate my life. During high school, Mom would frequently remind me that I needed to take care of my teeth, my mouth was worth a lot. She would sigh, reminding me of their stress to pay bills; I'd study more, hoping to earn scholarships for college.

Now, my mouth is in shambles. My lower front teeth have been damaged and there are holes where teeth once were. The teeth on the bottom that are still standing are broken or chipped. Below my teeth, on the left side of my chin, a pinching pain radiates. It feels like someone is stabbing a fork into the side of my face. This is where my mandible split in two, where the oral surgeons carefully and permanently drilled two screws to keep the bone together as it heals. They showed me the X-rays and explained the surgery they did at a follow-up checkup. These pins in my jaw will be part of my body from now on; I will always remember the pain that is clenching into my face now.

* * *

In bed, staring at the ceiling, my cell phone rings. I'm thrilled to hear Peg's voice. She sounds emotional, affectionate. "Julia! I've been so worried about you! Are you OK?" My heart flutters, amazed that she's calling me from the other side of the world. She's in Uganda interning for the summer as part of her graduate studies in public health. I try to speak clearly through my teeth, without moving my jaw.

"Ebeth called and told me what happened to you! How are you feeling?" Peg says. She sounds like she's trying to hold back sobs. Then she adds that she and Ebeth are sending me things they believe will cheer me up. "Do you already have copies of *The Sound of Music* and *Mary Poppins*?"

But I want to talk about something else. I ask the question that has been on my mind for a few days, and my breath gets caught in my throat as I speak, because I already know how she'll respond. I ask Peg if I would have survived if my accident would have happened in Uganda.

She sighs, pauses, seems reluctant to answer. But then she tells me, no, she doesn't think I would have survived, with the terrible roads, with how long it takes for ambulances to get anywhere, there's so few. She says that when people get in accidents there, even car accidents close to the road, they don't survive because the ambulances can't reach them. "If you had fallen off a cliff in rural Uganda there would have been no way for anyone to reach you," she explains. Her voice sounds sad, apologetic.

I think of the volunteer ambulance driver who picked me up at the farm in Iowa. I know I'm lucky that my accident happened in a part of the United States where healthcare is good for most. It's unfair that geography and poverty determine if people live or die. "Everyone in the world deserves good healthcare like I've been blessed with!" I say, angrily, into the phone, feeling my eyes moisten with tears.

"I know, Julia. I know..."

Why did I survive when others die? I hate this. I don't believe the inequity is how God wants it.

* * *

Every day a pile of cards, care packages, and gifts arrive in my room. I thumb through notes, caring messages of encouragement. I'm learning lessons about love. My chest warms with gladness, appreciation. People I don't even know are telling me that they've added me to their church prayer list. Others write that they're holding me in the light. As a person who often intends to send kind messages of support and care to others, but often fails to do so, I'm amazed by the generosity, effort, and time that people give to express all this love.

There is something about love that invites an incarnation, a bringing of the emotion, the spiritual into the material world. Whether it's expressed through physical touch, the movement of a body bowed in prayer, or by signing one's name, putting a card in an envelope and dropping it in a mailbox, we long to express love tangibly. It's beautiful and natural for us to show love through gestures, ordinary and profound.

Lying in bed one afternoon, I feel queasy and restless, unable to nap. Around the quiet room: a thick stack of mail is waiting for me on the desk, more cards for me to read and pray with. Many are already taped up on the cupboard, thanks to one of the CNAs. I feel dizzy as I take in all that people have sent.

So many other gifts, too. The milkshakes in the freezer. The balloons, gifts, and flowers filling ledges. So much love and support surround me that I'm nearly smothered, breathless with the pressure of it. But it's so messed up. I'm so broken. All this energy and money put into me—not others—is all my fault, my clumsy fault. Why was I so stupid to think I could climb down the cliff without hurting myself? Because of my foolishness, all these people have been inconvenienced, their lives disrupted. So many people in the world are suffering more than me but might never experience such a beautiful and generous outpouring of love from so many strangers, friends, family—community. It's so unfair.

I stare at the brightly colored cards, thinking how it's all paradox: injustices with beauty, brokenness with blessing. Everyone deserves to be flooded with unconditional love like this. It's awful that others are isolated, aren't as connected and supported as I am. And, knowing about this injustice *and* the imperative to extend the goodness I'm receiving to others, seems to be shredding my gratitude into strips. The love is beautiful, but I feel crushed by the consciousness, the droopy heartache clouding over my gratitude, because so many people aren't embraced by an endless network of support.

* * *

I'm sitting up in bed and Sister Anita is with me, listening as I share updates about medical appointments and treatment plans. I have more appointments ahead in orthopedics for my hand and follow up appointments in oral surgery. I'm starting regular treatments in physical therapy for my chronic dizziness. Apparently, my ear crystals were bumped out of place when I hit my head, I tell her, so that's why it feels like the room is spinning so much.

I tell Anita that I'm feeling overwhelmed by the injustice of surviving my fall, the injustice of getting good medical care when others in the world don't and can't. The injustice of being loved and supported when others are not. I think of the young adults I worked with when I lived in Casa Jane, who were homeless because they didn't have a loving support system like I do. I'm so uncomfortable that's it's become hard for me to be grateful for blessings.

"Anita, I deserve it no more than them! This makes no sense to me. Why do I get to be so loved while others aren't?" My jaw and heart both hurt from saying all this aloud. I start to cry.

She knows what I'm talking about. She's traveled the world as global educator, as a woman who has taught others how to do social analysis of systemic problems. She pauses and seems to be thinking about how no answer will satisfy me, how there is no good answer. She lifts her dark eyebrows when she finally speaks. "I don't know, Julia... But perhaps you could think about how the rest of your life is an opportunity for you to share all the love you have experienced? To work hard so others can enjoy and experience the privileges and blessings you have known?" Her voice is encouraging, empathetic.

Later, I feel a space open inside me as I reflect on what she suggested. I'm learning how important it is for people to send gifts and messages of love and support as I recover and heal, that these gestures are often how people put their prayers into action. I can settle in and relax, absorb the love and positive energy they are sending toward me. Then maybe I'll be strengthened to serve, to move out of gratitude and into a space of solidarity and action.

Looking at the pile of get well cards on my dresser and those taped onto the white cabinet, I allow myself to feel the love, to think about how hundreds of people all over the country—the world?—are praying for me. It's OK that people hope I'll heal and be able to serve again. It's good. I visualize the faces of those who have sent messages. I visualize my name on prayer lists in church bulletins, in emails, on Facebook. A map of the United States floats through my mind, with colored dots on it, as if seeing all the places where people are thinking of me, praying for me. My moist eyes are pressed in prayer, my chest warms with affection. My tense, aching body finally relaxes.

This love is a gift, a strengthening. The love of my friends, family, and community is a sustainable, deep well from which I can drink the healing waters of Christ. Each of their gestures of kindness and care is God's healing love poured over me. I hope I can love as well as others have loved me, no matter what my future holds.

20

I listen to the prayers, readings, and songs of daily Mass coming through the Villa intercom every day at 9:00, but I don't want to sit with my elder Sisters in the chapel during the service. My throat clenches, my gut aches. I don't want to be with my Sisters if I can't join them at the altar to eat. I'm so hungry for the Eucharist, I want to consume Christ; I'm craving the feeling of the papery bread on my tongue. But I can't open my mouth; I can't eat solid foods; I can't chew. I can't receive Holy Communion.

The chaplain notices that I'm not attending Mass, and she comes to check on me. I tell her it feels too painful to be close to the Blessed Sacrament and not receive it, to not participate in the liturgy by receiving, communing. I tell her that I can hear all the prayers through the speaker. She seems to understand yet wonders aloud if there is a solution. I tell her I'm fine, that she needn't worry about me. But I'm still hungry, lonely.

Another day, I'm sitting in the recliner and listening to Mass with my eyes closed and suddenly I'm filled with an urge to be near my community. But I don't want to make a scene, to expose my tardiness and interrupt the devout, punctual Sisters by coming into the chapel in the middle of Mass and trying to find a pew. I want to absorb the vibrations of music, the energy of the prayers. I know, believe, that to sit in the presence of the service will nourish and strengthen me: will heal me from the outside in, just as holy community does.

I get up from my chair and begin to pace in the hallway, still listening to the service trying to decide what to do, where to go. I end up sitting on wicker furniture in a sunroom off to the side of the chapel. I keep listening to the prayers. I'm only separated by a thick brick wall from those in the chapel. The holiness, the bread of the Eucharist feels closer—but yet too far.

My heart is aching for the bread. This longing feels like another gap in me, another type of brokenness, another way I am wounded from my fall. I can't open my mouth and consume Christ like I've done thousands of times since my first communion in second grade. I don't think I can drink the wine either, with all the medicines I'm taking.

I feel deprived, unable to let the Body of Christ transform my own flesh from the inside out. I wonder if this gap, this denial, is slowing my healing process. But my teeth are locked together, my jaw is wired shut. There is a tiny gap between my upper front teeth that is slightly wider than the edge of a card. Could I stick a crumb into that crack, a little piece of Jesus? No, I decide. I'm not sure why, but even thinking about it feels sacrilegious, like an insult to my love for Jesus, even though the whole design of Eucharist is based on *broken* bread. So I sit still and stare at the grass out the window and listen to the sounds of Sisters singing, processing forward, receiving Communion. The priest's microphone is still on: I hear "The body of Christ," "Amen," "The body of Christ" "Amen," again and again. I walk slowly through the long white hallway back to my room, tears filling my eyes.

* * *

After a couple weeks, I move from the Villa into the motherhouse—St. Rose Convent, where there's assisted living nursing care provided for Sisters who need it. I'm now allowed to freely roam the building without having to tell the nurses where I am. I can tell the receptionist that I'm going out for a walk. I don't have to ask a nurse to go with me. I can even go to some of my appointments by myself.

Cups of puréed food don't show up in my room three times a day anymore. Eating is now a complicated chore. I go to the dining room at mealtimes and fill my tray with bowls of food. Then, I take my tray up to a kitchenette on the residential floor to purée the food in the blender, adding milk and water to turn solids into liquid. Once the food is the right consistency, I sit by myself and slurp my goo through a straw. No matter how much I slurp, I never feel satisfied. I'm so hungry.

Walking through the long hallways of St. Rose Convent, I catch a glimpse of myself in a full-length mirror, but I'm barely recognizable. My flowered knee-length skirt and magenta t-shirt are loose and saggy, my frame is thin. My brown shoulder-length hair looks ragged around a bumpy, crooked face. There are bright red scars on my eyebrows, nose, and lip. I'm not swollen, bandaged, and bruised, but I look disfigured.

* * *

Sisters have been telling me that they want to eat at my parents restaurant sometime and I get an idea. With my wired teeth clenched together, I speak to the administrator of the convent, a Sister who plans outings. "Do you think we can arrange a bus trip to my parents' restaurant for lunch one day?" To my surprise, she agrees, seems to think it is a great idea.

Now a cloudy and muggy day a month after my fall, I'm with thirty Sisters in a charter bus, riding over the country roads between La Crosse, Wisconsin and Gunder, Iowa. Earlier, Sister Dorothy loaded her walker under the bus before she gripped the handrails and wobbled up the stairs and plopped into a seat at the front. Around the bus, canes are tucked next to Sisters and their seats.

The bus winds up and down the rolling hills, over river bluffs and through cornfields. Cheerful voices float throughout the space as Sisters chat, excited for the opportunity to get out of town and eat a meal in a restaurant. I hear Sister Anita's laugh and notice that she is changing seats, as she jovially visits with different sisters during the ninety-minute ride.

I sit up near the driver telling him which ways to turn. At noon, we all spill into the restaurant and Mom splits us up into smaller groups, tables of four or six. Sisters order hamburgers, Reuben sandwiches, and Philly steak sandwiches. I'll hear praise about this for years following: "That was the best sandwich I ever ate!"

I sit next to Sister Dorothy, hungry and sipping water through a straw, halfway listening to the conversations. In front of me is a puréed grilled cheese sandwich in a clear plastic cup that Mom set down. I put my lips on the straw. I'm grateful Mom made this, but it's gross—a cold bready soup. I tell her when she asks.

She insists that I let her try again. "I found some leftover lasagna! Try this," she says, placing a bowl of warm, creamy lasagna goo in front of me. It takes me a long time to suck it all up with my straw, but the Sisters keep chatting, happily, waiting for me to finish.

Soon, half-eaten sandwiches go into boxes and we all load back into the bus. The driver agrees to take a slightly different route back to La Crosse. I grip the microphone and stand in the aisle, trying to be a bit of a tour guide along the way.

The bus rolls down the steep hill from Gunder to Elgin. When we cross over a little bridge that crosses the creek I fell in a month ago, I feel my throat tighten, my heart pounding. "Sisters, upstream from here a mile or so is where I fell off the cliff and broke my face," I say through clenched teeth, without moving my jaw.

Then, my voice turns cheery, as I share with my community and find the fun in playing docent. "The farm I grew up on is down that gravel road, about a mile up that hill," I say as the bus passes the place where my parents still live. I'm smiling and exposing my wired jaw as I continue to point out landmarks. The bus loops through the little towns. "There's where I went to high school." "There's my home parish!" Soon, we return to La Crosse, to the place that is slowly becoming my new home.

21

My days now seem to be filled with appointments. I feel like I'm always sitting in a waiting room in a different clinic or physical therapy center. Oral surgeries, hand surgeries, follow up appointments, physical therapy for my hand, physical therapy for my vertigo. I'm poked and examined practically every other day as my broken body heals, shifts, takes on a new shape.

My mouth still has wires and brackets holding the jaw in place. In a physical therapy center focused only on the healing of hand, I'm studying the gallery full of black and white photos of hands on the wall; pictures of large hands, small hands, pale hands, dark hands; hands holding other hands, hands cooking food, hands reaching out, hands folded in prayer. My sore hand is resting in a sling on my lap.

I'm thinking about how much my body has been broken and then transformed over this summer. It crosses my mind that the human body is very sacred and good. I wonder if it feels like an act of prayer for these physical therapists and assistants to help hands heal and gain strength all day long, considering all the incredible things hands do, how hands allow lives to be full, blessed.

I close my eyes and take a deep breath as awe swirls in my heart. *God, thank you for the awesomeness of our human bodies, for your designs, for how you work wonders in us each day. Thank you for giving me such excellent healthcare and helping me heal. Thank you, Jesus.*

Journal
August 5, Sunday night, 11:30ish p.m.
(still recovering at St. Rose Convent)

God, Holy, Pure, Burning, Awesome, Guiding God!
Holy Spirit, precious Jesus. Sacred Humanity & Divinity—
 Something is turning within me.
 Holy all in all, I sensed a deep click in contemplation earlier this evening. Thank you. But as is so often my nature, I got distracted and forgot precisely what the shift was before I could record it. I think it had something to do with my doubts, with my questions surrounding lifestyle, love, companionship, and community. I think I felt a strong desire for male companionship unlike what I've experienced before. I don't necessarily desire love or a lover in a different form than now, but I would like to have male companionship on a daily basis.
 This is true and this scares me. Is it about more than Mike? Sure. I suspect there could be 1000s of compatible men out there living life the way I want—in communes and intentional communities; working with the poor; loving, living, giving.
 Jesus, I know these things tonight—Holy Spirit I'm sensing that you're showing me these clear spots:
 I'm called to live a life of working with the poor.
 I'm made to be an advocate for the environment and the poor.
 I'm called to live in community.
 I love children.
 I'm called to union with you and holiness—a path of prayer is essential.
 I'm a Franciscan.
 I really like the freshness of the new monastic communities.
 The roots and tradition of FSPA are sacred.
 The Eucharistic spirituality of FSPA is sacred to me.

Do the stability of FSPA—the institutionalism and bureaucratic feel of our structures—scare and concern me? The mystery of the roots and tradition and connecting with spiritual ancestors is beautiful. Are these traditions sacred to me though? I don't know. So now, God—with men, and other big confusing questions spiraling around me, I go to rest, trying to trust you'll reveal what you want for me gradually and gently—maybe in my unfolding dreams.

* * *

My eyes are half open and I'm stumbling through the long corridor, moving toward the adoration chapel on the other side of the convent. The pre-dawn light is dim through the windows. The halls are hushed and bright with security lights. I hear some Sisters snoring as I walk by their doors, and feel embraced by the silence, calm. It was only about 4:15 a.m. when I crawled out of bed wearing my t-shirt and shorts. I grabbed my journal and pen and began to move, my jaw aching, my body fatigued. My mind is stuck in a dream-state; cloudy, swirling. Yet, my body moves toward the chapel, summoned—the Christ energy magnetic.

In my dream, an elder Sister in a vintage blue suit wisped in front of me. "It's time, Julia," she said. I jolted awake, heart pounding, eyes open, and sat up. I stared into the blurry bedroom. "Time for what?" I heard myself say, while my heart knew. I must have fallen back to sleep, back into the dream. Then I heard another Sister—who?—respond. "Time to sign up for an adoration hour." I understood. But I resisted, staying in bed longer, dozing. I doubted my dreams. I made excuses. I was comfortable. I didn't want to move.

Then the nudge become unbearable, my body *had to* respond. I'm thinking of this, in the chapel now, my bare knees pressed onto the kneeler, my hands folded in front of my body. I sit into the chair and breathe deeply, still drowsy. I open my journal and begin to write thoughts that surface from the daze in my brain, my words becoming little offerings before the altar. I wonder why I make excuses. I wonder why I procrastinate on what I know is good for me. I remember the surprise I felt when telling Mayr on the phone the other day that

I have a feeling I'll stay with the Sisters. The feeling still lingers; I feel that I'll stay when I allow myself to connect with the deepest part of me. Although I'm uncertain and resistant, I suppose I know that this lifestyle is the best thing for me.

22

Weak and wobbly, and with my jaw still wired shut, I drive to the hospital alone and wander through the gift shop. I pick up trinkets and hold them in my hands. I study flower arrangements and boxes of chocolates. Nothing seems adequate for the gratitude I want to express to the ICU nurses who tended to me. I don't know how to reciprocate the kindness and love I feel. I'm thinking of the nurse Jesús, especially. How can I say thank you to someone who taught me how to love?

I settle on a blank card and a box of chocolate, tuck into a bench in the hospital hallway and write a thank you note, saying how deeply I appreciate their care and love. I write how their going out of their way to sit with me and provide for my comfort gave me strength and taught me important lessons about how to love and be with someone who is suffering and hurting, lessons that are changing who I am and how I'm a Sister. I sign my note with hearts and smiley faces, with promises that I'll pray for them and everyone they serve. Then I ride the elevator to the floor where the ICU is, feeling my heart palpitating. I'm confused and slightly wobbly as I approach the nurses' station.

A nurse with blond hair looks up from a pile of papers with a tired expression. I explain who I am, that I was there earlier in the summer, and they cared for me. She is unfamiliar, yet seems thrilled. "I remember you, but I didn't recognize you. You look amazing! You have gotten so much better!"

I'm eager, insistent. "Please make sure that all the nurses, especially in the evening shift, get to see this and enjoy the candy." She assures me she will, that they will all share it. She thanks me for the gift.

"Can you especially tell Jesús how grateful I am? Can you please make sure Jesús sees this?"

She looks at me with confusion in her eyes, curiosity, and concern lining her face. "There is no one named Jesús who works here..."

I'm surprised that she doesn't know the names of everyone in her department. "Um, maybe there's a maintenance worker named Jesús? Or a custodian? Or maybe someone who works in food service is named Jesús?" I suggest.

She shakes her head and apologizes, insists again that there is no one who works in the hospital named Jesús.

"Well, thank you," I say. "Thank you so much for your care and helping me get better!" *And then my heart sinks* as I watch her set my card and chocolate on the counter. I feel so unsatisfied.

Walking back to the elevator, I'm doubting the nurse knows what she is talking about. I doubt she knows everyone who works in this giant hospital. Then I think of how amazing the love was that flowed out of Jesús, about his warmth and kindness. I feel my shoulders soften, my spine relax, my breathing slow. Still, I continue to wonder. How could she not know Jesús?

23

Here's what comes to mind when I think of perfection: dust free furniture, people who are always punctual, and their hair and skin and clothing all tidy; eating a well-balanced diet, each meal at exactly the right time; healthy snacks with all the right doses of fruits and vegetables. Everything is in the right place, everything done on time, everything in order. It's all about appearances, I suppose, but there's a rigidity to the structure of perfect lives, as well, an inability to budge, to be flexible, to make room for neighbors, for strangers, for me.

I asked one of my friends what comes to mind when she thinks of perfection. Here's what she said: unchangeable porcelain, because it's hard and cold.

In the images of convent life I carried with me when entering community, nearly two years ago now, I imagined the Sisters with politely grinning faces, perfect posture, immaculate clothes, polished shoes. I visualized hands folded in prayer, a uniformity and conformity that created structure for every day, each minute. Everyone right where they are supposed to be, on time, in the right mode for the activity: in the right pew meditating in the chapel, kneeling at the right moment at Mass, knitting with other Sisters in the parlor, reading books in the library, washing dishes in the kitchen, walking to the quaint Catholic school nearby. Everything orderly, just right and predictable.

I imagined convent life that way, but I didn't expect it. I knew it was some mythical image from an era gone by, or possibly a reality in another convent community far away. But it certainly wasn't what I felt called to, nor wanted. Such a lifestyle was far from what I believed would have been a healthy, authentic match for me. I had no desire to be perfect. I didn't want a life of conformity.

It made more sense that God was calling me to be authentically myself, the person who God made to be me. But yet, the strange images from days gone by hover over, and crush, me with thoughts like, *Good nuns aren't late for prayer*, or *A real sister would never do that*, or *I should be more grateful for this*.

I should, I should, I should.

24

Roaming the long, carpeted corridors of St. Rose Convent, I pause and study the artwork: oil paintings depicting saints and scenes from the gospels, wooden carvings depicting the mysteries of the rosary, giant crucifixes dotted with bright red paint—blood. I think of how the images express the faith of the people of God, people who have understood the narratives and traditions in unique ways throughout history; each generation had its struggles, sins, horrors, heartaches. In each era, the Church caused harm. The Church is broken now, and it's been broken for its entire history.

Majoring in history during college, I examined the dark underbelly of Catholicism through an objective microscope, unfiltered by theology or devotion. I read accounts of the bloody battles of the Crusades and felt nauseated. I memorized facts about the Spanish Inquisition for an exam and felt my head ache. In class, we discussed the doctrine of discovery and how white supremacist colonial Christianity destroyed cultures and civilization and I heard my voice become strong, my body shake with rage. When I learned how the Catholic Church was complicit with slavery, sorrow and shame settled in my bones and I wanted to disown my faith. I tossed and turned in my dorm room bed, wondering how I could be Catholic, let alone religious. I walked around campus in a daze, wondering if disgust for the sinfulness of the Catholic Church could make me into a Protestant, perhaps a Lutheran. By the time I graduated college, I felt little pride in being Catholic, in being part of a church that inflicted oppression upon the poor and vulnerable for centuries. I felt empathy for others who decided to leave religion altogether—I understood how associating with the Catholic Church could get in the way of authentic following of the Spirit and boldly standing up for peace and justice. I thought about church membership as similar to being part of a dysfunctional family failing to heal from trauma, at best, a nation waging a civil war, at worse.

If it hadn't been for such a persistent curiosity—a calling—to Catholic Sisterhood, I probably would have left. Countless times I wanted to. But whenever I prayed about it, I arrived at the same conclusion: it's Catholic Sisterhood I want. The saints depicted in these oil paintings likely felt this too; I hope to stay devoted, faithful to Jesus, no matter how messy and complex fidelity may be.

* * *

It's the Feast of St. Clare of Assisi—my first as a Sister. But I'm not with them on this joyful day to celebrate the first Franciscan woman. Instead, I'm going to my friend Luke's profession of vows in the Society of Jesus: the Jesuits.

I drive through the streets of St. Paul, Minnesota and it's only been two days since I had my jaw unwired. Besides walks around La Crosse, and visits to various doctor's offices, today will be my first time being around people who don't know what happened to me. Still, my jaw is sore and tender. I can only open my mouth a crack. I still have to speak through my teeth. Although the wires are gone, brackets line my teeth; it doesn't look quite like braces, just bizarre and ugly. And although my face is healing, red scars are visible around my eyebrows, nose, lips, and chin. I hurt.

My jaw, neck, and shoulders are tense. A stranger who sees me will probably wonder why I look the way I do—or have feelings of revulsion. Thinking of all this, as I park the car I pause, pondering how ugly I feel, how deformed I am. I care for Luke, and am excited that it's his vow day, but I'm not sure I want to go into the Mass and be around strangers. My heart is pounding.

Walking from the car to the church, I look down at my outfit: green and white sundress, wide floppy straw hat, dusty hiking sandals. When I got ready earlier, I tried to wear something to shield my broken body, but now I wonder if my clothes will draw attention, which I don't want today. I wore my Tau cross necklace to identify myself as a Franciscan. But do I want people to know I'm a Franciscan Sister today?

Behind big heavy doors I find that the church is crammed full, and the service is about to start. I meander to the balcony and awkwardly slide my body between people in the front I don't know, where I can lean over the railing and look down. The worship aid is crisp in my hands; I find Luke's name. I think about how he and I have a lot in common. We met at the airport on the way to JVC orientation in California and afterwards we both came back to the Midwest and entered religious life. I'm so grateful for our friendship. Looking into the church, I see Luke and his classmates walk up the aisle together and take spots in the front pew wearing black suits and white collars. I feel my face grinning, my shoulders relaxing. I know people have complicated feelings about priests, but it crosses my mind that the six of them look like a lineup of baby holy men, of good ones who could do a lot of mending and healing for the hurting world, and our broken Church. I trust that Luke will.

Later, the gifts of bread and wine are brought to the front and I sing the offertory hymn from my heart, free and happy. Then I remember how I look today: broken and ugly. Who are these people around me? Their clothes look expensive, fashionable; they seem beautiful, perfect, wealthy. I'm ugly, broken, and poor. Are they judging my beat-up, floppy, straw hat? My faded sundress and dirty sandals? Do they see these weird brackets on my teeth? Scars on my face? I feel their stares on me. I shrink, hushing my singing voice. I fold my hands and gaze toward the altar. I'm here for you, Jesus, and for Luke, not for these people.

There are a few priests presiding at the Mass. Together they bring the bread and wine to the altar draped with a white cloth, and place the ordinary items upon it, next to an open prayer book. The priest in the center picks up a gold plate, the paten, with the bread on it and holds it in front of him, reciting the prayer: "Blessed are you, Lord God of all creation, for through your goodness we have received the bread we offer you: fruit of the earth and work of human hands, it will become for us the bread of life."

"Blessed be God forever." I hear my voice recite the response with the rest of the people, although my teeth remain clenched together, my jaw achy.

The priest picks up the gold chalice filled with wine and holds it in front of him as he speaks again: "Blessed are you, Lord God of all creation, for through your goodness we have received the wine we offer you: fruit of the vine and work of human hands, it will become our spiritual drink."

"Blessed be God forever." My voice sounds strong, mixed with the crowd.

"Pray, brothers and sisters, that my sacrifice and yours may be acceptable to God, the almighty Father," the priest says.

"May the Lord accept the sacrifice at your hands, for the praise and glory of his name, for our good and the good of all his holy Church." The body of believers speak, including me. The rhythm of these prayers, this sacred liturgy, is comforting. My body relaxes. Muscles let go, and my breathing slows.

The priests hold their hands in front of their bodies, palms turned downward over the altar, and pray over the gifts, invoking the Holy Spirit. I watch them pray over the offerings on the altar, a sacrifice of thanksgiving. Prayers I have heard hundreds of times in my lifetime, prayers that are as ordinary to me as bread, water, air, light.

We sing together, our diaphragms moving up and down. We exhale, we inhale, we share the same air, and our bodies—each broken and imperfect in some way—move together and make music. In this common space, we are on holy ground—just as every community gathered around an altar is, no matter where they are.

I sit next to the people who were bothering me moments ago—strangers I was certain were judging me. Though I'm weak and imperfect, I desire to give God my respectful attention, my love. I lean on the railing and look around the church, my hands folded. I listen to the priest continue the prayers, prayers of thanksgiving, prayers of mystery. With the words, we are reminded of our tradition, our beliefs, our hope that these offerings could please our God, and help bring peace and healing where needed. We are reminded of our relationships: praying for the local bishop and the pope; we name Mary, the Blessed Virgin; we hear a litany of saints. We remember our belief that the holy ones of eternity are gathered with us around this altar in this moment; we are in communion, connected to the heavenly reign of God.

We are reminded of how Jesus taught us to do this, at that holy Last Supper about two thousand years ago, the night before he was killed on the cross. Holding a piece of the bread, a round host that resembles a large white wafer in front of his chest, the priest says aloud, "The day before he suffered, he took bread in his sacred hands, and looking up heaven, to you, his almighty Father, he gave you thanks and praise. He broke the bread and gave it to his disciples and said…" The priest pauses, begins to speak more slowly.

"Take this, all of you, and eat of it; for this is my body which will be given up for you." Then he elevates it above his head as bells ring, marking this moment as the holiest part of the Mass. He uplifts the host, his body becomes a monstrance, like the one that honors the Blessed Sacrament on the high altar back in the chapel at St. Rose Convent, where I poured out my doubts in the middle of a quiet night. The priest kneels, genuflects, behind the altar before he picks up the chalice filled with wine and holds it in front of him, praying more words of consecration. He holds the cup higher as bells ring, before placing the chalice on the altar and genuflecting.

I feel my body fill with strength, calm, and joy. I think less and less about my broken appearance. We join voices together and pray the Lord's Prayer, and reach out to our neighbors and touch their bodies, exchanging signs of peace. "Peace be with you," we say, touching hands. Some people embrace.

Then, I don't know what's happening, Mass becomes different from anything I have ever experienced. The priest isn't summoning us to communion; he asks us to kneel or sit. I kneel down with the others near me and watch a man put a kneeler in front of the altar. The priests stand behind the altar, elevating a consecrated host and the chalice, facing forward. Another man puts a microphone next to the kneeler. Then one by one, Luke and each of his classmates take a turn kneeling in front of the bread and wine, each holding a little card as he speaks.

When Luke speaks, I lean in, smiling. He reads from the card in his hand. "Almighty and eternal God, I, Luke Jeffrey Peter Paul Hansen, though altogether most unworthy in Your divine sight, yet relying on Your infinite goodness and mercy and moved with a desire of serving You, in the presence of the Most Holy Virgin Mary and Your whole heavenly court, vow to Your Divine Majesty perpetual poverty, chastity, and obedience in the Society of Jesus; and I promise that I shall enter that same Society in order to lead my entire life in it, understanding all things according to its Constitutions. Therefore, I suppliantly beg Your Immense Goodness and Clemency, through the blood of Jesus Christ, to deign to receive this holocaust in an odor of sweetness; and that just as You gave me the grace to desire and offer this, so You will also bestow abundant grace to fulfill it."

Wait? What!? Did Luke just profess *perpetual* vows? Did he say that he is doing this for *the rest of his life*? I can't believe it, so I listen to the next man profess his vows and realize, that wow, yes, they are actually professing perpetual vows today. They are joining the Jesuits for the rest of their lives in this moment!

I'm confused because I didn't expect them to do this, didn't know this is how it works in other communities. Luke and I have been in our communities for about the same amount of time. Yet, *I'm* still two years away from *first* vows, I figure, and *so very far* from ready. If I *do* decide to profess FSPA vows in two years, they'll be temporary, for three years, and likely renewed for three more years after that. My final vows as a member of the Franciscan Sisters for life would be eight years from now—if at all. But Luke just joined the Jesuits *forever*. I'm surprised the Jesuits ask for this level of commitment so early in the process. It's amazing that Luke and all the other Jesuits are agreeing to it.

I think about all this as I watch each man kneel before the Blessed Sacrament, proclaiming dedication to God and reliance on God's grace, and I feel my confusion turn to admiration. I feel a desire bubble up in my gut, my heart: I *too* want to be bold with my love for God, to trust deeply in God's goodness. I'm thinking of that powerful love I felt in the ICU from Jesús: I want to love God's people like Jesús loved me. I want to give my whole self to God, like Luke and his classmates. I think I want to make vows, too. I think I do! Eventually. Maybe.

* * *

After Mass, I'm in a giant ballroom with a crowd. A reception. I find Luke's housemates from JVC and spend the day and evening with them: we go from the reception to the mall, then to a bar. In each interaction, I feel my body tense with insecurity, apologizing for my appearance and struggling to explain it adequately. Then, I feel badly for putting people in an awkward conversation on what is supposed to be a joyous day. It's a dramatic story to tell people—yes, I fell off a cliff and broke my face about two months ago; how is life going for you?

All the socializing feels trivial and dumb as jarring thoughts float through my mind: I could have died this summer. And, Jesus, I think I really *do* want to make vows one day. Around the bar that night, I find myself ducking out of pictures, cozying up to the edge of the room, choosing to be an observer instead of a conversationalist. My jaw is sore and I'm tired. I'm eager to go see Sisters Sarah, Eileen, and Linda, so I leave. Back with my community that night, I relax; my broken face no longer an embarrassment.

A few days later I'm in the adoration chapel snuggled into a chair with a prayer shawl draped on my lap, my journal resting on my knees. I fill the pages of my journal with prayers, questions. Thinking back to the gathering in the bar with Luke's friends and family, it occurs to me: I'm becoming less interested in bar scenes. Am I mellowing? Has the accident caused me to age? I suppose it's only going to become tougher to relate to people my age, now that I'm more interested in the activities of my Sisters: prayer, reading Scripture, meditation, deepening relationships. Is this normal, or is it sad?

I don't know what's happening, but I do know that I survived a great fall, felt great love, and now I'll never be the same. I'm becoming a new person. I'm not sure how to talk to people who haven't been close to death, who don't seem as enamored by God's love as I do. When people seem petty and superficial, it's tough for me to be patient and kind. I suppose this is another way I'm broken. Mixing with people even while I adjust to all these changes in myself: I don't know how to love like that.

25

I was bound to hear from Mike again. And my questions about staying and going, continue.

G-Chat
August 15, 2007, 9:53 a.m.

Mike:	i'm so glad that you're in as good of shape as you're in. i'm sure i don't need to tell you that you're pretty lucky.
	it could have been much worse.
Julia:	mike, i gotta tell you
	last week i almost called you when you were in milwaukee
	i was struggling with some huge hard discernment q's and i thought you might have been good to talk to about it
Mike:	really?
Julia:	yeah....
Mike:	i thought about getting over there to see you, but from the minute i touched ground it was run run run. i was insanely busy the entire time. but i was thinking about you and wish i could have gotten over there!
	what kinds of questions did you have? i don't know if i could have helped you! ;)
Julia:	the thing that i wanted to talk to you about is how it's occurred to me recently that i really desire male companionship in my life - on a daily basis and i never had that desire emerge in me before, so it was freaking me out

Mike: i had an old guy tell me once that the stuff you struggle with today will probably be the same stuff that you'll be dealing with 10 years from now.
these are the cards you are playing with, you know?

Julia: i don't know, mike
i just don't know
part of my confusion is the annoyance i have that i never met any people that seemed compatible until i came to religious life
i continue to think of you in that category, honestly

Mike: HA!
tell me about it.
yeah, i think a part of that is that like-minded people tend to be much more interesting!
i mean, i don't meet a whole lot of peace and justice catholics who are into contemplation and love hanging out with old brothers and sisters out here in the streets, you know?

Julia: right, and as my friends have reminded me, it's because i'm doing something that is more "me" now than ever before

Mike: haha
yeah. you're centered.
people are into other people who are centered.

Julia: which confuses me even more.... ok, if this is "me," then are the good guys i'm meeting also more "me"?

Mike: i have to admit, i STOPPED meeting people with whom i'm compatible with after i left.
it's like everything dried up.

Julia: ha, really!

Mike: i'm not sure i understand what you're asking

Julia: i'm not sure i do either
i mean, if this life suits me so well and introduces me to people that are so like me, then does that mean being a sister is the thing that is the best for me? the most like me?
i know i could never get married if marriage means buying a house and settling down
i want to be itinerant and available for God

Mike: i don't think so, necessarily. you're meeting a lot of like-minded

| | people because of your environment. that doesn't mean that you are a natural celibate.
you could do a volunteer program and meet the same folks.
(you probably know that) |
|----------|---|
| Julia: | i'd only say i've met 2-3 people, though, really
and, i never met any in JVC that were quite the same |
| Mike: | i'm going to tell you a story.
:-/
[that's my "i don't know if this is a good idea or not" face.]
so I was really torn and ambivalent when i was discerning too. and a lot of that had to do with celibacy, obviously, and specifically my relationship with my ex-girlfriend. i was miserable for three years. i couldn't make up my mind and i prayed and prayed for guidance and answers, and i never got them. then one day it happened. i had an epiphany. but it wasn't the kind of epiphany that i was expecting.
the epiphany was this: |
| Julia: | da-duh! |
| Mike: | i had been waiting for god to show up in my life and make everything ok. i was waiting for him to give me peace and joy about my decision, about my life there. i was waiting for confirmation, maybe. it was like i was waiting for my "knight in shining armor" to show up and save and redeem my life and my choices. and i realized: there is no such thing. god's not coming. i'm on my own. he's not going to give me guidance or peace or confirmation. and actually i'm fucking miserable. and I knew then that my discernment was over, and i walked away.
that's it.
of course by then it was too late to go back.
i may be even more miserable now! |
| Julia: | ugh. that's shitty, but don't worry, that's not my experience
i'm not miserable, i love my community and i don't want to leave them at all
and, i think Christ has already come and given me lots of clarity.
i know i can live the vows and be happy.
i know i can do what i want to do with my life (and feel called to do) |

	from within this community
	but, i also know i'd be a great mom and wife
	and i know that the new movements of the spirit - like the new monastics movement with shane claiborne - are more attractive to me than tradition a lot of the time
	and, i know that i'll always be falling in love with people
	i fall in love way too easily, because i recognize the beauty and goodness in people quite quickly
	soooooooooo......
	i think deep down, i know i won't be leaving
Mike:	if the new monastics are more attractive to you, would you ever want to try that out instead of the more traditional stuff?
Julia:	oh yeah, absolutely
	i have thought about living with them once i'm done with formation
Mike:	like a catholic worker house?
Julia:	well, yeah
	or something newer like the simple way community
Mike:	why don't you just go now, before you take vows?
	it's a nice in-between world.
	you could be a nun, but not.
	that's kind of what i'm doing.
Julia:	are you suggesting i leave and go try it out now?
	why is that what you think?
Mike:	here's what i'm observing.
	you are doing this thing, but you have all these questions about being in a relationship. there are two resolutions to these questions: either go date and get more info so that you can be more at peace with your decision down the road, or - pardon the harshness - get over it. (i don't mean that in a mean or rude way, but that's the other option and i don't know how else to put it.) you are also obviously attracted to living an "apostolic" lifestyle - something like the new monastics - but for some reason want to take vows in a community first. that simply doesn't make sense to me.
	obviously, i can't make your decision for you. i know you love the sisters, i'm sure you can live the life and be happy, but maybe there's a way that's "tweaked" a little better for you. fine tune your

	vocation. and i think a good way to do that is to spend time "out there." go live with shane and company, at the simple way.
	that way you can live the vocation of a sister without the added confusion of a traditional formation
	you can date if you feel the need
	and you can always come back!
Julia:	community means more than the group i live with
	it means being a part of the whole congregation
Mike:	i know.
	yeah, i know that.
	i'm just saying, there's more than one community out there,
	more than one way to be a "sister"

I suppose Mike is right: I could choose something else, I could leave community if I want to, I have that freedom. But I *really* want to continue with the novitiate process and see where it might lead me.

26

Weeks later, I'm with Sister Lucy Ann in the car, the backseat and trunk filled with suitcases and boxes stuffed with favorite books, saint statues, photo frames, art supplies, clock radio, CDs, clothing, quilts sewn by my grandma and aunts. We're on the highway to move me into the Common Franciscan Novitiate in Joliet, Illinois, five hours south of La Crosse. Yesterday I wrote in my journal that I'm apprehensive and anxious about a new living community. I wrote that I don't know if I will make it through the year. I'm thinking about Mike and my aching jaw and mouth. I feel scared about all I don't know. I'm thinking about the possibilities and uncertainty, the hopes and doubts, as I stare out the car window, the radio humming as we make our way along the interstate, watching the rows of corn and soybeans dance in the wind. Moving toward the novitiate, I think of what I said to Sister Eileen the other day, "I'm riding the train of discernment, unsure of where it will lead."

Although the fears and uncertainties are real, I'm glad to go away too. I hope for spiritual deepening and growth. Ever since that awesome prayer experience in the hermitage during my pre-novitiate retreat, encountering Jesus there—and Jesús in the ICU—I've felt pulled to sit in the chapel for hours, soak up God's love in silent contemplation. I imagine that there will be opportunities for this now, away from La Crosse, where I feel compelled to socialize. I hope I'll get along with the other Sisters I'll be with too, and I'll gain new friends. I understand there's going to be five of us who are novices; the other four are from congregations with motherhouses on the East Coast.

Two directors will facilitate our program: months of living in community together, volunteering, studying, praying: being sisters. It could be good.

Sister Lucy Ann was gracious enough to call and tell the two Sisters leading the novitiate about my accident, saying I'll need soft foods for the first few months. Recovering from my accident will still fill my time. I have to find doctors in the Joliet area. I have to find a place where I can continue my physical therapy for my hand; I still can't make a fist or stretch out my fingers. The weight of all the looming tasks of healing that are ongoing puts a pressure on my chest. Whatever happens, I hope my medical appointments, broken jaw, and soft food diet don't become a burden to the novitiate community. I hope all the strangeness of this summer, of being broken, won't get in the way of being in the present moment, of being a sister to those around me. I hope that when the new Sisters meet me, that they aren't repulsed by my crooked smile, broken teeth, and scars. I hope I'm not as disfigured as I feel.

I feel the sadness of saying goodbye to my Sisters and other friends around La Crosse. I remember how I crossed paths with Earl in the hallway inside St. Rose Convent, saint icons hanging beside us. His blue collared shirt was loose on his once-round frame, his skin pale, his cheeks concaved. He was weak and wobbly, leaning against the wall. I hadn't seen him much—at all?—since he played the guitar at my novitiate entrance ceremony in the early spring. He said he heard about my accident; he asked about my recovery process, wondered how I was feeling. Then he said "Julia, I'm not sure if you heard, but I am dealing with terminal cancer." My eyes filled with tears and my glasses steamed up. No one had told me; I've been absorbed with my own accident, recovery, and discernment. I noticed last spring that he was getting thinner, but it hadn't occurred to me that he was losing weight because he was deathly ill: why would I have thought that? I wonder if I never heard because people figured I was dealing with enough. I asked Earl some questions, told him I'd pray for him, thanked him for his kindness. He asked about my novitiate, promised to pray for me too. I reach out to hug him, saying goodbye, feeling his bones under his drooping clothes.

I feel my body fill with a prickly sorrow. More tears fall down my cheeks. I look at Sister Lucy Ann, her focus on the road. "Lucy Ann, do you think Earl will die before I come back at Christmas?" I hear my voice whine a little.

She exhales, makes a little moaning noise. "Yeah, he might, Julia. It's so, so sad. I feel so much for Marci, and their kids!" She tells me that no, I won't be able to come back for his funeral, or any Sister's funeral, for that matter. I must stay focused on the novitiate program, be where God has put me. She promises me that we'll stay in touch, and I can talk on the phone and write emails; no one will forget about me. I understand, but I feel very sad.

* * *

"Well, I don't know what I expected, but I don't think this was it," I say when Lucy Ann pulls into the parking lot. On top of the hill, in the middle of suburban Joliet, we've arrived at a giant, three-story 1920s institutional building that will be my home for the next nine months. Guardian Angel Hall, owned by the Joliet Franciscan Sisters, is on a triangle of land next to strip malls and shopping centers. There's a small grotto in the yard, a nearby bench overlooks grass, asphalt and concrete.

I'm carrying my laundry basket full of quilts and clothes as I enter the main door with Lucy Ann. I see a reception desk and mailroom on one side, a chapel on the other. In the hallway, I meet two women with glasses and short hair, Sisters Naomi and Lisa, the on-site directors for the five of us who are novices. They smile politely, their eyes looking tired. This will be an interesting nine months, I think, the high ceilings and wide tile-lined hallways looming around us. Walls are painted bright colors, yet everything in here feels institutional: old school.

"We'll show you the classroom and our offices down here later," Sister Lisa says. "Everyone else is here. You can go up and find your bedroom on the third floor. I'll show you the way."

The second floor of the building is off limits, I learn, housing a domestic violence shelter and other social service agencies. Although Sister Lucy Ann and I have traveled the shortest distance compared to the other four novices who came from Pennsylvania and New York,

I'm the last to arrive. I end up with the smallest bedroom. The other novices come to greet me while Lucy Ann and I unload my stuff. Each is wearing a modest blouse and khaki pants, but I'm in a t-shirt and shorts. I'm the least nunny one here, I think. I want to hide. Yet, their warm smiles and friendly hellos help me relax.

At dinner that night, I see platters filled with grilled burgers and brats, and a giant bowl of chips. So much to bite, chew. I pick at the bread, cheese, and tomato slices on my plate, although I'm hungry. Didn't they get the memo about my need for soft foods? Yes, I've learned, the other Sisters have all heard about my accident, and are kind and empathetic. They simply didn't know what I could eat. I look at each one around the table happily biting into burgers, chomping on chips. They ask about my accident, but I deflect their concern and ask them questions. How did they come to their communities? What did they do before they became Sisters?

Within days, it becomes clear to me that we're all very different. I feel like the oddest: the youngest, the only one who grew up on a farm, the only one from the Midwest. I'm interested in drinking, going out, and using the internet; they don't seem to care when I talk about these things. Someone says, "If this is the common novitiate, I'd really be interested in what the uncommon one is like." We must share space, studies, meals, reflection, prayer, chores—the ins and outs of our daily lives; I feel tense, feeling more uncertainty. I wonder how this could impact my choice to stay a Sister, or to leave.

* * *

Sitting on my bed, journal on my lap, I draw a line. At one end of the line I write, "Stay with FSPA." At the other end, I write "Leave FSPA." Then I draw notches along the line, and a star on the continuum. Some days the star is closer to "Leave," and other days the star is closer to "Stay."

When I'm being honest, I can admit that I'm thinking more about leaving than staying. My mind wanders and I daydream about other forms my life could take, other ways that I might live the Gospel. I daydream about the Catholic Worker movement, thinking of communities I've encountered since graduating from Loras. Maybe that's what God wants from me.

Then there's the new monastic communities. I study a website that lists houses all over the country where people are living in prayerful, service-minded, intentional communities; something amazing is happening and I think I want to be part of it. God is up to something. There's so many households of faithful young adult Christians serving their neighborhoods in cities throughout the United States. I'd be up for that too. My shoulders tighten as I feel the longing to live my faith more boldly, radically. What am I doing here? How does this daily life have anything to do with what Saints Francis and Clare envisioned and established? I don't want to sacrifice my ideals only so I can fit into this community, contained in tradition, and tied to institutions.

Despite all the questions storming within, I feel God nudging me to stay. Plus, this is where God has me now. I'm part of the Franciscans; it feels clear that God led me here. I'm supposed to be here, I think.

I was emailing with Andy about these doubts and he echoed what others have suggested: now that I'm here, in the canonical novitiate, I ought to stick around, see what I can get out of it. I agree, so this is my plan. I'll stick around longer. Maybe I'll discover that this is a good fit for me. Maybe I will come to a point where I'm happy and want to be a Franciscan forever: no more moving the star around on the continuum of doubt and desire. Or, maybe not.

***

It's a Tuesday morning and I'm in a classroom in a northern suburb of Chicago, sitting at a table, listening to a theologian priest lecture, filling my notebook with words: poverty, detachments, possessions, solidarity, freedom, itinerancy, Tradition. I nod enthusiastically and slurp black coffee from a giant travel mug. The fog of morning drowsiness has cleared and my mind is energized. I'm happy to be learning about the history of religious life from this scholar, to hear an intelligent presentation on a topic that has captured my imagination for years now: what does it mean to live the vow of poverty in this modern world?

The classroom is full: forty novices and twenty novice directors, men and women from different parts of the U.S. and the world. Different religious orders too: Maryknollers, Redemptorists, Salvatorians, members of the Society of the Divine Word, Holy Spirit Missionary Sisters. I've looked ahead in the syllabus and am curious about the topics we'll study throughout the year: each of the vows, addictions, sexuality, the Second Vatican Council, personality types, mental health, prayer, social justice, spirituality, the history of religious life.

I'm animated and engaged as I consume all the information, delighted by the chance to learn. Each new theological principle, every tidbit of history, every close read of a Church document, every story about a Franciscan saint: each morsel of information provides more to consider as I discern if I'm called to stay. It all becomes like breadcrumbs nourishing my search, pilgrimage, through doubts and closer to vows.

Hours ago, in the yellowish-orange light of sunrise, all seven of us crammed into a van and sat in Chicago traffic for two hours. Along the way, a contemplative quiet filled the space: some of us rested, some prayed. I looked out the window at billboards and passing cars, thinking about how going to the Inter-Community Novitiate program is my favorite part of being a novice. I enjoy Tuesdays because I enjoy learning *and* I like the people, especially the men.

Later, in a dim basement dining room, eating the applesauce and peanut butter sandwich from my sack lunch, I'm sitting with a group at a round table. Next to me is a handsome Navy-vet-turned-novice named Tim. Near his muscular body, I feel alive, energized. I feel pulled toward his strength, confidence, friendliness—and am tempering my tendency to touch his arm while we talk, all while I keep leaning in to hear his thoughts about the morning lecture, about the vow of poverty, a grin wide across my face. I hear my loud laugh echoing through the dining room. I feel light.

Tim feels safe and familiar, like someone I've known for years, someone I'm meant to have in my life for a long time. It could be our similarities that has him feeling like a fast friend, as he grew up in rural Minnesota, near the Iowa border. Over the weeks, it doesn't take long for me to feel like we're bonding, building a real friendship. And it doesn't take long to wonder *how* he likes me; to feel confused about the attraction I feel. As the weeks and months of the novitiate go on, the questions linger, and the excitement for Tuesday classes persists.

Journal
September 21, 9:00 p.m., in my room at the CFN

Good God,
My clarities today have been these things:

It's my nature to *share*. I very much want to share my body, like with a person, in a sexual way. I just love sharing all I am and giving.

I really like religious life and this week I want to stay and am hoping it will work.

I do really like Mike, and I think about him way too much. I keep catching myself fantasizing about dating him if I were ever to leave. And, I secretly hope that no girl ever works out for him so that if I were to leave he'd be available. How awfully SELFISH of me! That's not love & care! So help me God!

Amen!

27

"Can you play chess?" the nursing home volunteer coordinator asks as we walk through a bright linoleum hallway.

"Well, I know how, but I haven't done it in years... And, I don't think I'm very good."

"One of our residents here, Fred, loves to play chess but doesn't have anyone to play with. Maybe that can be something you do when you come each Monday."

"I'm willing to try. He'll probably enjoy winning over and over!" I laugh a little, and make a mental note to review the rules of the game before returning next week.

Before moving to Joliet, I sent my resumé to the novitiate directors. Though I'm only twenty-six, I have already done a lot of things: jail ministry, teaching, working with the homeless, accompanying pregnant women, tutoring, helping with youth ministry, volunteering in soup kitchens and shelters, advocating for justice and peace. I hoped that my weekly service experience would lead to my being assigned some work among the marginalized in society, like in a jail.

But when I learned I'd been assigned to volunteer in a nursing home, I wasn't surprised. Sister Lisa said that medical and elder care seemed to be the main ministry area where I lacked experience. I nodded, understanding, while my stomach turned into knots. I just spent the whole summer on the receiving end of medical care, so this feels a little too close to home. I decide not to tell her I volunteered regularly at a nursing home during high school; just cooperate and accept the assignment.

Yet I'm concerned it will be painful to be around others who are sick and weak; it will remind me too much of my own brokenness.

It doesn't take long for me to start looking forward to going to the nursing home each week. As I get to know the residents and spend time with them, I try to be a loving presence—much like Jesús was to me when I was in the ICU. When the suffering I encounter makes me uncomfortable, I try to offer a smile and a gesture of kindness. As I hear about the lives of the elders I get to know, I'm encouraged and strengthened to embrace my own struggles—to allow suffering to be a teacher, a beautiful mystery. With each encounter, I'm reminded that every human has scars. We each have a story of brokenness and pain. As I listen, crack jokes, and quickly lose at chess each week, I hope I'm honoring the sacred dignity of each person. I hope I'm adoring the holiness of their pain.

> *Journal*
> *September 22, Saturday, 10:00ish p.m.*
>
> God that is all, in all, and of all—I love your presence in all of your creation, especially trees and people. Tonight I acknowledge your presence in the good, holy man of Mike, who has still been on my mind—a lot—through this day. Thanks for him, and for all the people I'm getting to know here.

> *Journal*
> *September 23, 9:20ish a.m.*
>
> God, beautiful God—the one I deeply love and live for. Suddenly I remember and wonder: Did I dream last night that you asked me to proclaim that I live for you? Wow!
>
> Well, I do know of one of my leftovers from my dream: I live for you, Jesus, in this life, not life after death. And this was being challenged. I was fighting and arguing—with who? She said my theology was all wrong and in fear and insecurity I waved my theology credits around and said "the reign of

God is here and now and our call is to help the living! Not the souls of the dead!"

All that aside, this is one of those days that I feel restless and yet lost in things I desire and crave—such as this silence and stillness.

What's my mood? What's going on inside me? Is it an internal sorting day? Or a day when I'll get lost in my longings again?

Speaking of longings. Mike. I know I could really deeply fall in love with him. I'm tempted to avoid him for a while, to remain safe and try to focus on this life, Sisterhood. This is where I am. Can I be here with all my heart? I may have dug myself into a hole the other day—a deep dark, muddy, smelly hole—when I told him how much I believe in honesty and live by it.

Since then I've realized how dishonest I really am with him. And I wonder if I should be honest. It could be disastrous and disappointing and embarrassing. I can practically hear him respond to me, "Oh Julia, I'm sorry. I wish I could say I felt that way about you, but I don't."

I sure am sighing a lot. A lot.

If I had freedom right now I would fly to Denver and stay with Janie and visit Mike and see how we really are when we're together.

But I don't have freedom. This is where I am. This is my life. And I must accept it and live it fully.

It doesn't mean I don't have freedom to be fully honest with him. And myself.

Honestly.

These are my questions: Would I be happier with him? Would he date me if I were available? Does he think about me a lot too? How do I face the attraction to a choice that isn't really a choice right now? How do I admit my attraction when it's not as clear how I'll be responded to? Do I need to admit it?

I don't know.

Help me redirect my love and confusion into my relationship with you, Oh Christ, because that's what you're calling me to focus on now. I believe.

Help me Jesus. Amen.

2:00ish p.m. (that same day)

Today at Mass I sat behind a middle-aged mom and I thought "that's not the life I want. I don't want to be thought of as somebody's mother."

So, Sisterhood may fit me best, after all.

Yet, vows seem uncomfortable and like a bad idea for me. Especially when I daydream about other possibilities so much.

I wonder what I'll learn during the next two years. Maybe if I'm still thinking of him in two years then I'll know that I should pursue your love in a whole different form. There's many ways to live a life of love.

I've been attracted to him for a year and a half, already, which is a long time to be attracted to someone.

Amen!

Journal
October 7, Tuesday, nighttime

God! Good God! What is it going to take for me to ever have peace about relationships?

Could I ever be able to do as I desire: see the beauty of people, thank you, bless them and move on?

Jesus, there's so much going on in me. And I don't know what I'm learning, what I'm growing into... So I've just been reading the Bible for prayer, as comfort. Am I procrastinating on praying through my hard uncomfortable emotions, manic thoughts, exhausted dreams and questions, though?

So God, Holy Lovely Jesus, I just give it all to you; my inspirations, dreams, gratitude, affections and attractions, emotions. And I trust you're taking care of me, even when my heart and mind and body seem disconnected.

Amen!

28

Mike and I are G-chatting again, nearly every day now. I'm trying to not get too sucked into the conversation, too distracted from the Franciscan history homework I should be reading. When I asked Mike how he was doing, though, he said that he was lonely and down, that he wishes he had some significant, meaningful relationships in his life—in his part of the country.

My heart goes out to him, and I want to help. I sometimes daydream about leaving, and then trying out dating him, but I also wonder if I should try to set him up with my college roommate, Janie—who is already in Colorado.

I've realized that I've been developing more feelings for him through all our chats. I wonder if I'm falling in love. I'm not sure, so I'm not admitting this to anyone yet, not even my spiritual director. Maybe my chest warms with a happy energy when we G-chat simply because I enjoy connecting with a like-minded friend, because he helps me laugh. How can you be in love if you have spent so little time in-person with someone? But whatever the feelings are, something is happening and I'm trying to be open and free, while being a Sister who is getting ready for vows.

I want to convince myself that I'm not being possessive of Mike, that I'm detached and am OK with him dating others, that I won't be jealous. It's good for me to love like Jesus, selflessly. To care for others no matter the costs. I care for him and want him to be happy. Right?

If these feelings are romantic, I doubt the feelings are mutual, anyhow. Unlike me, he's too grounded to allow things to get big in his head.

G-Chat
Nov. 3, 2007, 1:35 p.m.

Julia: you're online on a saturday!
i was just about to sign off, but how can i not say hello to you!?
Mike: hey
i'm just trying to figure out how to get to janie's house
Julia: i have to share something with you
ok i hope this is not freaky to you
but i think it's funny
so i'm going to email you an essay i wrote the other day
Mike: ok
an essay?
Julia: well, or something like that.
just something i wrote kinda for the fun of it
here it comes
oh god
Mike: ok
Julia: i hope i don't regret that
Mike: i'm waiting
what?
Julia: i e-mailed it
Mike: i just got it.
you sure you want me to open it?
Julia: lol
Mike: i can still delete it if you want…
;)
Julia: i don't care
Mike: ok
here i go…
Julia: i can't be anything but honest with you
Mike: awe…

Julia:	oh god
Mike:	hahaha
	are you freaking??!?!?
	haha
	don't worry...
	i think it's good to be open and honest.
	that's what's made our friendship so great, right?
Julia:	riiiiiiiiight
Mike:	haha
Julia:	gawd
Mike:	i kind of had a sense about all of these things...
Julia:	i knew you did
Mike:	i know that it was probably really uncomfortable for you to set me up with your friend
Julia:	uh huh
Mike:	thank you, though...it really is an act of selfless love.
Julia:	you can see right through me
	yeah, yeah, yeah
	i don't care
	it is also self-torture
Mike:	and don't worry...i'm not ready for anything serious now, anyway, so it won't get serious.
Julia:	all right
	it's my problem if it does, anyhow
	i'm the one that needs to learn how to deal with it
Mike:	are you ok?
Julia:	yeah, i hope so
	just embarrassed, probably
Mike:	(don't worry that we haven't brought you up yet...your ears will be burning later on)
	;)
	why?
Julia:	lol
	right
	do you think you like her?
Mike:	i don't know

	i haven't even met her
	i mean, her emails seem nice...
	you know?
Julia:	yup, totally.
Mike:	but it's hard to judge by just that
	and there haven't been that many emails either
	so it's hard to say
Julia:	well, i hope you don't regret going
Mike: :	so.....you know that i have a hard time with disclosing, right?
	remember? we talked about that one time
	anyway
	i feel like a jerk too
Julia:	yeah i remember
Mike:	because i don't "disclose" very much
	i'm a pretty private person.
	(as you're aware)
Julia:	right
Mike:	(PS - this IM conversation is copyrighted.)
	hahahha
Julia:	lol
Mike:	but i wanted to thank you, i guess
	i mean, over time we've gotten to know each other pretty well
	and you're definitely a close friend
Julia:	of course. you're very welcome.
Mike:	and one of the few people who "get" me
	and i value that a lot.
Julia:	yeah, i'm really grateful for you too
Mike:	i think, in a way, it's like a real spiritual friendship...
	i don't know what the term for that is
	but anyway,
Julia:	i think it's soul mates?
Mike:	i think you're right
	(maybe anam cara?)
	i don't know
Julia:	what does that mean?
Mike:	soul mates has too many connotations

Julia:	lol
	yeah
Mike:	i think it's like gaelic or something for "soul friend"
	it's celtic
	there's actually a really good book about it
	but anyway
	i got off track there...
	haha
	so
Julia:	yeah, anyway! yay God that we're friends
	oh
Mike:	hahaha
	yay god!
Julia:	there's more? you're not supposed to be mr. disclosure! ;)
Mike:	lol
	...
	...
Julia:	press enter
	!
	;)
Mike:	i just wanted to say that, thanks for being such a good friend,
	thanks for letting our "relationship" develop the way it has,
	...and stuff
	(god i suck at this stuff!!!!!!)
	anyway,
	i know it's hard
Julia:	it's all good
Mike:	but thanks for being such a loving person
	ya know?
	;)
Julia:	ha, you're welcome
Mike:	you seem happy now, or at least happier
Julia:	:) that's good to hear
Mike:	it seems like you're feeling that god really wants you there
Julia: :	you're quite loving to me, too
Mike:	;)

Julia:	well, or at least i want to be here more than 1/2 the time
Mike:	ok, question: are you sure you want us to go on this date?
	you sure it's not going to be too upsetting
Julia:	ha, yes
	of course
	my community mates are also anxious to hear how it goes too. :)
	they saw my agony last night when i thought it was going on
Mike:	ha…greeeaat…
	hahaha
Julia:	and they are ready to walk me through it again!
Mike:	hhmmm…
	ok
Julia:	seriously! go!
	you need to meet her!
	and receive some of her lovin!
	and have fun!
	she's wonderful
	and somewhere within me i actually hope you click really well
Mike:	receive some of her lovin'?!??
	hahaha
	lol
Julia:	yes
Mike:	how about we start with coffee?
Julia:	GOOD
Mike:	i'm beginning to wonder if this is a "set up" or a "hook up!"
	hahaha
Julia:	(this is why you shouldn't marry her)
Mike:	MARRY?
Julia:	lol
	well, yeah
	that would be annoying
Mike:	like i said, i think we'll start with coffee and see how it goes
Julia:	it's a good place to start
Mike:	it would be annoying if i married her, huh?
	hahaha
Julia:	lol

	well yeah, today it would be annoying
Mike:	so...?
Julia:	so, even though we're not really on the subject anymore
	i just gotta ask, because it has bothered for me for some time
	is it tough for you to know that I have feelings for you?
Mike:	that's kind of a strange and complicated question (no offense)
Julia:	i know. i'm sorry.
Mike:	short answer...no
	the thing is, when we first met in chicago, of course there was energy and we clicked
	that's obvious, otherwise we wouldn't still be friends
	but i think that over the past year and a half we have grown alongside each other as friends
	you're in your situation, i'm in mine
	and we've kind of fallen into roles
	like "soul friends" roles
	and you're doing your thing, and seem happy and fulfilled
Julia:	right
	and i am, i'm happy
Mike:	so, in my mind, this is maybe the best of all possible worlds
Julia:	good answer :)
Mike:	and like you said, just because a person loves someone, there are a lot of ways to love somebody
Julia:	right!
Mike:	so it's an awkward situation sometimes
	but i think we got a good thing goin'
Julia:	oh yeah man
Mike:	i don't know if that makes any sense
Julia:	no, it definitely does
	it's how i feel too
	but sometimes i'm afraid that when you're all in one of your "no one will ever have me" moods and i'm thinking "i would so have you if i could have you!" it's jerky for me to have feelings for you, because you can't have me
	if that makes any sense
Mike:	haha

Julia:	it's lame. because it assumes you want me, and i don't think that's what you want
	you want things as they are
Mike:	yeah, it's maybe jerky for me to say that
	it IS jerky
	i guess that's not what i really mean when i say that...
	anyway, sorry if i come across like that
Julia:	i know. it's all good
	i just want to make sure that it's not annoying that you can't have me
	lol
Mike:	hahaha
	i think we both know that this is the best way to go and i'm just grateful to have you as my friend
Julia:	whew
Mike:	(and matchmaker???)
	hahaha
Julia:	i'm glad we got that cleared up now
Mike:	yes
Julia:	whew!

PART THREE
HELD

29

Sitting in a quiet chapel on a cool November afternoon, I stare at the cross hanging above the altar, its shadows long. My jaw still is sore, my teeth ache, and my mouth hurts. Every tooth has moved while my jaw has healed, while the brackets and wire held everything in place. The teeth are loose, shifting around while the jaw regains strength. Gaps between teeth are different, new slants to each tooth, and my gum line is not my own. I don't know my mouth anymore.

Before all this, my most complimented physical feature was my smile, thanks to all those painful orthodontic adjustments during the adolescent years. Now, though, my grin feels crooked, hideous. Before my accident, I would walk down the street smiling at ordinary things: the beauty of trees, clouds, street art. People I didn't know would say, "You have a beautiful smile!" Surely that will never happen again.

Even so, I still smile a lot. I have a lot to be grateful for, and the goodness of God's creativity continues to impress me. But with these gaps between my teeth, with my lips curling up differently and exposing more gums than before, I suspect my smile looks a little crazed, goofy. Certainly crooked. When I catch a glimpse of my smile reflecting in a panel of glass, I don't recognize the face, it doesn't feel like mine.

I wonder if the men I'm getting to know at the novitiate classes—Tim especially—find my face attractive at all. Or are they all grossed out? Do they like me? I wonder why I care.

Even as my face is mending and healing, my teeth will forever remind me of the truth of my brokenness; the failure of my body to stay on top of the cliff, or at least climb down carefully. This new mouth helps me know that I have been wounded, that my body can't forget what I've gone through. No matter how I heal, I'm pretty sure that from now on, I will always feel broken. In front of me, an image of Jesus hangs on the cross.

* * *

Since joining the Sisters, I've heard them say that community is a life of "perfect joy." I've also heard some say this about being part of the Catholic Church itself. Now that I'm studying the Franciscan documents, I'm starting to understand.

> Brother Leo asked St. Francis: "What is true joy?" Francis said: "I return from Perugia and arrive here in the dead of night. It's wintertime, muddy, and so cold that icicles have formed on the edges of my habit…. I come to the gate and, after I've knocked and called for some time, a brother comes and asks: 'Who are you?' 'Brother Francis,' I answer. 'Go away!' he says. 'This is not a decent hour to be wandering about! You may not come in!' When I insist, he replies: 'Go away! You are simple and stupid! Don't come back to us again! There are many of us here like you—we don't need you!' I stand again at the door and say: 'For the love of God, take me in tonight!' And he replies: 'I will not! Go to the Croisers' place and ask there!' I tell you this: If I had patience and did not become upset, true joy, as well as true virtue and the salvation of my soul, would consist in this."

St. Francis knew and felt it too: living in community has always been difficult, challenging. Toward the end of his life, he was rejected as leader by his brothers, the very community he founded. No matter who we are, each of us comes to community to love; to be loved and to love others, to know belonging and meaning. Yet, we all are fumbling humans, each of us so imperfect and weak. We fail ourselves and each other, we hurt and harm. When the waves of our siblings' inner brokenness and sin spill out on us, when the wounds of others disturb any sense of contentment that might have settled into our skin, we feel the crush of collective trauma. A Sister's defensive tone of voice, a snide comment: all bad behavior can ignite resentment, betrayal, and fury. We may have good intentions, but the impact matters more. And more than I would like, the impacts I have on others can be awful, destructive.

I'm learning that the causes are complex, but there's a lot of reasons why life in community is tough, why we bump into each other and get bruised; behavior causes bonds to splinter, break. I'm learning that our diversity of personalities, experiences, preferences, and perspectives can offer invitations to growth. With each conflict we have a choice. Love *is* messy, and Christian community is often the place where the messiness of love manifests, in bitterness or bickering. We fail to show the world that our religion is designed by love, for love. It's not a mystery why people don't stay.

Yet, in all this mess, a deep, perfect joy *can* persist. I often feel it, in the deep and quiet part of me, where my heart widens and cracks for the pain of the world, where I feel love for others. It's like the powerful love I felt from Jesús when I was in the ICU, silent and strong. It is the broken part of me that is ironically beautiful, like photos of decaying buildings, or rusty cars turning pink in the evening sun. The love is grounding, illuminating. The sparks of joy in the love create rays of hope and transcendence. It insists that all this Christian love, all this messy community living, is meant to imitate Jesus Christ, a man whose resurrected flesh bore the wounds of love.

* * *

I think of how my novitiate has taught me a new vocabulary, one I didn't expect: dental implants, periodontics, bone grafting. Thinking about my complicated treatment plan, the long schedule of surgery-heal-surgery-heal that has been outlined for me, I feel conflicted. I'm glad to be alive and grateful for the good healthcare. I'm impressed with what's possible, for how I will likely have a toothy smile again in eighteen months. But I'm also disturbed about the expense, the privilege. This process isn't cheap: do I really need new fake teeth?

I feel tense, wondering if there is another way to use the funds, to help those with greater needs. I wonder whether it is just to have all this medical care at my disposal. Is going through oral surgery helping me to live closer to the poor, to be poor in the way that Jesus was, that St. Francis and St. Clare were? I doubt that.

30

It's early Advent and I'm putting items in a suitcase, thinking about what's coming in the weeks ahead. I am dreading having my broken teeth pulled, having oral surgery. Yet, I feel excited to celebrate Christmas with my Sisters in La Crosse, to attend Mass with them, to pray adoration hours. Besides my JVC year in California, I've never been away from my family for Christmas. I'm glad I'll get to go to my parents for a couple days between Christmas and New Year's Day—also Dad's birthday. I'm glad Mom and Dad still live on the farm; they're now scheduled to move to Gunder, nearer to their restaurant, in the spring. Sitting on the bed, I organize toiletries into my travel pouch. Then my cell phone rings. I answer, and hear Sister Linda's voice.

"Julia, it's us. Sarah and Eileen are with me. We're on our way to La Crosse. Earl died last night."

"Oh no, oh no, oh no!" I cry. It feels like a cyclone is swirling through the room. I rub my face; my shoulders shake. I take a deep breath, try to steady myself, find words, ask questions. I groan, but no tears fall.

"We decided to pull over to call you. We knew you'd want to know. Marci called us and asked us to come, and we got in the car right away. She wants to gather with a small group in her house, she hasn't told very many people yet. We don't know much more. We'll find out more when we get there. We'll see you in La Crosse."

Two days later, I am sitting in a corner of San Damiano chapel on Viterbo University's campus, Sister Karen beside me. We came early to find a seat, and found some of the last chairs open, glad to sit together. The overflow has to watch Earl's memorial across campus in the Fine Arts Center.

I look around, noticing familiar faces: Sisters, single and married affiliates of our Franciscan community, a reporter, some students I recognize from the theology classes I took at Viterbo before becoming a novice. I watch more people come to the door and ushers greet them, tell them how to find the overflow space. Voices are hushed, many people have their eyes closed, heads bowed. Soft piano music fills the church. Then the music shifts, and everyone stands.

I sing along with the choir and the crowd, glancing up and down from the worship aid in my hands. Along with the priest, Fr. Tom, I watch Earl's teenage daughter and son and Marci enter the church, approach the altar. Marci is carrying a small metal box in her hands—an urn. My eyes fill with tears and my neck swells with heat as I watch Marci place the urn on a wooden table in front of the altar, then sit in an empty chair in the front row. Along with the crowd, I cry, sing, pray, and listen. The motions and the meaning of the liturgy are familiar, safe: a comfort. I find my mind and my spirit resting into the rhythm. After I receive communion in my hands and mouth I return to my chair, wipe tears from my cheeks, close my eyes, rub my forehead. I don't sing; I focus on what's stirring in my gut and heart. God, why did Earl have to die while I got to live? God, I hate this.

* * *

Early February I'm back in my tiny bedroom in Joliet, talking to Sister Lucy Ann on the phone. She says I must attend a community meeting in Colorado Springs in June, after the Common Franciscan Novitiate program is over. When I hear "Colorado" my gut starts to do flips, feeling anxiety and hope. Could it be possible to visit Mike while I'm out there?

As this year has gone on, I've become more honest with myself and others—Sister Lucy Ann, my spiritual director, other Sisters—telling them about my attraction to Mike. I've become convinced that everyone is healthier when we're transparent and honest. I'm learning to admit my doubts and desires out loud to those I trust; this act allows the tangles in my head and heart to unravel.

It feels important to visit Mike while in Colorado for the meeting. I don't know how else I can gain clarity and proceed as a novice if I don't; I feel I must see him so I can live this life wholeheartedly. I want to know what it's like to be in Mike's physical presence. I want to know what will happen in my body—in our bodies. I want to know what's real.

I tell Sister Lucy Ann that I'd like to visit Mike after the FSPA meeting and I'm surprised she agrees to it. But I think she understands this is a part of my process, that experience helps me know answers. I think carefully about how to make the trip affordable and have boundaries, so I also reach out to my cousins who live in Fort Collins and arrange a visit. I tell her that if it works for Mike and me to go camping as we hope, his friends will join us. Mike and I chat about how we'll spend time together too, just us. Our G-chats are playful as we talk about beers I'll try, breweries we'll visit, and where we could hike and kayak. I squirm with excitement and nervousness as the days get closer.

Journal
February 22, 9:00ish a.m.
(on the train to Chicago, for a day at the museums)

Sweet God,

Can I detach myself from my desire to be admired? It was so flattering to hear another novice say that Tim has a crush on me yesterday!

Even though I want this life with you (and I really do feel called to celibacy, at least right now), I still daydream about romance with Mike. And sometimes Tim.

I'm not sensing more guidance in either direction. I wonder if you even care what I do.

I mean, God, I know you care and you have a will for me and it's perfect, but I wonder if some things are totally up to me, all choice and free will.

I want to be loved by a man who I also love. I want to know what that's like!

Guide me good God, you are sweet and I know you are all I need.

Also, I hope that all I want is within your will and way for me.

Guide me today. Teach me how to listen and live in your love.

Thank you! Amen!

* * *

Alone in the quiet chapel again, gazing at the corpus of Christ on the cross in the midday light, I think about what it means to have an embodied faith, about how Jesus knows what it's like to have a body full of pain and emotions. And desire. As far as we know, Jesus didn't exactly profess public vows, but he was poor, chaste, and obedient. Studying the vows this year has helped me understand how radical and bold it could be to give my body to God as a vowed Franciscan Sister. In a world obsessed with sex—and frequently oppressing the most vulnerable in society because of the obsession—a vow of celibacy could be an act of resistance to the sex industries. I can proclaim a radical "No." Living in a community of strong women means I'm coming to grips with my own independence, that I can see how together we don't need men as partners, paths to power or freedom. I suspect—and hope—that I'll be able to have my needs for intimacy met in other ways.

Maybe that's what my relationship with Mike provides: a lesson about what's possible. I'm learning and seeing how celibacy will allow a freedom for me to not cling to people, to love anyone who comes into my life, to be broadly available to serve and care. Even if this is my call, my choice, it will be a challenge. I'll continue to develop feelings for people, but I think the sacrifice will be worth it. I won't be tied down to any place or person. I'll have a true freedom to go where God needs me. I feel my face relax, thinking these things. I've found joy in the freedom already.

The vow of poverty is about freedom too. Living with few possessions could mean that material goods won't lock me into a certain place; attachments won't get in the way of going where God needs me.

The freedom that comes from common ownership of goods (and no private ownership) has always felt radical to me in a world obsessed with consumerism and trends. I must put effort into resisting being materialistic, but I've been inspired by the description of the early Christian communities in Scripture: *"All who believed were together and had all things in common; they would sell their property and possessions and divide them among all according to each one's need"* (Acts 2:44-45, NAB). With my Sisters, I have experienced this: we share our money in common, and then each woman has enough funds to pay for her basic needs. A lot of money is left over because we live simply and this is given to the poor, often in the form of grants.

As for the vow of obedience, I can see how the input and perspective of others in my community can help me see the big picture. Sisters reveal things to me that are in my blind spots. They can name my gifts and talents—and weaknesses—in ways that I cannot, and help guide me toward the future. I understand now that my personality type means I can easily distract myself: I love trying new hobbies, getting immersed in projects and going on adventures; I'm free-spirited, can lack focus and direction. I think my gut and heart know that the vow of obedience is good for me and will ultimately provide a container that will refine me, force me to serve better. Accountable to other Sisters, I'm less likely to flounder and be impulsive. Instead, I'll live from a grounded connectedness to God and community. My culture is obsessed with independence—"do what feels right" or "do what you want." For me to turn to community—and God—for guidance and direction is a better way.

I press my knees into the kneeler in front of me, fold my hands in front of my body, close my eyes tightly, bow my head in prayer. Jesus, I don't know if you had all your questions worked through before you went to the cross. I don't know if I will ever have my questions worked through. But I know I love you and want to give myself to you. Do you want me to profess the vows of celibacy, poverty, and obedience? Is this the way for me to give myself? Will I really do this? Help me know and have courage, dear Jesus.

31

Along with the other Sisters in the Common Franciscan Novitiate community, I lug my suitcase and backpack out of the van and walk up to a house—a small convent. Short, bright, green grass dotted with violets and dandelions bursts through the soft soil along the sidewalk. We're in Stevens Point next to the shore of the Wisconsin River. We trekked here for a week together, a time to integrate all that we've learned these past nine months, we're told.

Settling into a simple bedroom, I look out the window at blue sky and notice I'm feeling grateful to have time to sit with all I've wrestled this year: the men I love and who I believe love me—Mike and Tim—in tension with the love I have for Jesus and my Sisters. I feel a longing that won't go away: I want to be a Sister, serve, and give my whole self to Jesus. The desires are deep in my heart, but I'm not feeling the certainty and confidence to match.

On day two of the retreat, we gather in a musty living room and listen to a Sister who is also a scholar lecture on details of the San Damiano cross, the icon crucifix before which St. Francis prayed eight hundred years ago in the little dilapidated chapel near Assisi, where he heard Christ say, "Francis, rebuild my Church which is falling into ruins." I fill a paper with notes and ask questions. But my heart and mind feel restless. I want quiet and solitude so I can process all that I've learned, all that I've been through since I started the novitiate, fell off the cliff, met the amazing nurse Jesús in the ICU, grew closer to Mike, met Tim, and realized that I want to be a Sister; I simply am not sure about the lifelong commitment part.

During the open, reflective time, I'm eager to be alone, to think and pray, but I don't sit still. I sit in the dim chapel, then go to the simple bedroom for a nap. I take long walks along the Wisconsin River, sitting on its shore and filling pages of my journal with pieces of poems, questions, prayers—and watercolors. And I scribble lists of hopes, of what I've learned during this first year as a novice, lingering questions, reasons why I want to remain with the Sisters, but also why I want to leave religious life. I'm still trying to understand and embrace how my fall off the cliff, only ten months ago, has changed me. My body is wounded and made new, my living is acute with an awareness that any stumble, mishap, or fluke could end my life: be my last moment.

I notice that my floppy attempts at prayer keep being interrupted by thoughts of Mike. I miss him. I want to call to hear his voice, his laugh. I long to sit at a keyboard and G-chat with him, to joke about dumb things. I think about how I gave up G-chatting during Lent, hoping some distance would decrease my affection for him, but it didn't. In fact, my fondness and longing might be intensifying. Every time I see something beautiful—like birds playing in the river or light streaming through the budding trees—I want to share the beauty with Mike. I long for him to be close and see what I'm seeing.

Before I came here, my spiritual director asked what I get from my relationship with Mike. I didn't know how to answer, but now in the quiet and solitude, I'm trying to find one. I think it is somewhere deep in the folds of my heart, in the eyes of Christ, and the time ahead. God is my retreat director, and I'm guessing that God wants this retreat to be about getting ready for my upcoming visit to Mike in Colorado. In my prayers, I'm telling God the truth: I want the visit to be romantic. I want Mike to desire me. And, I think it will hurt if it isn't, if he doesn't, if I feel rejected. Is this a betrayal of my Sisters? Of where I am now? I don't know. But I feel like God hears me, receives my struggles, and is guiding me forward.

Walking along the river path one afternoon, everything I see seems to be screaming that celibacy is a bad idea. It's unnatural. The ducks have mates, the herons, the turtles. It's according to God's designs that all have companionship, communion. Every person that I encounter is with someone else. Why is God asking me to be so different? To dedicate myself to loving God's people in this bizarre way—a life of inevitable loneliness and longing? This vow might not be a good match for me. Especially when I love people so, so much.

Sitting on a bench and staring into the flowing river, I wonder what my time with Mike will be like. I remember the few intimate experiences I've had with men in the past. There was the night with Brandon while I was in the Jesuit Volunteers in Sacramento; I muttered surprising words to him between kisses: "This is my body given for you"—the same words that I've heard priests pray hundreds of times over the bread on the altar during Mass. Years later, in a sacramental theology class taught by Earl, I finally understood why I said those words to Brandon. "The sacrifice and communion that occurs between a husband and wife in their wedding bed is as holy as the sacrifice and communion that happens on an altar during every Mass.... Both acts of love ought to mirror each other," Earl said.

Why am I giving up the chance of experiencing something so sacred? What do I really want?

32

After another oral surgery, then a road trip across Iowa and Nebraska into Colorado with two of my Sisters, Sharon and Lucy, I'm at the retreat center in Colorado Springs. My gums are sore, and my mouth is full of stitches where bones were grafted. I still must eat soft foods and can't wear my fake teeth now. But the pain isn't too bad. It feels a bit funny to meet Sisters I've never met with a giant gap in my mouth, like a toothless kindergartner.

About twenty Sisters from my community who minister in New Mexico, Arizona, Idaho, and Washington are here. Going through a process called a "cultural audit" together, our meeting is full of prayer and conversation; I quickly find myself thinking, I love these women. I'm easily engaged and enjoying building relationships. A lot of them seem to be down-to-earth, relaxed, accepting, nonjudgmental. I feel a total freedom to be who I am: to crack jokes, ask questions, and voice my opinions. And when I do, I feel like I'm being heard, honored, respected. Off and on I find myself thinking the same prayer again and again: God, I love these Sisters, and this is such a good community. With them I feel at home, thank you.

At the same time, I think about Mike. If he doesn't have any luck rounding up people to go camping with us, will we be OK? I'll be forced to face the truth of whatever we are, whatever's going on between us. We'll be alright, I think. I'll be safe with him and we'll enjoy each other. I feel a trust swelling in me: being with Mike after being with the Sisters, this will offer me clarity. I hope so! Whatever I discover, I hope I will accept God's will for me.

* * *

I stand outside the door of the retreat center in the crisp Colorado night, under a sky full of stars, waiting for Mike's best friend, Rob. Most of the Sisters are in their rooms for the night, or are playing cards together in the lounge. But I'm eager to get off campus and be with people closer to my age.

Mike called Rob and asked him to take me out, and although I never met Rob before, I thought it was a really nice gesture—sweet that he wanted his best friend to meet me—so I agreed. Now I look at my cell phone, hoping he shows up soon. Rob already called once and asked for directions.

I think about how I look: partly toothless, scars still visible on my face, but I don't feel as ugly and broken as I did after the accident last summer. It's been a long time since the name "Frankenstein" has come to mind when seeing my reflection. I think I'm getting used to who I am: a broken woman. My wounds and scars are normal; wearing the memory of my wounds is part of being human. I need not be ashamed of my past, or defined by it either. I'm not unique for my scars and brokenness. This whole healing journey has taught me that when it comes to woundedness, everyone has a story to tell.

Finally in the car with Rob, we start chattering while driving through Colorado Springs. Rob points out landmarks and tells me about the history and culture. He's brought his sister-in-law along. I'm polite to her, and she is quiet, but I don't know why she's here. Did Mike tell Rob that I can't be alone with a man? Rob mentions that he's trying to work things out so he can go camping with Mike and me in a few days.

On Boulder Street we go to two different, mostly quiet, bars. Rob and I talk about politics, religion, and his teaching job as I try out Colorado beers. I like Rob, who is a lot like Mike: knowledgeable, kind, caring, thoughtful. Rob holds opens doors, pours drinks for me and his sister-in-law before himself, pays for everything, makes sure we're not bothered by his secondhand smoke. Sitting on bar stools and sipping beers I lean in and ask questions about his teaching methods, my body sways, the room spins. Oh, that's right, the altitude: I get drunk fast here. I grip the table and realize I'm happy and safe: my muscles relax and my face flushes with embarrassment.

Feeling uninhibited, I ask questions about Mike. Rob vaguely tells me about Mike's history with women, that he's had a lot of bad luck. It feels good to talk with someone else who knows and cares for Mike.

"Mike has a girlfriend now, right?" I ask Rob, knowing that things with Janie never really took off, and he's been dating others.

"Eh," he says, shrugging his shoulders. "Mike's really digging two women, actually. He thinks whatever's going on with Charlotte is going to fizzle out."

"Gosh, how come Mike doesn't tell me about this stuff?! I didn't know there's another woman. Who's the other woman?!" I practically spit out my beer. My guts turn into knots. I'm annoyed Mike has hidden this from me. But Rob doesn't say anything, and never answers those questions. Now I can't stop thinking. Am I the other woman that Mike likes?

* * *

The following morning, I wake up early and sit in bed, writing in my journal about a dream I've just had, full of images of death and denial. Of people bloody and dead, tortured and hanging in a convenience store. I woke up saying, "I would die if I stay here."

Several hours later, walking with Sister Eileen in the afternoon sun, with mountains looming bright on the horizon, I ask her about her life in Minnesota. I tell her about my plans to visit Mike here in Colorado. She asks why I'm going to see him and I admit that I hope for some sort of "internal click" about the relationship, so I can move on from all my unresolved questions. Eileen is empathetic and accepting, encouraging me to keep listening to my heart, referencing movies we watched together and teasing me. I laugh and feel a softness in my chest, a warmth, gratitude for her compassion.

* * *

I say goodbye to the Sisters and drive my rental car through the Garden of the Gods Park before leaving the city. I study the jagged landscape, peaks of red rock surrounded by blue sky. Seeing the boulders hanging on the edges of cliffs, seeming like they could roll down and crush passersby, I feel my heart pound. It hasn't yet been a year since the accident. The hardness of the rock has stirred up a terror in me. Never mind, I will not park and hike here, as planned.

I leave the dangerous terrain, grip the steering wheel tighter, turn around and drive towards Fort Collins. Going through the foothills of the Rockies, through Denver and Boulder, I wonder if the tension I felt in the Garden of the Gods wasn't so much about the way that the steep rocks reminded me of where I fell. I wonder if my recent dreams about danger could be about my accident. Probably not. I'm nervous about seeing Mike after all. And, I feel conflicted about being away from the Sisters.

I must be careful, no matter what's ahead. I want to focus on remaining faithful to God, to surrendering to Jesus' guidance and love.

33

I'm sitting at a table on the sidewalk in front of a coffee shop in downtown Fort Collins when I finally see Mike. I've been people-watching for a while, looking for him where we agreed to meet. I finally spot his kind, round, grinning face, his balding head and muscular body, and my heart flutters.

He's wearing a t-shirt and jeans but still has that jolly monk-look that I first thought was cute, even without the Franciscan habit. I wave, smile, and holler "Hello," awkwardly bumping into the table as I stand up. I see a wide smile through his bearded face. His kind and gentle eyes seem to sparkle behind glasses. I feel myself blushing.

Soon, we're hugging each other, a long and quiet embrace. I feel my body warm next to his, the solidness of his muscles. I had forgotten how much bigger he is than me, how small I feel next to him. It's a type of smallness I like, a kind that helps me feel safe, protected. Standing on the sidewalk our embrace is slightly awkward—but definitely joyful.

I turn quiet as we spend the afternoon and evening together, walking around downtown Fort Collins, tasting beers in different brew pubs before kayaking in Horsetooth Reservoir. The whole time, I'm trying to pay attention to his body language, looking for clues as to how he feels about me. My body easily gravitates toward his. I sit close to him on bar stools. I touch his arm while we talk. I lean in as we walk along sidewalks. Behind him in a tandem kayak, I imagine touching him more, but remain reserved, keeping a tight grip on my paddle.

During dinner and drinks later, we don't laugh as much as I

thought we would, as much as I do when we G-chat. We keep falling into silence that is half-awkward, half comfortable, light and controlled conversation. He's being polite and thoughtful, like he really wants to be good to me. But when I ask about the girl he is dating, he says little. I wonder why he doesn't want to tell me about her. I wonder if he would rather not think about her when he is with me. And I wonder if the quietness between us is a tension (sexual tension?), if we both feel unsure about what we can really say and do.

After dark, I drive the rental car to the neighborhood where one of my cousins lives with her husband, and chat with them a while before turning in for bed. Before sleeping, I pray and write a quick prayer in my journal.

> *Journal*
> *June 1, Sunday, 11:30 p.m.*
>
> Good God…I just don't know. Get me out of my head and help me to listen with my heart, to love and bless. Am I going to be disappointed if nothing drastic happens? I know I'm a little ridiculous. I need to stop wanting to solve stuff and just be, especially when nothing is wrong. So, help me God. Amen.

I eventually fall asleep, deciding that I'll just go with the flow tomorrow, when we go camping. I'm glad it worked out for Rob to come along too, that feels healthy and good—and my Sisters would probably like it much better. I'm grateful for this little adventure, and am trying to remain open to however God is leading, to whatever happens between us.

* * *

The next night, we go to bed in three different tents, all spaced equally apart throughout the campsite. The fire smolders. Smoke lingers in crisp, mountain air. I lay in the sleeping bag I borrowed from Mike, listening to the subtle sounds of wind rustling trees and coals crackling in the fire ring, thinking back through time spent with Mike and

Rob. I rest into the gratitude I feel for them, for how respectful they are to me, how they've thoughtfully checked in about my comfort and needs.

I remember when we traversed along a cliff overlooking a creek, Mike read my anxious body language, moved his body protectively closer to mine, assured me I was OK. The heat of his body and his kindness relaxed me; I did feel better. With both of these good men, I feel completely safe at this remote campsite. And I feel very happy to finally be in the woods again—nearly a year since my fall.

But I'm also disappointed. I want more. I want Mike to be affectionate. It bothers me that he is being standoffish. Would it have hurt him to put his arm around me? Would it have been so bad for him to grab my hand and hold it? My sense is that he'd like to touch me, but is trying to be careful, to keep to a safe distance. "Uh, it's complicated" is all he could mutter the other day when I asked about the other woman he likes. If I'm that woman, he's exactly right. Whatever's going on between us is *very* complicated.

Earlier tonight, I wanted him to sit closer while the three of us drank beer, whiskey, and smoked old fashioned pipe tobacco around the fire. "I could get really into this, it's a good thing that smoking is so expensive or I might become a serious addict," I told them. If Rob weren't around, I probably would have snuggled close to Mike on the same stump or log. It's really a good thing Rob is around: God is taking good care of me, I decide, as I drift to sleep.

But not for long.

When I wake up my body is shaking, my teeth chattering. I have never felt cold like this before. Maybe this sleeping bag isn't insulated well. I must not have enough warm clothes on, and I don't have anything else to put on. I reach down and rub my toes. I rub my hands together, rub my arms, rub my hands over my chest. I try to warm my body and relax so I can go back to sleep.

It is so cold, though. My body rolls around in the sleeping bag; I twist and turn on the hard ground. I'm restless and can't stay still, can't get warm, can't relax. I tuck my head deep into the bag and curl into a ball, shaking with the chill. I roll and roll, not getting warmer. My teeth continue to chatter. Nothing seems to work. This trial goes on for what feels like hours. Chattering, rolling, rubbing, curling up, and shivering. And instead of getting warmer and relaxing, I'm growing colder, and frustrated.

If I were sleeping closer to another person, I'd be a lot warmer.

Now, another layer of agony is tangled into my chilly discomfort in this dark tent. I start to wonder what would happen if I crawled into Mike's tent, and if I would sleep. I think about all the possibilities. We might maintain our boundaries, we might not. We might sleep, we might not. I'm not sure what I want. I have a lot of questions. The questions bounce in my brain, as my body rolls around in my sleeping bag and I continue to shiver.

I'm uncertain, yet eventually feel my body preparing to rise. I fumble and find the zipper to the tent, grab my pillow and sleeping bag, and make my way across the gravel of the campsite. I feel stones on my icy, bare feet. I feel like I'm turning blue and can't I stop my jaw from chattering.

"Mike," I whisper as I unzip his tent. He mumbles some sort of sleepy response. "I'm so cold, I can't sleep." I tuck my head into his tent. "Can I just sleep in here to get warmer?"

"Oh yeah, OK. Sure." He shifts over to the side and makes room. I crawl in, zip up the tent. "God, you really are shivering. Why are you so cold?"

"I don't know. But thanks."

I lay out my sleeping bag next to his, his body big and round beside me as I crawl in. He looks at me sleepily, smiles, and then closes his eyes and falls back asleep within minutes.

Even though I'm now only a few inches away from Mike—there's only layers of our clothing, sleeping bags and some open air between us—I'm not feeling any warmer. I relax a little, from the gladness of being near him, but I'm still shivering, down my legs, up my arms, through my spine and shoulders. So many parts of me are shaking and shuddering. My jaw continues to chatter. How can I relax?

Besides, lying this close to Mike, sleeping away, snoring some, my mind and body are far from calm. I trust him completely. I'm not going to make a move. I *want* to make a move, but I don't know how.

And I'm a Sister! I'm supposed to be living as if I have vowed celibacy right now. I'm probably breaking every sort of rule and behaving very un-celibately by being this close to a man in the middle of the night. And it isn't even helping me get warmer, or get any rest.

Yet, I feel completely safe. There are few men I would allow myself to become this close to. There's few that I would trust enough, feel comfortable enough with, that I would ever consider being next to them. I don't think I'm going to try anything on Mike—but I sort of want him to try something on me.

Will he? Does he want to?

I don't know. But I'm still *so* cold. My teeth have stopped chattering, but I feel cold to my bones, as if I have ice in my veins. I curl into the sleeping bag again, my head tucked toward my chest, my body a little ball. I'm trying to be still and quiet, not wanting to wake Mike with any of my noisy movements. But I want to sleep, be warm. He seems like he is sleeping so well.

I wonder if he might have another blanket or sleeping bag somewhere? An extra sweatshirt? He must have an idea of how to make me warmer.

If only I could be closer to his warm body, then maybe I would relax. Then maybe I could sleep. If only. "Mike," I whisper, reaching out and touching his shoulder.

"Mmm," he stirs. He rolls over and looks toward me. He is close enough that I can make out a small smile.

"I'm still freezing. Do you have an extra blanket anywhere or anything?"

I can feel his concern as he reaches and touches my shoulder gently and studies my face. He is quiet and thoughtful. I know he's being careful and wants to be respectful. I'm trying to be patient in this long pause while he considers what to say.

"I don't have any other blankets or anything. Sorry. How about you climb in here?" And then he starts to unzip his bag. I smile. I sort of hoped that's what I'd hear. Yet, I'm not so sure it's right.

I also don't know what else to do. How else can I get warm and sleep? "Do you think I will fit?" I give him a chance to change his mind, to say we better not, that we're crossing a boundary. Maybe it would be better for us to go start a fire and sit by it for a while. But he begins to make room inside his sleeping bag, scooting over. I feel warmth coming out of him, inviting me close.

I crawl inside his sleeping bag and we get situated side-by-side. Mike tucks his legs, arms, and chest around mine and wraps his arms around me. He zips up the bag, our bodies spoon, snug together. "You *are* cold!" he says as he squeezes me tight and gently rubs my arms, like he is trying to warm them.

"Sorry. I hope I don't make you cold."

I feel his skin touch my skin and I begin to get warmer, an energy flowing through me. But my mind wanders to thoughts of God. Did God have me get cold so that I'd get into Mike's tent, into his sleeping bag? Maybe this is God's way of clearing up the confusion in my heart.

"No problem, no problem. Let's get you warm," Mike says, sounding not annoyed at all. He even seems to sound glad that I'm close. His kindness is a relief; it doesn't take long for me to relax, to feel warm again.

As he squeezes me tightly, I feel my body react, wanting more. I know what my body wants. But what's going on in *his* body? I'm too inexperienced to have any idea.

For the rest of the night, we don't say anything as we lay together. I doze off and on, but never too deeply. Each time I awake and feel myself wrapped inside Mike's warm body, I'm thrilled. Yet, I wonder what Rob would think if he knew Mike and I were sharing a tent, a sleeping bag. *And,* I feel my chest tighten with a sting of guilt, like we are betraying others: Mike, his girlfriend; me, my Franciscan community. Or, we would be, if we let ourselves do anything else besides spoon like this.

As I lie there thinking off and on through the rest of the night, between little naps, I feel Mike is awake too. His breathing shifts and we lay together very still, each lost in our thoughts, trying not to disturb the other.

After a while, I decide that I do want him to kiss me, that I would allow it, welcome it. But I'm not going to kiss him; I'm not going to make a move—mainly because I'm still unsure how much he likes me and why he's been so standoffish. I wonder if respecting me and where I am in religious life is more important to him than enjoying physical connection. Maybe his desire to honor my process and discernment is more important to him than showing me love.

My body and mind feel electric with a longing for a kiss, a longing to know what's going on in him. I'm not sure if any of my guesses are right. I'm not sure if he will decide it's worth it, if he will start to show me affection. I'd like to know his body more intimately, but I don't know what he wants.

The thoughts of desire, the endless questions, turn through my mind, intensifying the longing. I stay still and try to enjoy what I *do* have, what I can have: the body of a man with whom I feel safe, that I love, wrapped around me through the night. It feels really good and my body relaxes with comfort. Eventually, I fall asleep much warmer and more relaxed, my heart still pounding with a little hope.

I never got the kiss I hoped for, after all.

* * *

When dawn arrives, I return to my tent so that Rob won't know where I've slept. Mike and I pretend as if nothing unusual happened as we eat breakfast and pack up. And my body and heart droop with disappointment.

I don't feel rejected, exactly, but sad that nothing more happened. I'm also sad that our time together is ending. I'm not going to fly back to the Twin Cities until tomorrow, but Mike is leaving for a vacation with his girlfriend in the Grand Tetons this afternoon. I feel a bit resentful—jealous?—that he's not making himself more available to me. But it's probably all healthy and good. I'm not his girlfriend, after all. I'm a Franciscan Sister! And a friend. I need to stop trying, wanting, to be anything else.

Through the gloom, I try to come off as kind and understanding. I hope I'm not coming off crabby. I hope that I love him unconditionally like a friend and Sister ought.

We say goodbye to Rob, and Mike and I go back to his apartment where I left my rental car. He unpacks and repacks his clothes and camping gear and I sit on his couch and study his books, art, CD collection, saint statues, even the way he's arranged his things. It all resonates. I feel at home, comfortable. Mike and I *are* a lot alike; we could have been a good couple. Being in his space helps me understand what I'm saying no to by saying yes to God and religious life: no to chances of being with a man like him. With him.

He has to go meet his girlfriend, the woman I've heard so little about during our time together. The relationship Rob said Mike expects to "fizzle out." I never figured out what he is hiding from me. But it's time for us to part. Whatever we're not talking about, I must say goodbye. I need to let him go. I need to go back to my Franciscan Sisters, to my life as a novice preparing to profess my vows.

So I help Mike reload his truck and we hug goodbye in the parking lot, a much longer and sadder hug than before. A few tears fill my eyes. I don't want to let go, and refuse to be the first to do so. When we finally do drop the embrace, I realize that though everything about saying goodbye to Mike feels awful, it also feels right.

* * *

I stay another night in Fort Collins with my cousin. Flying back to the Midwest, I gaze through the thick window glass of the airplane into green fields below, lost in thought and feelings. Blue sky is dotted with cheery white clouds, separate unto themselves, not unlike the sorting I feel happening in my head and heart. I take a few deep breaths and relax into the present moment, feeling grateful for how things went with Mike.

There is so much that we didn't say to each other, so much we left unsaid, undone. And although I'm disappointed, and a bit hurt, I'm also relieved. Now it will be easier to follow the urgings from the deepest part of my heart.

I lean into the sense of calm; a relaxed gladness warms my chest and slows my thoughts; a joy falls into a new opening forming. Where there was once a crack that I had hoped Mike would fill, I sense God's quiet presence rushing in. And with the quiet, a peace. I want to deeply listen. I'm eager, hungry, to be more devoted to this goodness. I want to hear God, to follow God's will for me. As everything shifts in my heart, feelings of anxiety evaporate. This great letting go is allowing me to become someone different.

I feel grateful for the love I feel for my Sisters, and for good friends like Mike. The more that others accept and love me, as broken and complicated as I am, the more I can accept myself. I feel less ashamed of the broken parts of me, even the parts that are disfigured. The shadows in my being I'd rather keep hidden, the parts of me that are weak and needy are embraced and allowed. Even the parts of me that want to know what's it's like to be physically intimate with someone beautiful, someone I love, are drawn toward the light, toward a place of wholeness.

I don't really want to get married. I want to be a Sister more than I want that type of intimacy. I feel deep in my being that living as a Sister will allow me to continue to grow in health, happiness, and holiness, as I hope. I'm at peace with the possibility of being with the Franciscans for the rest of my life. I really am.

All of this jolts me to attention; I'm surprised to hear myself. But yes, I mean it. I really would be fine being a Sister forever. I smile as I gaze into the rolling farms fields below. This is who I am.

Who I really, really am.

34

I live with two Sisters in their sixties who are professional listeners. Sister Beth, a spiritual director, is petite with short curly brown hair, a simple gentleness, and fierce strength. Sister Fran, a blond psychotherapist of short stature, wears her clothing in an air of refined sophistication, with a flare of warm joy. Together we make a small community in a modest home in a northwestern Chicago suburb, spending evenings together eating homecooked meals at a small kitchen table, praying evening prayers, and relaxing in the living room. I ask them questions about how they understand the vows of poverty, celibacy, obedience. What is it like to be part of a community that has been in flux since they entered, shortly after the Second Vatican Council? How do they live out the Franciscan charism?

I tell them about my feelings, questions, and doubts. I share my dreams and tell them about the ongoing medical appointments. How my mouth is changing, how my body remains nervous and tense on the edges of stairwells, curbs, balconies. I say that I'm adjusting to a new face, am less self-conscious about the scars around my eyebrows, nose, and lips. I'm getting used to wearing false teeth, even when I must take them out to eat around people I barely know, people who don't yet know what happened to me.

I still feel broken and messed up, but my disfigured look doesn't stop me from smiling and laughing and exposing my strangeness to others. As I see it now, my fall off the cliff was one of my greatest teachers, yet I'm not sure I'm getting all the lessons. Sisters Fran and

Beth ask loving questions and nod as they listen, as they hold the space I need for my struggles.

On school days, I take the blue line train and two buses to the high school. During the hour-long commute, I grade papers, lesson plan, journal, and pray. I catch myself thinking that I really love my life. I feel excited about who I'm becoming. During times of solitude, I notice that my attraction to Mike has simmered. Has visiting him in Colorado allowed me to detach from my affection for him? Maybe. I still wonder what would have happened if he had kissed me. Would anything have changed? Maybe God wants me to learn how to freely live as a celibate woman. Or maybe God wants me to be fully aware of what I'm giving up, what I'm choosing as I move toward vows. Do I want to take these vows? What does God want of me?

Now that I'm working at the high school during the days, I rarely G-chat with Mike anymore. Yet, we chat on the phone some nights and email back and forth. He tells me about his breakup with his girlfriend and his struggles with dating. We never talk about our feelings for each other or the night we shared in a tent in Colorado.

After a breakup, he brings up the topic of celibacy:

G-chat
October 24, 2008, 4:24 p.m.

Mike: want to see my 13 reasons (so far) for choosing celibacy?
:)
Julia: YES!
omigosh, i so need to see those right now!
Mike: well, they're MY reasons. i'm not arguing for anyone else.
so they may not apply to you
but here they are...

Reasons to be celibate:
1. Feel lonelier in romantic relationships
2. I like being single; it's my status quo
3. Fiercely independent

4. No one to disappoint, no one to leave me
5. None of my paired friends are any happier than I am
6. Need private space and time
7. I feel most complete and "whole" (not divided) alone
8. Don't want to let anyone that close to me
9. Don't want anyone else to be an authority of me
10. "Love" goes away
11. Can't find a match, partner
12. Dating stresses me out too much, feel smothered
13. Every relationship I've been in I want out of

i'm writing down all my reasons and then going back and looking at them to see what i think of the reasons
i'm not sure all of these are totally healthy
:-/
but they're my reasons

Julia: my reasons:
1. sex is overrated
2. i don't want my identity to be wrapped up in one other person - i don't want to be known as someone's wife or mother
3. marriage and mothering wouldn't allow me the same quiet/prayer/individual time as i enjoy now
4. i'd rather be able to love everyone inclusively
(no exclusive love)

Mike: right
i just added two more
14. Friendships are my strongest, safest kind of relationship
15. Want to be open to loving everybody
that's what you just said!

Julia: 5. a family and a home is likely to tie me down to a place
6. i think our world is over-sexualized and i want to show that happiness is possible without sex
7. i hate the sex industry and celibacy is a form of protest
8. i doubt that there's anyone in the world that would want to live life the same as me

Mike: right...

	(except religious)
	have you thought about New Monasticism?
	my thing is that i would be much more open to going back, but i also don't really believe in taking vows
	i can't promise that i won't change
	or that something different would come up down the road that i'd want to do
	i think that the only time a person should take vows is in marriage, and i'm not even real sure about that all the time
Julia:	wow
	um, yes i thought real seriously about leaving and doing new monasticism about a year ago
Mike:	i remember that
Julia:	but as i learned about the history of religious life and tradition and stuff, something happened in me very deeply that helped me to know that this where i belong
Mike:	what's that?
Julia:	hm. i don't know
	like a deep spiritual knowing? or an assurance from God?
	something like that
	9. i don't think i'm made to be part of a couple (i'm still thinking here)
	10. i'm too independent and strong-willed for most men
Mike:	hmmmm

35

Most days, though, I wait at the bus stop feeling satisfied and grateful: I'm offering my gifts of creativity, knowledge, and passion. I'm serving those on the margins of society, contributing to the mission of the Church that I believe in. This is what I wanted to be as a Catholic Sister: helping others know God's love through experience, relationships, and encounters. This is why I'm here, and I'm happy.

I share a basement office with the other high school campus minister, and the athletic director. We have put a foosball table and a couch in the room, and hang cheery posters about God's love, wanting to offer a relaxing space for teenagers. Once a day, I carry a bookbag and laptop up three flights of stairs to teach. I'm busy and working hard, I rush through the dim building and begin to feel an ache of sadness, a weight pressing down on me. I trip and stumble often. My body is spotted with bruises.

One day, going back to the basement office, alone in the stairwell, I trip and fall down a few steps and land on my butt with a thud, sliding down a few more. When I come to a stop, the gray stairwell swirls around me, my shoulders shake. My breathing feels quick and shallow. I think of the blur of limestone cliff, tree branches, dust, creek water. I taste blood in my mouth. I close my eyes and curl my knees to my chest, trying to breathe more slowly. My body hurts. But I'm in a high school stairwell, not at the bottom of the cliff on the farm in Iowa. And my mouth is not, in fact, bloody. I tell myself this.

I want to scream, or groan, but instead I slowly stand, steadying myself with the handrail, and return to my office where there's work to do.

* * *

It crosses my mind: do I need therapy? I have been falling a lot, feeling dizzy, like my body and mind are losing control. At night I wake up sweaty, feeling like my whole body is falling from a ledge. The room sways, my heart races, a restlessness vibrates through my arms and legs. My breathing is a pant, rushed and shallow. I often stay awake for much of the night, letting the quiet of the house surround me, summoning me to calm down. Sometimes I rise and snuggle next to the wall in a corner of a room, tuck my knees next to my chest, and rock back and forth. I pray for Jesus to come and free me, to relieve me from the tremors and terror.

During a phone call with my new novice minister, Sister Karen, I say that I've been falling a lot and am having trouble sleeping. She suggests I ask Sisters Beth and Fran if they know of anyone who might be good for me to meet with. A psychologist who can treat PTSD maybe? Do I have PTSD? Maybe that's what's wrong with me? Maybe that's why I've turned into an insomniac and am clumsy, why I can't even trip a little without having flashbacks to my fall off the cliff.

Sister Fran knows someone. I call and leave a message and then one day, while I'm in the middle of my commute home from work, my cell phone rings. The voice on the other end sounds compassionate, gentle.

"What type of trauma did you suffer?" she asks.

"I fell off a cliff and broke my face—my nose, jaw and hand, actually. I was on my parents' farm in Iowa."

She asks more questions, as if she's assessing my symptoms, and then tells me she would like to meet. She explains how she specializes in treating trauma, using something called EMDR—eye movement desensitization and reprocessing—to reset the memories in the brain somehow. I'm curious, and feeling desperate. I'm sick of falling, of the insomnia, and feeling that I'm losing control.

The Friday morning in November of my first appointment I pray with a devotional written by Patricia Livingston centered around the Jesus teaching, "Whoever seeks to preserve his life will lose it, but whoever loses it will save it" (Luke 17:33). Livingston's reflection reads:

> I strain to find a connection with hope rather than fear. I find it in the idea that in order to save your life you must lose it. I can hold on to this because I have seen it happen again and again. Some kind of radical disruption comes to the life we are used to: illness, accidents, losses, endings. Part of us moves on, but part of us is left behind. But if we can move forward…what lies ahead is transformation. The scarred beauty of the life that is saved can have depth for joy missing in the life that was lost.

Transformation. Scarred beauty. Depth for joy. I hope there is a way that my survival of trauma might become a bizarre gift that I can offer to God. Could the tension in my body, the disfigurement, I'm carrying around and exposing to others every day actually become a way of blessing others?

* * *

After several months of therapy sessions, I begin to think of how these weekly meetings with a psychologist concerned about my mental health *and* vocation are a blessing. I find comfort sitting in the soft chair in her sunlit room, talking about my questions and nightmares, while her basset hound softly snores on the rug. She's a devout Catholic and gets where I'm coming from, as I sort through all my conflicting desires: Catholic Sisterhood seems right for me, but I'm still uncertain.

The therapist and I go through the story of my fall off the cliff many times and she repeats the EMDR therapy when she notices I am getting stuck, when she hears how the PTSD symptoms interrupt my days with terror. She's a good teacher and I'm glad that I understand more about what's going on with me and my moods. I now understand that my mental state is fragile and must be tended to along with my broken body.

I am starting to feel better, even while I accept that I'll need a therapist to help me heal and grow for years to come. Like God, the human mind is a glorious mystery and there is much beauty and potential mixed with what's hard. I'm learning how caring for our minds, trying to avoid mental breakdowns, is part of what it means to care for the broken body. Showing up for another session, week after week: doing this work is another way to show devotion.

36

"Why won't you commit to me, just so I can have the experience of having a boyfriend?" I asked Brandon once, when we were alone in my bedroom in Sacramento.

"Because I want to have sex, and I know you won't have sex unless you're married," he said.

Another time I asked, "Why can't I be your girlfriend?"

I heard, "Julia, I know if I let myself get close to you, I would fall for you. But you would choose God over me. I gotta protect myself from that."

I remember feeling hurt, even though I knew he was right.

I don't know why I've stayed in touch with him since leaving California, but maybe it's because he broadens my awareness and reminds me what I'm giving up. Like how a different height can reorient one's perspective, knowing Brandon forces me to name my beliefs and vantagepoint—to explain why I see the world as I do; it's a clarity that few other relationships offer me. He's unlike anyone else I know in my circles; he forces me to claim who I am.

* * *

Darkness is thick on the winter solstice and I'm back in a hermitage on the edge of the bluffs near Villa St. Joseph (where I lived with the infirm Sisters during recovery). Amid the frenzied pace of ministering at the high school, I felt a nudge from God to come here, to be alone and quiet during winter break. But now I am not sure why I'm here, looking out at the snow-covered valley.

As the days approached for this time of retreat, I began to dread coming. Lonely, anxious. This is my first private, non-directed retreat—only me, God, silence, and the blank pages in my journal. It should be a formula for joy and bliss, for union with my love, Jesus. But I feel far from bliss.

Praying in the chapel with the Sisters a few days ago it dawns on me that coming back to La Crosse and into St. Rose Convent feels like coming home. Praying in the adoration chapel, visiting with Sisters Anita and others—all of it offers me rich wells of belonging and acceptance that I know I can drink from for years to come. And then, while with my new local community Sisters—praying, laughing, and reflectively sharing our lives—it occurs to me that this group is like a Franciscan version of Casa Jane. We're committed, bonded, and supportive to one another, and centered on the same values. Much of what I lacked and longed for at the start of my time with the Sisters is now available to me.

Yet, questions linger. I'm not completely decided about vows, even as I move towards them, most of the time with some confidence and joy.

Why did God nudge me to take this retreat? Is it simply to quiet down? To discern the vows more deeply? To integrate?

Before coming out here, I spoke on the phone with Brandon. I was reminded how dating him during my time in California was rocky: our relationship was off-and-on, complicated by our conflicting morals and beliefs, and my attraction to Catholic Sisterhood. I was drawn to Brandon's playfulness, creativity, honesty, and tendency to challenge me. My Casa Jane housemates repeatedly said that he wasn't worth my time and energy, but I kept going back to him like an alcoholic to the drink. I remember how my feelings about Brandon flipped between giddiness and guilt that whole year. I still feel conflicted about getting involved with him, staying in touch with him. But there's no reason not to talk on the phone.

* * *

"How's your job going?" I say.

"Um, I got a new job. I'm working for a porn company now," Brandon replies.

"WHAT!?"

"I needed more money. There just isn't enough money in teaching for me to make my rent out here, Julia. It pays really good."

"I don't get it. How could you even do that? Something that hurts so many people?!"

"Well, I don't think it's hurting anyone. It's a good job. I like it."

I listen, trying to be curious and kind. But I am horrified and when we end the call, I feel nauseated. My face clenches, my shoulders shake in revulsion, my throat is tight with anger.

I feel so sick.

* * *

I journal some of my questions before going to sleep. Why were Brandon and I ever in a relationship at all? How can it be that he—a man that now sells porn, and me—*are friends*? Is the connection that remains between us anything at all? Brandon called it "mutual fascination" when I named the contradiction, and if that's all we have, it's OK to be sick.

I see now that I dated Brandon because he represented everything I needed to reject in order to enter wholeheartedly into religious life. As much as I wanted to join the convent, I was afraid. Seeing him as he is now, is horrifying, but also clarifying.

I feel gross. Simply knowing Brandon, being associated with him, I feel as if I've been forced to encounter what I most despise, that which I want to protest and resist. I can't hate the people who are involved with the sex industry, because I don't hate him. Instead, I'm on the edge of the evil; I feel it in me. The reality of what I'm near stares me down and makes me shudder. The slime of my selfishness also crawls on my skin. I'm appalled and disgusted with myself, repulsed by the ugliness that is part of me too. I feel slimy with shame, nauseous.

I can see now that although I have been in love with God and on a path of holiness for most of my life, I'm not exclusively a "good girl." I'm capable of making the wrong choices, "being bad." I can't be secure in who I am. I'm disturbed by the terror of the truth; now that I can see this ugly side of myself, I start to cringe, to shrink with sorrow and shame. How could I allow myself to get so close to ugliness? I'm afraid of myself, of what I'm capable of.

I'm unworthy of living my life as a Franciscan Sister. I'm too gross, too disgusting to be holy enough to make vows, to give my whole self to God's mission. I doubt I will ever be good enough.

37

Journal
January 28, 8:40 a.m.

GOD! I ask you to bless and help these parts of me:
- the part that wants to rebel, even against you! (Help me be obedient.)
- the part that wants to have sex, be desired, have union with another person. (Help me be celibate!)
- the part that wants and tends to cling, possess, consume, take and hold. (Help me be poor!)

Forgive my failures. Help me be ready for these vows and want them for the reasons that are healthy and glorify you.

Have mercy on me, Sweet Jesus, for my sins. Give me the graces I need to be honest and genuine and listen to you in my heart. Heal me, shape me, hold me, create me, deepen my love for you and my desires to follow your way. I want to learn and grow into a Sister who is present, caring, supportive and loves warmly, deeply, attentively—in community and in ministry.

Bless another day with my students and coworkers. Amen.

* * *

It's a quiet Saturday morning in February and I go to the mailbox. Among the junk mail I find an envelope addressed to "J. Walsh @

C.F.N." It's been forwarded from my old address in Joliet, with a Philadelphia return. What is this?

Last year I wrote Shane Claiborne and thanked him for writing *The Irresistible Revolution*. I forgot I did that; I don't think I expected him to actually write me back. My hands begin to shake, my heart pounds as I take in what I hold. As quick as I can, I sit down and open the envelope.

On the back side of a piece of scrap paper (what I'm guessing is a page proof for another book he is working on) there's a hand-written response:

> January Something 2009
> Sister Julia :) —
> Your letter warmed my heart. Thank you.
> Sorry for the delay, it seems I stay behind on letters, but love writing—after all, it's an important Christian past time.
> I admire your hope and discontentment—and certainly the Church needs both—it is a beautiful thing to hear in your words the fiery passion of Francis and Clare—and the humility to submit and seek the wisdom of elders. I'm also on an unfolding journey of spiritual direction and discernment as I seek our Lover Jesus. Our communities and "new monasticism" has its charm and fresh charism it also has its challenges and vulnerabilities—and I think stability and supporting celibate singles, formation…are all things we still are figuring out. So pray for us—I certainly will keep you in my prayers as you continue the work of Francis and Clare "repairing the ruins of the Church." :) You are a gift to the FSPA. Send my love to all the saints and sinners there. May we continue to become the Church we dream of.
> Your brother—Shane Claiborne

Tucked inside the envelope I find a prayer card—with the classic peace prayer of St. Francis printed on one side and an image of Francis on the other—a tiny little plastic baggie filled with about a teaspoon of sand, and a rectangle of white paper with words printed on it:

This dirt is from outside San Damiano in Assisi, where little brother Francis heard God whisper: "Repair my Church which is in ruins." And he started working. May the repairs continue in us.

I want to scream with joy, to run around and tell all the neighbors about my mail. But I sit still, reading the letter over and over, soaking in its message of encouragement along with the affirmation of what I've been praying about: I'm here, I'm a Franciscan Sister, not because the community or the Church is perfect, but because, somehow, it is home. In this home, I get to serve. I give of myself and try to help the suffering parts of Christ's body be healed, repaired. I hope I do; I hope I can.

38

I wake up aware that I have a giant task today: write a letter to our congregational leadership team requesting that I profess my first vows. If approved, I'll make those vows in July.

It's another quiet Saturday morning, and as I drink my morning coffee next to a burning candle, I journal about making those first vows, but also about feeling unsure about all that remains unresolved in my heart and mind. The shame of darkness I encountered surrounding Brandon's new line of work still haunts me. And I'm still not sure I want to relinquish the chances of being married, having children. I definitely don't feel holy or pure. I feel unworthy of being a woman of God, available for God's purposes. Is any offering we give to God good enough?

In the shower later, I think of how I'm still broken. I still have one more oral surgery to go through, so I'll have implants and it will look like I have lower teeth once again—it should be done by the end of April. I remain very clumsy, and practically *always* have bruises on my body or a swollen ankle from a trip down the stairs or off the curb of the street. Taking care of my mental health and recovering from trauma feels like another exhausting full-time job, but I'm glad for a good psychologist. I'm starting to become more observant of my thought patterns and feelings, and am learning how to cope and grow. Yet, I hate how much I regularly wake in the middle of the night with a racing and pounding heart, short of breath, my body shaking. Now that I'm more clued into how screwed up I am, I wonder if I will have to keep seeing a therapist for many more years—if not for the rest of my life. I suspect so.

In other words, I'm a mess. Weak. Tense. Unsure. Stressed out. Any snide remark from a student or another Sister can push me into a cave of self-doubt and anxiety. How can I possibly be an effective minister? I'm unsure how I will ever fully integrate the trauma I've experienced; I doubt I'll pull myself together. I'm unsure if I will be faithful and holy enough to be consecrated to God.

As I dry off and get dressed, I continue to think. Maybe I don't have to pull myself together. Maybe I don't have to be good enough. Maybe the point is to submit to God and allow God to work with my brokenness. Perhaps if I offer God my broken, weak, and incomplete self, then God will transform and heal me. God can make of me whatever God wills. I know for sure that I can only be whole, complete, as part of Christ's body. In this broken body, my shattered and weak self can be a gift I offer. With God's light and grace, every scar, crack, and fragment of who we each are can help manifest God's beautiful love. I brush my hair and my shoulders relax some, thinking about this.

Next to my desk, I see my bag from work: a stack of papers to grade, the teacher's textbook. I sit on my bed and think about teaching at St. Greg's. The beautiful and complicated teens I get to serve have no interest in someone fake or perfect; they need an authentic example. Since my fall, I've learned that everyone has brokenness story to tell. Each of us has vulnerabilities, weaknesses, pain; our imperfect bodies and minds carry the memories. And our hearts carry the longing for wholeness. In a culture and Church that loves "picture perfect" scenarios of devotion, perhaps the most radical and countercultural offering I can make is my flailing imperfect self. I know that's the best I can do. I'm discovering there's a freedom in accepting this, in trusting that God will figure out how to use me, cracked and all. Showing up to serve as a broken and imperfect disciple will be OK. I may have a mood swing, I may overreact. The smallest thing could cause me to feel tense. I may trip or fall. I certainly will wear my scars and slightly crooked face, my false teeth. But that's OK, it is who I am—who I'm becoming.

Wearing these imperfections might demand that I become a healthier member of my Franciscan community too. I will have to admit my weaknesses and shortcomings to others. I will have to ask for help. I will have to be honest and vulnerable. If I'm leaning on my

Sisters to help through the tough stuff of being imperfect and lacking, then I will probably come to experience the wholeness that is meant to be offered in the body of Christ. Broken people, uniting into one, serving one another, tending to our wounds, accepting and embracing our needs, only becoming whole through our devotion to our common body: this is the Church that I'm in love with now. This is where I want to devote my life. So I sit down and begin to write.

Formal letter submitted to the FSPA Leadership Team
March 19, 2009, St. Joseph's Day

Dear Sister Marlene and Leadership Team,

Greetings to you in Christ! It's been two years since I've written a formal letter to you requesting to move forward in the process of incorporation into FSPA. On this Holy Day, I write to you again, transformed by the experience of novitiate and with all new awareness. I write to you expressing my desires to make my first profession of the vows of poverty, consecrated celibacy, and obedience to God as a FSPA.

> Lord, fill my life with you alone.
> Empty myself of all that's my own.
> Lord, fill my life with you alone.
> Jesus, keep my eyes on you.
> Help me stand, help me stand for what's right.
> Help me walk, help me walk in the light.
> Help me run, help me run for the prize.
> Jesus, keep my eyes on you.

Those are the lyrics to a song from Bible camp, where my major faith formation began. Nearly every day during the past decade of my life I've prayed this song. When I was studying at the Common Franciscan Novitiate, I learned that the flavor of the prayer-song is very Franciscan and this helped me understand my identity as a Franciscan. I've learned that Franciscan life is about emptiness and following Jesus.

In following Jesus' example of emptiness, I desire poverty. Francis and Clare were empty and poor like Jesus was. They stripped themselves of ownership in order to be more available to God. I desire that same emptiness and life of discipleship. I want to stand with the poor, for the poor, as a poor child of God without clinging to any idea, property, person or vision. I want to live simply for the benefit of earth and global community. I want to rely only on God, as the founders of FSPA so bravely did.

I desire God as manifested in FSPA community. I have been blessed to be a part of the FSPA community for the past three years. I've been embraced, affirmed, encouraged, challenged, loved, cared for, received, celebrated, questioned, held, understood and heard by the community. Thanks be to God for the ways I've come to know God's love! Community is all about loving relationship. To choose life in our congregation over all the other options that are available for me—a young American woman of the twenty-first century—is about a whole other way of living loving relationship.

During my novitiate, I've had to sort through questions and struggles about my choice to remain unmarried. God has companioned me in these struggles and sent me great signs about what life is best for me. I recall a dream that God gave me when I was confused about my attraction to a friend of mine. I prayed for a dream that would give me clarity. I had a dream that I was helping with a Mass with the entire FSPA community in the Mary of the Angel's Chapel at St. Rose Convent. The Mass was transformed into a fantastic potluck meal with food on every altar around the tabernacle and flowing through the sacristies and onto the altars in the adoration chapel. Folks from the street and from Place of Grace Catholic Worker House joined us in enjoying the greatest banquet I had ever been a part of, and I was elated.

I desire Eucharistic Love. I desire consecrated celibacy. FSPA fulfills my desires and allows me to serve God and community while helping me to fully become the woman that God calls me to be.

I desire obedience. I desire to listen to and follow God, as an empty, poor, celibate, loving member of a Eucharistic community. Recently, I've been singing another Bible camp song, one about being a holy sanctuary for God. It feels like God is calling me to consecration.

The songs and the dreams of my heart reflect my desires and joys. I'm very blessed to have been a part of FSPA the past three years. I desire to make my vows and more fully become a member of the community. I have included my self-evaluation which elaborates on how I have prepared for this step. I'm grateful for your prayerful consideration and appreciate all your support and service to so many, including me. Be assured of my continued prayers for you.

Thank you!
Peace and Love,
Julia

* * *

It's the middle of the night, and I'm rolling around in bed, my heart pounding and mind racing once again. I sit up, trying to catch my breath and relax, but keep shaking. I'm wide awake now, so I turn on my lamp, pull on my glasses, and grab the novel *The Shack* by William P. Young from the lampstand. I read pages and pages in the silence of the night, hooked by the story. As I do, I gradually relax, while Sisters Beth and Fran continue to sleep in their bedrooms across the hall. The book is about a man who encountered God during an accident; a story that I can relate to. I read for hours through the night, tucked under the blankets in my bed, then I open my journal and begin to write about my fall off the cliff and the hospitalization afterwards.

I muse on the memory of Jesús visiting me in the ICU. I remember the glowing warm love I felt from him beside me in the quiet; his presence, how he said little but taught me how *to be* with someone when they suffer, how to offer my loving presence to others. I know I am very loved, yet the love I felt from Jesús remains the strongest, most powerful love I've ever felt. I felt wholeheartedly embraced. Accepted. Unconditionally loved. After being with him I felt stronger, healed: internally and externally transformed. How could he do all that? And why? Who was he? Why did he feel so familiar? I was so weak, so broken, yet this mysterious man sat with me and taught me how to love, taught me what love really is.

I think about how strange it was that the ICU nurse didn't know that she worked with someone name Jesús, when I brought them a thank you note. I feel my face frown, confused and sad for her, still wondering who Jesús is.

Wait, what!? Is Jesús actually Jesus Christ—not a male nurse? Of course. Yes! That's absolutely true! Wow, I was visited in the hospital by JESUS, the love of my life! My body is shaking now. I feel like I'm floating, illumined. Every part of my body is delighted. Tears flow. I sob into my pillow, feeling my body shake my bed. Tears and snot flow from my face, my voice groans out muffled wonder, joy. I try to quiet my vocal cords, to cry quietly so I don't wake Sisters Fran and Beth snug in their beds.

I cry and cry, snorting, shaking. My skin and my sheets: all are soaked with tears. It feels like every cell in my body is releasing relief that my mind finally caught up with what my heart and body knew all along. Jesus visited me! Jesus *himself* came to sit by me and taught me how to love. Jesus is with me! I think the phrase again and again—feeling shocked, feeling awe—making the mantra into a formula to believe the unbelievable.

I'm also amazed it took me so long to figure this out.

Much later, I'll start to put some pieces of my story together. Yes, Jesus visited me in the ICU, when I had tubes down my throat and couldn't speak. But we had a conversation. And I remember the conversation clearly. Maybe Jesus and I didn't physically talk, but the memory is imprinted on my heart at such a depth that it might be the only experience in my life that I'm completely certain about. It feels truer than anything else I have ever been through, than any other story I have told. Learning how to love from Jesus is the realest part of my life.

39

The broken body I have grown to love is bigger than my own. My bones crushed and shattered, the teeth extracted and replaced with permanent implants, the hand forever bearing the scar next to my knuckle, the artificial tissue in my now tiny nose clicking under the pressure of a finger; my smile now slightly crooked, the scar under my chin, where my face was split open for surgery. I now love all these broken parts of me. Or at least I have grown to accept them, embrace them, allow myself to carry around these wounds as reminders of what I've survived, been through, of the miracle of God's love that has reformed, reshaped, and reclaimed me.

This broken body I love is also Jesus. It is the connection I felt while on my retreat before entering the novitiate, tucked away on those bluffs near the Villa St. Joseph. It is the Jesus who visited me in the ICU and taught me how to love, how to be loving presence unto others, who said "This is who I am," so biblically.

It is the holy bread become Jesus reverently secured in the monstrance and placed on the high altar in our adoration chapel at St. Rose Convent—love, quiet and present. It is the bread at the center of my dreams, the overflowing and expanding potluck, inclusive and open to all who have need. It is the courage that I have gained to say yes to God with my life, through the approaching profession of vows.

The broken body I have grown to love is also every human who held me in my misery, who tended to my wounds, who held my hand during surgery or sickness. It is the people of God, close friends and distant strangers, my Franciscan Sisters and my family, those near, those thousands of miles away.

The broken body that I love and am eager to dedicate myself to—includes every person living. It is those who profess they are children of God, and it is those who never consider it, and those who have turned away from God. It is those who flaunt their wealth and oppress the poor *and* those who are living on the streets, under bridges, in the corners of cities. Those who are hungry, in jail, or barely getting by. It is the farmer who is going bankrupt. It is the woman who is fleeing her abusive husband. It is the teen afraid to tell their parents they are gay, that they are going to venture out on their own. It's the children in crumbling, poor schools and those living in villages without a proper well.

The broken body of Christ that I love is the people of God on the margins of society, who know they are broken and feel the pain of being broken as they struggle through every ordinary act. It is for them that I will imitate Christ. I will offer my body as a sacrifice too.

I will give up allowing anyone to love my broken body in the ways that are natural, normal. I will not get married; I will not have sex. I will renounce the pleasure and pain and mystery of knowing what it is to share my broken body with another human, to bond in the most intimate of ways, to celebrate the communion of the wedding bed; this renouncement will unleash the power of my love, allow my expansive love to be given to the greater good. I'm not worthy of this, but I believe that through my surrendering to God's grace, good can come.

* * *

Journal
June 28, Sunday, 7:55 a.m.

Oh my GOOD GOD, increase my love for you.
    Give me the graces I need to let go of men and all other "what if's" and live deeply, joyfully into what is Now: the reality I'm in.
    Yesterday was a hard day. I was a mess about it all—I

felt sadness and pain in my chest and stomach. I ached with longing. I was lost in my confusion. It's so hard to be friends with someone I'm in love with. I'm surprised that I've been thinking about Mike a lot lately. Is it just because I'm about to make vows?

You didn't design discipleship to be easy. You made me a passionate person on purpose. I want to be free. I want to freely love. Most of the time, I feel free, and do love with freedom. Thank you.

Thank you for the good sleep. I'm amazed at how you can shift things in me. I went to sleep so upset about the confusion regarding the future and men. I was praying an important mantra: "Jesus, help me love you more than Mike and other men, more than anything."

I still pray this, aware that if I do love you most, it'll give me the graces to joyfully follow you anywhere, to whatever. And love is a grace, a gift. It's the most important one. I desire to live more fully in love with you. And I'm glad God, so blessed, that I awoke with a little clarity: I know what I need to do today, and all the tasks are about preparing for vows. I'm excited!

Bless me, Good God, with what I need to know your way and then follow it. I do want to make these vows and consecrate all I am for you. I'm your child, your daughter, lover, and friend. It's beautiful to commit to love, freedom, emptiness, and following you.

40

After hearing that I was officially approved to profess my first vows, and filled with an electric joy, I'm now excited to plan a Mass that will include my favorite readings and music, symbols and colors. Based on the dream about the overflowing potluck in our adoration chapel, I'm framing all my choices around the theme, "Come to the Table!" That's what I want the celebration to be about: an open table of love.

The liturgist at St. Rose Convent and I are working together on the design for the ceremony's worship aid, but she says it's my job to design the cover.

I pray about who—besides Jesus—I'm going to commit myself to through the vows of consecrated poverty, obedience, and celibacy. I find photos of people I love sitting around tables and make a photo-collage: my Casa Jane housemates; the wild and laughing Walsh family: Mom, Dad, Hans, Ellen, and Colleen; the Sisters at Chiara House from last Christmas—Anita, Mary Louise, Linda, Eileen, Kristin, and Amy. I include a picture of Sisters holding protest signs after the immigration raid in Postville, Iowa; a picture of Sisters in the dining room at St. Rose Convent; a cheery photo of my friends Dana, Hillary, and Angela taken before my jaw was broken; a picture of students at St. Greg's High School; and another showing some of the children I met as a college student in South Africa. I realize something is missing and add a photo taken from the edge of a cliff, the branches of a bare tree outlined by a bright sky, a stream of water below. I study the image and feel pleased: along with God, many people and places have prepared for this moment of consecration.

I think about Masses I've attended where a priest invited children to stand in a circle around the altar as he prayed over bread and wine. I search online and find an image of adults and children holding hands around an altar while the priest uplifts his hands in prayer. A loaf of bread (that looks like my tattoo), and a chalice are on the table, a cross hangs above. God's tables are wide and plenty—many places and people offer God's love. I print the clipart in the middle of the collage, hoping everyone who comes to pray at my vow Mass feels included and welcome.

* * *

I'm in Hiawatha, Iowa now, praying in a straw-bale hermitage at Prairiewoods, a spirituality center sponsored by my community. I'm here for five days to prepare to profess my vows. My days are filled with walks and runs on the trails through woods and prairie, attending daily Mass at the local parish, and meeting with a spiritual director.

I lay on a blanket under the summer sun to read what Sister Karen assigned me for this retreat: several sections about commitment and celibacy in a book called *Selling All: Commitment, Consecrated Celibacy, and Community in Catholic Religious Life*, by Sandra Schneiders.

Later that day, I write another letter to God:

> *Journal*
> *July 13, Monday, 8:20 p.m.*
>
> In the mix of many blessings today, God, I've been wondering what it means to get ready for first vows. What do I need to do to prepare? What do I need to pray about? Deal with? Face? How do I get ready?
>
> And now, an answer, thank you God. A big answer: I must completely close the possibility for marriage.
>
> I realize now, I haven't fully said no to marriage and chosen celibacy. I've asked to make these vows because I want to

remain with FSPA. I want to keep going and move forward and I want to be a full member. But I've been aching for sex lately and feeling annoyed and upset and frustrated that I'll never get to know that pleasure. I'm mad at you sometimes, God, because I don't get to have sex.

I thought earlier today: is there going to be a point during this retreat that I'll weep with grief because I won't get married?

Last night, when I was reminded that the first vows are only for three years, I felt relieved and grateful.

About a month ago, I admitted to Sister Linda that I still think about Mike. She asked me to play with the scenario of Mike suddenly proposing to me. She challenged me to consider if I would be able to say "no" to him and "yes" to FSPA. Honestly, I'm not sure. I'd like to think so. But I know I love him and would be very happy with him. It would be hard, but this is hard too.

I think it's going to be a struggle to always be clear to myself and others that I'm not even interested in the possibility of marriage and sex. Certainly, I must still be loving, completely and radically, not limited to one person or way—just eliminating physical and married ways. I love. I always will.

Can I be free from the temptations to flirt, possess, engage, and unite with others? Probably not. But I could become disinterested. And I need a sense of humor, so that if any person whom I'm in love with and would like to marry ever does propose I can simply smile and lovingly say, "No, thank you."

So, Good God, help me to live into this and embrace the challenges. I want to fully close the options of marriage and sex out of my life. I know I can only do this with your help, by your power of grace and love. You have given me great strength to overcome temptations, struggles, pain, and suffering. You've blessed me abundantly and I trust you and your faithfulness. I trust in your ways and consistency.

Jesus, unite me to your love and help me to grow more

fully in it so that I can get grounded deeply in my commitment to you. I want to love you more and more. More than anything and anyone else. More than any other way or path or option. I love you, Jesus. So help me say NO to all other dreams.

Thank you. Amen.

My spiritual director invites me, then, to ritualize my renouncement of men, sex, romance, and marriage—so that I can fully embrace a commitment to celibacy. Thinking about her challenge, I realize that my body wants to throw something, to let something go, to leave something behind in a place where it will no longer be accessible to me.

So, one afternoon, during a prayerful walk I find a rock that fits in the palm of my hand. It's round and flat and multicolored, an ordinary piece of dusty granite. I take it back to the hermitage and sit with it, praying and thinking about all the people and things that the rock needs to represent. It still feels tough to let go of Mike, I realize, so I pick up my journal again and pour out my affection for him in a goodbye letter that I never actually intend to send.

Journal
July 14, 5:30ish

May this be the last message I write in my journal for Mike.
Dear Friend,

As you go swimming on your way, may God bless you. No matter what you decide, no matter what you do, may the ocean of love, found only in Christ, whirl around you.

When the currents and tides pull you away to shores you'd rather not go, may you have the strength to be free and submit to the powers beyond you.

May the beauty of God's glory and goodness always ripple out from you.

May waves and splashes of grace and mercy mesmerize you.

May you have no fear to swim to the great depths of his glorious love where light is still found glowing in the mysterious creatures.

And when you rise to gasp for breath and feel lured and tempted by the glamor of sin, may you have the strength to turn away and rush towards the love that accepts you always, cling to that shore, and unite yourself with that Holy water as you drink in what's been poured out for you.

May you be blessed by the Ocean of Love named God no matter where you go, no matter what you decide to do. Amen.

Goodbye. Goodbye. Goodbye. Amen.

With my paints and markers, I decorate the rock. I write the initials of men I love, have loved, each in different ways: Greg, Brandon, Mike. I use colors to represent sex and marriage, dating and romance, the chase, the obsessions and infatuations. I color hearts and squiggle lines, representing the passion I will never express physically, the normal and intimate communion with a lover that I must renounce. I layer colors and lines upon the stone. I study the rock in my palm: a symbol of my complex desires. I feel the rock heavy in my hand, pressing into my skin, as I consider what it means to let go and say goodbye to the chances to know that sort of love. My throat tightens, my mouth droops, my stomach aches, a swirl of sorrow moves through my body. I feel so conflicted about renouncing the goodness of men, marriage, and sex.

It's getting closer to sunset. I need to do this, ready or not. Will I ever feel completely ready? Do I have to force myself to let go of the longings and potential? I grip the stone and move into the muggy air, looping through the trails, between tall prairie grass, under oaks through an apple orchard. The stone is tight in my hand as bugs buzz in my ear, as a branch scratches my face and I walk under a tree. I walk and walk, searching for a place where I can drop the stone and never find it again.

Stepping over tree roots, I think about others who can't get married. I think of one of my aunts who has been single most of her life. I think of my friends who love being Catholic—and are faithful to the Gospel, but are gay, so they can't get married in the Church. I think of the women I know who have escaped abusive relationships and are moving toward healing, but doubt they'll ever take the risk of getting married again. For them—in solidarity with all who want to be married but can't be for whatever reasons—I renounce marriage and sex. I say "no, thank you."

Faces full of longing flip through my mind. I see people I've met in shelters, on the streets, the lonely and sick in nursing homes, hospitals. I see a divorced woman crying, full of anguish, and asking why she is not able to get remarried—why she is not supposed to receive communion in the Church anymore if she does so. I see the faces of my students, especially those who are immigrants and refugees, longing for hope, acceptance, and belonging. For them—in solidarity with all who have longings that may never be met for whatever reasons—I renounce marriage and sex. I say "no, thank you."

I feel my throat clench as I think of women who have been beaten, sexually assaulted, raped. Women who try to raise their voices and demand equal rights, but are called horrid names, talked down to, manipulated, silenced. I think of homeless youth I know who were gang raped. I remember my students who have cried in my classroom, telling me how their boyfriends, dads, grandfathers, and uncles have hurt them; I despise how reporting abuse is an ordinary part of a teacher's role. I worry about the women—and men too—who are being damaged and destroyed by the sex industry and human trafficking. I think about my allegiance to the Catholic Church and how the body of Christ I love so intensely has caused harm. Priests have abused nuns, young girls, boys.

Practically every woman I know has a story of a man taking advantage of her, hurting her. Could my vow of celibacy be a form of resistance, a type of feminist act? Yes, of course, sexual energy is good and sacred, able to produce union and love, to heal—but it is also often dangerous, destructive, and harmful. For them—in solidarity with all who have been hurt by sexual violence—I renounce marriage and sex. I say "no, thank you."

My walk brings me to a cliff above a creek, similar to the one I fell from two years ago. My heart rate increases and my body tenses as I stare into the muddy water, listening to its gurgle. It's hard to tell how deep the water is. If I throw this rock in there, I doubt anyone will ever see it again. I doubt I'll ever find it.

I pause, breathing deeply, slowly. I pray for courage and strength. I study the rock in my hands, thinking about dating, marriage, sex: I must renounce it all. I must let go of the past and the potential so that I can totally give my whole self to Jesus. Only through a wholehearted "no" can I say "yes." I look at the muddy water and talk to God, but I'm struggling to throw the rock. I don't know if I have the strength.

The light changes, the bugs continue to buzz in my ear, and after an hour or so, I decide I need to simply let go. So, I grip the rock in my fist, lift my arm over my head, and throw the piece of granite into the water. It plunks toward the bottom, and the surface of the brown water ripples. I slowly walk back to the hermitage, my empty hand held open. I am surprised to notice that my heart feels lighter, my hope is stronger. I feel free.

41

Two years and two months after becoming Sister Julia, I'm standing in the threshold of the Mary of the Angels chapel inside of St. Rose Convent in La Crosse once again. Wearing a burgundy bridesmaid dress from Hillary's wedding earlier in the summer, I feel a little naked without the Tau cross necklace I've been wearing since becoming a novice.

My clumsiness hasn't stopped: I tripped and bumped into furniture often as this day approached. While getting dressed, Sister Linda and I tried to cover bruises on my legs with makeup, and when it didn't work very well, I felt amused, aware that even at this big moment I cannot hide my brokenness.

A lard light burning in my hands, my gaze moves across the chapel toward the white marble front altar. Pews are packed with Sisters, plus twenty-five guests I was allowed to invite. From the backs of their heads and shoulders, I recognize people I love, friends and family who have traveled great distances to gather around this table and be with me: Andy and his wife; Hillary and her husband and stepson; other close friends, Dana and Laura; all my Casa Jane housemates in green dresses: Peg, Trishy, Ebeth, Tines, and Mayr. I think I see my aunts who flew in from the East Coast sitting next to Mom and Dad and Hans and Colleen up front. Ellen and her new fiancé, Daniel, are with the other musicians, about to start singing. I feel a tinge of sadness, feeling the absence of Mike and Tim; Mike wasn't able to get off work and Tim couldn't get out of formation stuff with his own community.

I'm smiling widely, revealing the full set of teeth that I have had since mid-April. My thick-framed glasses hide the scars around my eyebrows and nose. My face has a new shape, a different look, than it did when I became a novice, but so does my life, my heart. I'm broken and scarred, and eager to give all my weaknesses to God—to allow God to complete me and change me.

Once the opening song, "Sing a New Church," starts to ring through the sanctuary I follow Sister Sarah and the cross she carries down the center aisle. People turn and look, their smiling faces and little waves offering me courage. Only because my community, my friends and family, lovingly accept me, mess and all, am I able to do this: I feel strength to move toward the table of God and dedicate my life to Jesus.

I carefully place the burning lard light on the little stand next to the ambo, where Sisters Dorothy and Cecy will proclaim the scriptures I selected for this Mass. The cantor, Sister Beth, will sing Psalm 40, the one that the hospital chaplain and I prayed together before my jaw surgery. After I set down the burning light, I bow in front of the altar and enter the pew next to Sister Karen. The community leadership team sits behind us.

Opening prayers and rites and the proclamation of the Word of God—all of it affirms that I have made the right choice, that this dedication is the best expression for my love of God and God's people. When the priest I've invited to preside—Father Paul, a family friend from Iowa—proclaims the Gospel (John 21:1-18) I want to stand up and respond to each of Jesus' questions out loud. Jesus asks Peter three times, "Do you love me?" *Yes, Jesus I do love you! And, I will happily do ask what you've asked Peter too: I will feed your lambs, your sheep, I will follow you!* But I resist that temptation. That'd be too over-the-top, even for me.

After proclaiming the Gospel, Father Paul makes a few remarks about the readings. Most of all, he says that I have arrived to this point because I have listened, I have heeded God's voice. Then he sits down, knowing that I've prepared a reflection that I want to share. Vibrating with joy and feeling everyone watching me, I leave my pew to stand behind the ambo and begin to read.

"You've come from far and near to celebrate and pray with me.

You've come and I'm very grateful. You've come to this moment in my life—to a table of God similar to the ancient places where believers committed themselves to the fire. Here at this table, like the table that the Prophet Isaiah preached about, you need not pay anything or do anything. Just be, God says, and I'll give.

"God has given me a lot. I'm so blessed and have much to shout praise about. I want to declare it before the assembly, like the psalm suggests. I'm here to do God's will, to make my vows and say yes again and again to that Great Love that I've known only in Jesus. It's been a journey to arrive at this vantage point, when I get to announce from this mountaintop that Jesus is indeed my All in All and he has done great things.

"Like in these scriptures, community carries the called. I'm abundantly blessed by the companionship and friendship from each of you. You all serve different roles in my life. Some of you have held my hand and helped me walk. Many of you have prayed with me and prayed for me. Some of you have cried with me. A lot of you laughed with me. Some of you have wondered with me. Others of you have been outright silly with me."

A few people in the pews, at this point, are chuckling, remembering. I go on.

"We're a bread breaking community with Jesus at the center. He calls to us 'Come, have breakfast!' There's no need to worry because we've been taught how to take care of each other. He showed us the way to be inclusive, open and inviting all to freely join us at the table. We share all, because all are one. Justice comes from understanding this. This table is so rich with praise and devotion. It is our joy to make more and more space so that every day folks can join us in our peaceful adoration. This table feels like a picnic to me, from this great view, where I'm about to yell out my vows and let them echo through the valleys. I'm so happy we're here together."

Then I pause, feeling my face flooding with emotion, seeing the next words on the page.

"Many of you remember that I took a leap of faith...."

People laugh.

"And then another time, I fell."

They laugh again.

"I fell into an awful pit. In the hospital, a chaplain spontaneously read to me today's psalm, Psalm 40, and we cried together in awe of how God had indeed drawn me out of the mud, set my feet upon rock, steadied my steps, and put hymns in my mouth. I sang and sang in the ER and overheard one nurse say to another, 'What pain medicines is she on?'"

The people laugh even louder.

"'None yet,' the other nurse replied. 'She's a nun.'"

Again, there's loud laughter. I'm smiling now, as I continue to speak.

"On this long journey of great surprises many have recognized my vocation even when I've tried to avoid it. Like in the psalm, though I'm afflicted and poor, Jesus keeps me in mind. He's my help and deliverer, never delaying to be present and walk with me. Creation knows, there's much to rejoice about."

I talk with my hands and nod as I declare the truth.

"So, although there's been great pain and some simple scrapes and bug bites, I've been healed by Jesus. When I've been thirsty, I've been given great drinks. When I've been hungry, the Bread of Life has been given to me.

"And the beauty and love has been abundant. The tiniest birds have modeled obedience to God for me, and the freedom that's found there. The trees and rocks have witnessed the strength in a life of poverty. And that glorious sun has burned me with the passion and fire of celibate Eucharistic Love.

"The path has been windy and steep. It's been rocky in places, and in other places it's been very smooth. There have been ups and downs. Sometimes I went in circles. When I've been exhausted, I've been permitted to rest. And when I've had a burst of energy it's been okay for me to freely run and dance on the holy ground.

"And we're finally here. Somehow you all met me here too. I get to shout out my love for God through the canyons and over the rivers. I get to declare my vows and then unite again and again with Jesus, whom I love.

"And, praise God, I get to have a banquet with everyone, including all of you. Come to the table, because dear friends, when Jesus asks us to love him, he then says, 'Feed my sheep.'

"So, let us be fed by the great yes to his love."

My face turns serious as I return to my pew, as the chapel fills with a sacred silence. It is almost time. Sister Karen takes her spot at the ambo.

"I call forth Sister Julia Walsh," she says.

Holding the wireless microphone and worship aid, I stand and respond from my pew. "You have called me, here I am," I say. As I listen to Sister Karen speak, it's hard for me to be still.

"Julia, you have discerned God's call in your life this far. Are you ready to deepen your commitment to live in loving presence and in service to others as a Franciscan Sister of Perpetual Adoration?"

"I am."

"Those of us who have journeyed with Julia, how shall we respond to her request to profess the vows of poverty, consecrated celibacy, and obedience as members of our community?" Sister Karen reads from the script.

All of my Sisters in the chapel then read their response in unison: "We affirm Sister Julia in her response to God's love and we will continue to companion her on our shared journey as Franciscans rooted in Eucharist and in communion with all God's creation."

The FSPA leadership team along with Sisters Cecy, Beth, Karen and I then move to the front of the altar. Sister Marlene, the community president, speaks.

"Sister Julia, by your baptism you have already been consecrated to God's service; are you now resolved to unite yourself more closely to God by the bonds of religious profession?" she asks.

"I am."

"Are you resolved to living your life following in the footprints of Jesus Christ, as did Francis and Clare, and living out your response to God's call to community as a Franciscan Sister of Perpetual Adoration?" Sister Marlene asks.

"I am."

Sister Marlene hands the wireless microphone to Sister Paulynn, the FSPA vice president.

"In vowing poverty, are you resolved to acknowledge and embrace your limitations and radical dependence upon God, recognizing that all of life's goodness is of God?" she asks me.

"I am." My face is solemn as I listen to each question and think about what it means.

"In vowing consecrated celibacy, are you resolved to live in covenant relationship with God and in right relationship with all of creation?" Sister Paulynn asks.

"I am."

"In vowing obedience, are you resolved to be attentive and responsive to the movement of the Spirit as revealed in the Gospel, prayer, daily events and persons around you?" Sister Paulynn asks.

"I am."

"May the One who has led you to our community continue to guide you in the footprints of Jesus as your faith journey unfolds," Sister Paulynn says.

A smile crosses my face as I look out at everyone watching from the pews. Together, everyone in the chapel says, "Amen."

Sister Marlene speaks again. I exhale while I listen. "Sister Julia, I now invite you to declare your intentions before God," she says, handing me the microphone. I smile and take a deep breath and then am surprised to hear emotion in my voice, to feel like I'm on the verge of crying, as I begin to speak.

"I, Sister Julia Walsh, vow to God Almighty, and into your hands, Sister Marlene, to live poverty, consecrated celibacy, and obedience in community for three years according to the Rule of the Third Order of St. Francis and the Constitutions of the Franciscan Sisters of Perpetual Adoration. I ask the help of God, the Blessed Virgin Mary, Saint Francis and Saint Clare, and you my Sisters. Amen."

I feel like I'm floating and filling with light, but I stand still. I'm stunned. My mouth hangs open a little as I hand the microphone back to Sister Marlene. I look at her face as she speaks to me.

"In the name of all the Franciscan Sisters of Perpetual Adoration, I joyfully accept your vows. Be assured, Sister Julia, of the love, respect, and gratitude of your Sisters as you share your life as a Franciscan Sister of Perpetual Adoration."

I whisper thanks to her, a smile big on my broken face. I turn and look around the chapel, seeing my Franciscan community, family, and friends. Everyone claps wildly. This love is amazing.

But it isn't over yet. Sister Marlene invites everyone to help bless the FSPA medal that I will wear from this day forward. Sister Cecy holds it up and we read the words from the worship aid together.

"Most gracious God, source of all good, we ask your blessing on this medal of the Blessed Sacrament. Grant that your servant, Julia, who wears it, may always strive to be transformed into the likeness of Christ, who lives and reigns with you now and forever. Amen."

I bow. Sister Cecy puts the silver necklace around my neck. It looks like a monstrance in front of my heart.

Sister Marlene speaks again: "Sister Julia, in the name of the Franciscan Sisters of Perpetual Adoration, I present you with this medal. Wear it as a symbol of our identity."

I smile, feeling the weight of the medal on my body. I listen and look at the faces of my community, these women I love deeply, and listen to them read the next words with enthusiasm in their voices: "Sister Julia, we join you in praising God. We celebrate with you the beginning of your religious profession. We deeply appreciate you and the gifts, talents and presence you share with us and all God's people. May God bless you."

As I go to the altar with a few Sisters to sign the official documents, marking this moment in history and establishing that I'm now a professed member of the Franciscan Sisters of Perpetual Adoration, I feel different, and I feel aware that God's timing is perfect, offering us exactly what we need.

42

When I made my final vows six years later, I was finally beginning to relax and rest into the life of being a Sister. I didn't have to agonize and discern about my choices anymore. I finally could enjoy and appreciate the goodness of vowed religious life. And I did.

At FSPA gatherings, I often feel so passionately in love with the life we live together that I'm emotional and enlivened—even if we're talking about ordinary community business, like finances and household matters. My relationships with my Sisters and the life we share sustains and defines me. Like any other loving commitment, the love we share is layered and textured, but the layers are deep. With my community I feel at home in myself and the Church. I feel like a wild tree growing from the depths of rich soil, reaching out and offering shelter to others.

Mike and I gradually drifted apart after my first vows, as my ministry teaching high school became more intense and my schedule became full, and as relationships with my Sisters deepened. It had been six years since we'd last spoken when I reached out to him again while writing this story. During that gap, he got married and I took final vows. He never attended any of my vow ceremonies. I wonder if I let him go after professing first vows because our bond reached a point where I knew it was unhealthy and unstable for us to be in contact. It could have turned into an emotional affair: my body remaining celibate but my heart and mind becoming too involved, attached, possessive. In many ways, I wanted him to be all mine and he couldn't, wouldn't.

It remains easy for me to feel attracted to good men, to become enamored by their beauty and glow. I won't ever stop loving men and having crushes, I am sure, because it is my nature to feel drawn to them like a moth to the light.

But living as a healthy celibate means that, over and over, I must track my desires and be honest. I must admit my struggles to other Sisters and to my therapist and spiritual director. I don't have secrets. I pray and aim to remain centered in the love of Jesus that I've encountered over the years, such as during my accident. The love of God is my home. This is the love that I'm *most* deeply dedicated to, so I thank God for the beauty of every man I develop feelings for—and then I let them go.

I have never felt a strong push or pull to leave FSPA because of my love for a man. My love for men remains a sacrifice I get to offer to God, a transformative heartache, allowing me to say yes again and again to the price I pay for giving my whole self—body, mind, and soul—to the God I love.

I continue to give my life to God as a consecrated celibate, as a Franciscan Sister, because I deeply love the broken body of Christ, the Church—as complicated and messy as commitment and love can be. It is for the people of God that I give all that I am; that I wildly, clumsily expose my brokenness to the world, often through creative offerings like writing and speaking. Christ compels me, again and again, to show my love to all of you through my raw authenticity. As freedom was opened through Christ's body, weak and broken on the holy cross, I hope that the mystery of communal bonds permits each of us to become a bit more whole. As we lean in and hold one another, we become bread for one another, giving our wounds and receiving tenderly what is blessed, broken, and shared. For all of you, members of the broken body, I give my life.

ACKNOWLEDGMENTS

The litany of gratitude begins first with God, of course, for saving my life and teaching me how my brokenness made me beautiful. Your nature of abundance, love, light, mercy, and relationship has been both teacher and healing balm. Thank you from every cell of your making.

There's no way I can express adequate appreciation to each person who God has worked through as an instrument, influencing my life and the turns it took. For everyone who had a part in my healthcare and healing journey, for every teacher along the way, for my earliest and most devoted readers, for those who held up mirrors to help me see the truth—blessed be every spiritual director and therapist who has accompanied me—you know who you are. Know, too, how thankful I am for your yes.

Thanks to my dear friends who have remained faithful and constant, no matter the distance or circumstances that could have created gaps between us: Laura, Hillary, Dana, Andy, Greg, Luke, Eric, Ted, Liz, Adam, Angela, Jessi, and all of Casa Jane: I count you each as my soul-friends forever.

To my community of "perfect joy," my family of call and choice: the Franciscan Sisters of Perpetual Adoration: thank you for encouraging me to write and then supporting each discovery of self and truth throughout the years; for allowing the practice of creative writing to form me. Thanks especially to Sisters Dorothy, Joan, Deb, Marcia, Beth, Fran, Carolyn, Roselyn, Charlene, Marlene, Paulynn, Kathy, Eileen, Sue, Dawn, Lucy, Julie, Georgia, Cecy, Corrina, Katie, Laura, Kristin, Amy, Laurie, Meg, Marla, Karen, Helen, and Michele. To Sisters Rita Rathburn and Anita Beskar—may you experience bliss eternal while you commune with The Word along with all other angels and saints. Sisters Linda and Sarah, I'd be nowhere without your input as I discovered what God wanted to do with my yes. Sister Maria, thank you for proofreading! And many thanks to each member of the expansive, borderless Sisterhood I have come to know through Giving Voice—for your constant unconditional love and holy commotion-causing as we work together to "afflict the comfortable and comfort the afflicted," 'til kingdom come. Over that Chicago pizza dinner in 2016 a handful of you forced me through fear and gave the nudge I needed to write this story: thank you!

Many thanks to the creative camaraderie I've known with the Sick Pilgrims, Muse Collective, Speaking of Writers, and to the Marywood Writers Group. Thanks to my colleagues and sisterly living communities and The Fireplace Community (especially Sister Sharon, Leslie, Cassidy, Abby, and Angela) for allowing me the space and time I needed. Thanks to every member of the Messy Jesus Business team, past and present, especially Jane, Jen, Charish, and Colin. Piles of gratitude to the community of creative folk in The Glen Workshop/*Image Journal* community. Amy Newman, you taught me to trust my poetic intuition. Kaya Oakes, you planted me firmly in the heartbeat of creative non-fiction. For the folks with me in the Spiritual Writing 2016 workshop who were the first to see part of the earliest draft of this book, thank you for saying you wanted to read more.

It is a marvel how many people God sent to cheer me onward as I spiraled through doubts about writing and sharing this story. Many thanks to Callie Bates, Rhonda Miska, Jessica Mesman, Hannah Bowman, Dorothy Fortenberry, Jennifer Grant, Gary Jansen, Liam Callanan, and especially patient and persistent editor extraordinaire Jon M. Sweeney (also an ideal companion for celebrating Christmas with Trappists!). Sabreena Croteau, thank you for helping me paint my portrait. A thousand thanks to Paul Cohen, Jon, and the entire Monkfish team for believing in this book and making it available to the world.

Lastly, thank you to my family: Mom and Dad, Hans, Ellen, Daniel, Xavier, Geneva, Colleen, and Peter and the expanding Walsh and Hanson clans—I would be nothing without your love; I am proud to belong to you.

PERMISSIONS

Living Faith, (Vol. 24, No. 3), Copyright © 2008 by Creative Communications for the Parish. Used with permission. The excerpt is from November 14, 2008, written by Patricia Livingston. Paul Frantsen, "Lord Fill My Life," *Cross The Sky Music* ©1998. https://www.crossthesky.com. Used by permission. "Bakerwoman God," poem by Alla René Bozarth. Used by permission. And thank you to my friend, Shane Claiborne, for permission to quote from a personal letter.

GLOSSARY

Adoration: More accurately known as Perpetual Adoration or Adoration of the Blessed Sacrament, this is a prayer form in front of Christ physically present in the Eucharistic host, either in a Tabernacle or during what's called Exposition on an altar.

Affiliate: In the Franciscan Sisters of Perpetual Adoration (FSPA) congregation, an Affiliate can be a single or married person who promises to share the community's *charism* with others through acts of prayer, ministry, and community.

Anointing of the Sick: Also known as Last Rites or Extreme Unction this ritual offers particular graces to a seriously ill person. With prayers and anointing with holy oil, the priest offers Christ's comfort and loving presence. It is one of the seven *sacraments* of the Roman Catholic Church and a Catholic can receive it any time they are sick or suffering.

Apostolic: The word means "sent forth" or "dispatched," as original apostles who followed Jesus were sent to serve. In the FSPA community, one year of the novitiate experience is Apostolic because it is the year the Sister is "sent forth" to serve. Similarly, several congregations of Catholic vowed religious are considered Apostolic because they are service-oriented.

Associate: In the *Franciscan Sisters of Perpetual Adoration (FSPA)* congregation an Associate is a pre-novice, or what was traditionally known as an Aspirant or Postulant. She is a woman who has been admitted into the early stages of Incorporation, is learning the *charism* of the community, and lives with the Sisters while remaining financially independent. In 2021, women in the stage of formation began to be called Candidates.

Blessed Sacrament: The belief that Christ is made physically present in bread and wine, *Eucharist* is one of the seven sacraments in the Roman Catholic Church. Once consecrated, the bread and wine are no longer called bread and wine but the Blessed Sacrament.

Body of Christ: A phrase with multiple meanings, all of which are closely interrelated. It refers to the *Eucharist*, the *Blessed Sacrament*. It also refers to the people of God, the faithful believers and members of the Roman Catholic Church. Plus, it refers to Jesus' presence still known and felt after his Ascension.

Catholic: Most simply, the word means "universal." It often refers to the Roman Catholic Church, a religion of which there are over a billion members worldwide under the leadership of the Pope in Vatican City, Italy.

Catholic Worker: Founded by Dorothy Day and Peter Maurin in New York City during the Great Depression, this movement of faith-based activists (with roots in the International Workers of the World, an early labor union) are centered on practicing radical hospitality, voluntary poverty, and practicing the works of mercy.

Canonical Novice: According to Church Law (also known as Canon Law) during this stage of entrance into religious life, the new Sister or Brother must be especially disciplined in their prayer and community. Restrictions from work and time away from community provide the freedom needed to discern and prepare for the profession of vows and deepen their contemplative life.

Capuchins: The Orders of Friars Minor (Franciscan men) that St. Francis of Assisi established in the 1200s went through a few divisions because of various reforms. The Capuchin reform dates from 1525 rooted in Marches, Italy where the Friars were isolated from the others and developed a more practical and mystical form of life.

Celibacy: Although every Christian is called to chastity (meaning only engaging in sexual expression appropriate with their form of life), certain people are called to be committed to the prophetic vow of celibacy, meaning without genital expression. This vow is prophetic because it points to the things of heaven—we can't fully make sense of it in this world, sort of how the prophets of the Old Testament did dramatic things to make a point. Jesus foretold that some of us would be needed to do this when he said that some have "renounced marriage for the sake of the kingdom of heaven" (Matthew 19:12). A healthy celibate sublimates sexual energy into a life of service, prayer, and community.

Charism: Particular spiritual gifts of a religious community often manifested through a unique manner of living the Gospel.

Christ: The universal, power, and presence of God's nature, revealed and hidden in all of creation. Also, more commonly, a title for Jesus the Nazarene because it is Greek for "Messiah" (or "Anointed One"), but transcendent of time and place.

Church: Again, this is a word with multiple meanings. It means the People of God, the Body of Christ, an institution, and a place of worship. It embodies the mission given to the people of God by Jesus Christ: to share the Gospel (good news) that God's love is for all, through its acts of service, prayer, community, and accompaniment.

Clare of Assisi: Raised as a member of a noble family in Assisi, Italy in the early thirteenth century, at eighteen, Chiara heard *Francis of Assisi* preach and was inspired to leave her wealthy family to join the early community of friars. He first placed her with Benedictine nuns and then helped her establish the *Order* of Poor Ladies, or Poor Clares, in San Damiano near Assisi. Known for her devotion to poverty, prayer, and her community of sisters, she became well-known for healing ministry and leadership of other women.

Cloister: The section inside a monastery that is isolated and separate from the public, where Sisters and Brothers live their quiet, contemplative life together.

Communion: Most loosely, this word means connection or oneness. Sacramentally (in the ritual of the Roman Catholic Church), it is usually prefaced by Holy as in Holy Communion, and is the reception of the *Eucharist*. The ingestion of the Body and Blood of Christ allows the faithful to become one with God and each other.

Confession: Another word used for the sacrament wherein a believer confesses sins to God and receives God's mercy through the ministry of the priesthood.

Consecrated Life: See also *Religious Life*. A vowed woman or man religious has dedicated their entire self—body, mind and spirit—to God and God's purposes. Something that is consecrated is set apart for God's holy purposes, so altars and churches are consecrated too.

Convent: Any place where men or women religious reside that has a chapel with a tabernacle containing the *Blessed Sacrament*.

Discernment: Related to judgment, a discerning person is able to distinguish between the sources of their thoughts, feelings, and desires in order to make clear decisions that best reflect their true nature. Discernment is often aided through spiritual guidance or direction and strengthened by prayer and reflection.

Divine Office: Also known as the *Liturgy of the Hours*, this is the daily prayer of the Roman Catholic Church. Cloistered monks and nuns frequently pause to pray the Psalms seven times a day. *Apostolic* Sisters and Brothers usually pray the morning and evening office.

Easter: The Christian feast that celebrates the resurrection of Jesus Christ from the dead.

Eucharist: Technically this word means "Thanksgiving." It is also the *sacrament* of bread and wine sacrificed to God upon an altar and miraculously transformed into the Body and Blood of Jesus Christ physically present.

Final Vows: After several years of Incorporation (or formation), preparation, and discernment the vows of consecrated celibacy, poverty, and obedience are publicly professed to God and community using the words "for the rest of this life and into the next." The ritual is sometimes called Perpetual Profession or Solemn Vows depending on the constitutions of the congregation.

Francis of Assisi: The late twelfth-early thirteenth century son of a cloth merchant in Assisi, Italy, Francesco grew up as part of the emerging middle class. He became a knight and was injured during a war and this trauma caused him to rethink his life. Eventually the people he once despised, lepers—the most marginalized people in his society—became beloved and beautiful to him. He turned away from his father's cloth business and began to dress like a leper and lived among them. A community grew around him and the Gospel life they shared was centered around begging, service to the poor, peacemaking and joyful proclamation of the Kingdom of God.

Franciscan: Followers of *Francis of Assisi* and *Clare of Assisi*. The Franciscan Order consists of three major branches. The First Order is the Friars Minor, established by St. Francis. The Second Order are the Poor Clares, who St. Clare and St. Francis co-founded as the "Poor Ladies." The Third Order consists of laypeople who blend into society, either as consecrated religious (Third Order Regular) or lay people (Third Order Secular). Simply put, the Franciscan lifestyle is based on the gospels. Franciscans are poor followers of Jesus Christ who live a community life centered on humble service to the marginalized, peacemaking, and care for creation.

Franciscan Sisters of Perpetual Adoration (FSPA): Based in La Crosse, Wisconsin, the community of Third Order Regular Franciscan Sisters was founded in Milwaukee in 1849 with Mother Aemiliana Dirr as their leader. In 1869 a group relocated to La Crosse, on the Mississippi River and began ministering to German immigrants, initially as nurses and teachers. On August 1, 1878 they began their practice of perpetual adoration which continues to this day. In 1965 the congregation membership peaked at with 1,158 members worldwide. In recent decades, under 200 sisters serve throughout the United States and world and mainly in Wisconsin, Iowa, and Minnesota.

Habit: The traditional attire of a monk, nun, Brother, or Sister that is simple and uniform, but varies in appearance or style from each community to the next.

Jesuits: An early nickname given to members of the Society of Jesus, an order established by St. Ignatius of Loyola in the early sixteenth century. Jesuits are to be "contemplatives in action," as the lifestyle of the men is centered around the Spiritual Exercises as they serve, study, and teach. Pope Francis is a Jesuit.

Jesuit Volunteer Corps (JVC): Offering one-year or two-year long service opportunities for young adults, Jesuit Volunteers (JVs) are full-time volunteers in places of high need. The life of a JV is centered around the tenets of service, community, social justice, and spirituality.

Lent: A season of prayer, fasting and almsgiving in the Christian calendar. Beginning on Ash Wednesday, it lasts for forty days and precedes the celebration of Easter.

Mass: A Catholic liturgy, or public worship, consisting of a particular pattern of prayer, Scripture readings, and *Eucharist* celebration.

Motherhouse: The headquarters and home base of a community of Catholic Sisters who have been sent out to serve.

Monastic: Contemplative monks or nuns whose life is centered around the rhythms of a particular monastery.

Monstrance: A transparent and decorative stand that exposes the Blessed Sacrament on an altar for veneration.

New Monastics: Married or single people of faith (usually Christians) who live in intentional community or singly as hermits and center their life around contemplation and service.

Novice: A new Sister or Brother in a religious order. They are living a life of prayer, community, and service and preparing to profess their vows.

Nun: A cloistered or monastic consecrated religious woman, such as a Poor Clare.

Obedience: Technically the word means "to listen." In the Roman Catholic Church, a person who is discerning their vocation is listening to the guidance of the Spirit to know God's will. They often listen to their hearts, other people, and the events of their lives, as these are all ways that God speaks. When a religious makes a vow of obedience, they are vowing to listen and follow God's will.

Order: A particular type of religious life, usually following the spirit, mission, or wisdom of a particular religious founder such as a saint.

Poverty: In Roman Catholic *Religious Life*, material and spiritual poverty is vowed. This means that a Sister, Brother, monk, or nun will not hold any private property but will share all things in common. Poverty is understood both materially and spiritually, so that the religious holds no possessions and is interdependent with others.

Religious Life: Consecrated men and women living a life of community, prayer, and service in communion with the Roman Catholic Church.

Rosary: A devotional prayer wherein series of prayers are said along a string of beads and the life of Jesus Christ is meditated upon.

Sacraments: As signs of God's grace (the free gift of God's supernatural help), ordinary elements are made holy and transform the believers. There are seven in the Roman Catholic tradition. Baptism brings the new Christian into the Church through holy water. Reconciliation renews the sinner's relationships with God and neighbor through blessings and the conversation with the priest. *Eucharist* transforms the bread and wine into the body and blood of Jesus Christ and builds communion between God and the community. Confirmation uses holy oil to anoint the believer to serve and represent Christ to the world. Holy orders ordains a person for priestly ministry and connects them to the lineage of the apostles in the early church. *Anointing of the sick* involves prayers and holy oil with which a priest offers Christ's comfort and loving presence to a suffering person. And, in matrimony the love and vows shared transform the believers into one body, united in Christ.

Saint: A holy person. Scripture says that we all are saints and sinners, but in order to be officially named a saint in the Roman Catholic Church, they go through canonization process after death in which their life is studied, miracles are attributed to prayers to the holy person's intercession, and they are remembered by others for their holiness.

Sister: A consecrated Roman Catholic woman religious who is out in the world serving God's people and living a life centered around prayer and community. The distinction between *nun* and Sister can be confusing because nuns also use the title Sister.

Tau: The nineteenth letter of the Greek alphabet, Scripture indicates that particular faithful people would be marked with a symbol like this (Ezekiel 9:4). Beloved by St. *Francis of Assisi*, he signed his writings with a Tau. The symbol was embraced by the Franciscan order as a new type of cross marking them as penitents.

ABOUT THE AUTHOR

Sister Julia Walsh is a Franciscan Sister of Perpetual Adoration and part of her congregation's formation team, serving women who are discerning their vocation. Along with another Franciscan Sister, she co-founded The Fireplace, an intentional community and house of hospitality on Chicago's southside that offers spiritual support to artists and activists. She has an MA in Pastoral Studies from Catholic Theological Union and is a certified spiritual director and secondary teacher. As a creative writer, educator, retreat presenter, and speaker she is passionate about exploring the intersection of creativity, spirituality, activism, and community life. A regularly published spiritual writer, Sister Julia's work can be found in publications such as *America*, *Living Faith Catholic Devotional*, *Living City*, *National Catholic Reporter*, and *St. Anthony Messenger*. She hosts the Messy Jesus Business blog and podcast and is on Twitter and Instagram as @JuliaFSPA.